COUNSELING GIFTED AND TALENTED CHILDREN

A Guide for Teachers, Counselors, and Parents

Creativity Research

Mark A. Runco, Series Editor

Achieving Extraordinary Ends: An Essay on Creativity, by Sharon Bailin

Counseling Gifted and Talented Children, edited by Roberta M. Milgram

Divergent Thinking, by Mark A. Runco

In Preparation:

Contexts of Creativity, by Leonora Cohen, Amit Goswami, Shawn Boles, and Richard Chaney

Creative Thinking: Problem Solving and the Arts Orientation, by John Wakefield

Creativity: Theories, Themes and Issues, by Mark A. Runco

Creativity and Affect, edited by Melvin Shaw and Klaus Hoppe

Creativity in Government, by Thomas Heinzen

Genius Revisited: High IQ Children Grown Up, by Rena Subotnik, Lee Kassan, Ellen Summers, and Alan Wasser

More Ways Than One: Fostering Creativity, by Arthur J. Cropley

Nurturing and Developing Creativity: Emergence of a Discipline, Volume 2, edited by Scott G. Isaksen, Mary C. Murdock, Roger L. Firestien, and Donald J. Treffinger

Perspectives on Creativity: The Biographical Method, by John E. Gedo and Mary M. Gedo

Problem Finding, Problem Solving, and Creativity, edited by Mark A. Runco

Understanding and Recognizing Creativity: Emergence of a Discipline, Volume 1, edited by Scott G. Isaksen, Mary C. Murdock, Roger L. Firestien, and Donald J. Treffinger

COUNSELING GIFTED AND TALENTED CHILDREN:

A Guide for Teachers, Counselors, and Parents

edited by

Roberta M. Milgram

ABLEX PUBLISHING CORPORATION
NORWOOD, NEW JERSEY

Printed in the United States of America

Library of Congress Cataloging-in-Publication Data

Counseling gifted and talented children : a guide for teachers,
    counselors, and parents / edited by Roberta M. Milgram.
        p.   cm.—(Creativity research)
    Includes bibliographical references and index.
    ISBN 0-89391-773-7 (pp.).—ISBN 0-89391-724-9 (cl.)
        1. Gifted children—Education.   2. Gifted children—Counseling of.
    3. Personnel service in education.   I. Milgram, Roberta M.
    II. Series.
    LC3993.2.C65   1991
    371.95—dc20   91-9372
                                                                          CIP

Ablex Publishing Corporation
355 Chestnut St.
Norwood, NJ 07648

This book is dedicated to my children
—with love, respect, and gratitude,

Shoshana, Wendy, Jonathan

מכל מלמדי השכלתי ומבני ומבנותי יותר מכולם

"I have gained knowledge from all of my teachers and
from my children most of all"   (Psalms 116:99)

Through them I have come to understand that giftedness
comes in many forms, and that its realization
depends on one's values and efforts.

Contents

Contributors

Robert S. Albert is professor, Department of Psychology, Pitzer College, Claremont, California.

Paul R. Daniels is professor of education, Johns Hopkins University, Baltimore, Maryland.

Ellen B. Goldring is lecturer, School of Education Tel-Aviv University, Ramat-Aviv, Israel.

Shirley A. Griggs is professor of counselor education, School of Education and Human Services, St. John's University, Jamaica, New York.

Lawrence J. Johnson is associate professor and chairperson, Early Childhood Special Education, University of Alabama, Tuscalosa, Alabama.

Merle B. Karnes is professor, Department of Special Education, and project director of Preschool Gifted Programs, University of Illinois, Champaign, Illinois.

Shoshana Knapp is associate professor of English, Virginia Polytechnic Institute and State University, Blacksburg, Virginia.

Elizabeth A. Mechstroth conducts a private practice in Dayton, Ohio. She is a lecturer, consultant, and co-author (with J.T. Webb and S.S. Tolan) of *Guiding the Gifted Child*.

Roberta M. Milgram is associate professor, School of Education, Tel-Aviv University, Ramat-Aviv, Israel.

Lita Linzer Schwartz is professor, Department of Educational Psychology, Pennsylvania State University, Ogontz Campus, Abington, Pennsylvania.

Joyce Van Tassel-Baska is Jody and Layton Smith Professor of Education, College of William and Mary, Williamsburg, Virginia.

Rachel Zorman is senior researcher, The Szold Institute for Research in the Behavioral Sciences, Jerusalem, Israel.

Preface

Gifted learners share the same basic guidance needs as other children and require ongoing developmental guidance and counseling in order to fully realize their abilities. In addition, however, because they differ widely in the type and level of their special abilities and motivations, in their learning styles, and in other personal-social characteristics, they require differentiated guidance and personalized counseling. There is a gap between the enoromous need for counseling services and research about the counseling needs of gifted individuals, on the one hand, and the limited availability of such services and knowledge, on the other.

This book is designed to give counselors, regular classroom teachers, gifted education specialists, and parents an understanding of the academic and personal-social needs of gifted and talented students, awareness of ways that they themselves may help these children, and an introduction to the available guidance strategies and materials.

Since the early 1930s there has been an awareness of the need for differentiated guidance for the gifted. Unfortunately, guidance has been narrow in focus, dealing only with academic acceleration or enrichment, with specific psychosocial problems, or with underachievement. There has not been a comprehensive conceptualization of giftedness to account for cognitive and personal-social development of gifted and talented learners to provide a sound thereotical base for counseling, and to serve as a catalyst for research. The counseling concepts and strategies presented in the current volume reflect a comprehensive conceptual model of giftedness developed by the editor.

This book represents an addition to the literature on gifted and talented children in the following ways:

1. It highlights the role of regular classroom teachers and teachers of the gifted in counseling the gifted and talented. This is important since much programming for the gifted takes place at the level of elementary schools where we rarely find counselors. Where there are guidance counselors, they are generally so overburdened in working with the average and below average learners that it is unrealistic to expect them to provide for the needs of the gifted and talented.

2. The book provides teachers, counselors, and parents with accurate, specific information about the wide variety of approaches to enrichment and/or acceleration providing full- or part-time special education for gifted and talented children.

3. It emphasizes the major role of parents in the development of their gifted children. Their influence in often highly positive but can also be negative. In the current volume major attention is given to provide parents with authoritative information about the nature of giftedness and their own critical role in its development.

4. The book stresses career education and guidance. Because of the widespread misconception that gifted and talented children will succeed without special help, efforts to provide special career education for them are rare. This book presents information on the career development of gifted learners and makes specific suggestions to teachers, counselors, and parents on how to help these children make wise academic and vocational choices.

5. Four chapters are devoted to important topics that have received very little attention so far in the literature: gifted girls, preschool gifted, disadvantaged gifted, and learning-disabled gifted. In the last two decades, there has been steadily increasing understanding that all four general categories—girls, preschoolers, disadvantaged children, and learning-disabled children—require special educational interventions. However, only recently have educators become aware that some of these children may require even more attention because they are gifted as well.

6. Finally, a unique feature of the book is a chapter in which fictional portraits of gifted and creative children are presented and analyzed. This material illustrates many of the concepts discussed in the other chapters.

The authors of the various chapters are highly competent scientists and/or practitioners. They combine excellent academic and research credentials with respect for and, in many instances, practical experience in gifted education. I have learned a great deal from each author. I thank the authors for their creative efforts, for their cooperation, and especially for their patience and understanding.

I acknowledge a debt to my children to whom this book is dedicated. My professional and personal life has been greatly enriched and my understanding of giftedness enhanced by my experience with them and with the second generation, my grandchildren—Avinoam Rimon, Rachel Heather Knapp, Nadav Moshe Rimon, Dashiell Ari Knapp, Talia Sara Rimon, Assaf Daniel Rimon, Genevieve Ilana Knapp, and Yael Rimon. They have led me to understand in a personal way that cognitive abilities and personality characteristics combine in an intricate pattern in each child and that giftedness and talent come in many forms. Finally, I thank my husband, Noach, for his help and support in preparing this book.

Part I
Counseling Gifted and Talented Children and Adolescents

Comparatively little attention has been devoted to counseling gifted and talented children and adolescents. In this book the attention of the reader is shifted from teaching to counseling and from cognitive and academic concerns to personal-social and affective ones. The first chapter is designed to give basic information on the nature of giftedness and an overview on the topic of counseling gifted children to counselors, regular classroom teachers, teachers specializing in teaching gifted, and parents.

In Chapter 1, Milgram presents her 4 × 4 structure of giftedness model in which giftedness is conceptualized in terms of (a) four categories, two having to do with aspects of intelligence (general intellectual ability and specific intellectual ability) and two with aspects of original thinking (general original/creative thinking and specific creative talent); and (b) four ability levels (profoundly gifted, moderately gifted, mildly gifted, and nongifted). Two other aspects of the model are learning environment (home, school, and community) and individual differences of age, sex, socioeconomic status, culture, subculture, and personality. This model will help teachers, counselors, and parents understand the specific counseling needs of each gifted child on the basis of his/her unique profile of assets.

Milgram sets the stage for the chapters that follow by giving an overview of the counseling needs of the gifted and discussing how and by whom these needs are to be met. She regards as unfortunate the exaggerated emphasis on social adjustment problems in the counseling of gifted learners. On the basis of research findings, it is concluded that most gifted children do not have adjustment difficulties, yet most, if not all, would benefit from counseling. Milgram suggests that counselors focus on the counseling needs of the large majority of nonproblematic gifted youth and their needs for information and understanding so as to develop their abilities more fully. Out-of-school activities conducted

1

at one's leisure constitute an important topic that has hitherto been neglected. Milgram recommends offering these children encouragement and opportunity to pursue a wide variety of leisure activities and weighing these activities in the identification and selection of gifted and talented children for special education.

We would expect the responsibility for counseling gifted learners to rest with guidance counselors. However, teachers in regular classrooms, special education teachers, and parents all counsel or provide information and advice to gifted and talented learners. This is especially true in many middle schools and high schools with very large pupil-counselor ratios and in elementary schools where very frequently there are no counselors at all. The different people who share the task of advising gifted children have the same goal, that is, to help the children make wise decisions. Despite the common purpose, each group has a legitimate and specific function.

In Chapter 2, Milgram and Goldring provide basic information about the 10 types of administrative arrangements most frequently used in special education for the gifted, and compare their relative efficacy. These options can be divided into two major categories: replacement systems offered in place of regular school hours for varying amounts of time, and supplementary systems offered in addition to regular school hours. Teachers, counselors, and parents can help gifted learners make wise educational choices by providing ongoing, systematic, specific, up-to-date information on the alternative models of special education available in the community. The authors highlight enrichment/acceleration in the regular classroom as a little-used special education option with many advantages. On the other hand, they conclude that there is no one best option for all gifted and talented children. The benefits and limitations of each option must be weighed in deciding which educational setting best matches the needs of a particular child.

In Chapter 3, Van Tassel-Baska outlines the psychosocial needs of gifted children and suggests specific strategies for addressing them. Gifted children differ in type and level of abilities and in personal-social development and characteristics. They have, therefore, special counseling needs beyond those required by their nongifted peers. A very high proportion of parents single out counseling services for their gifted children as the most critical school-related service they require. Unfortunately, because of the high counselor-pupil ration and the tendency for counselors to give most attention to problem students, most gifted children do not receive professional counseling during their K-12 school years. Van Tassel-Baska suggests that the teachers who provide special education for the gifted are not only available, but are the most appropriate agents to dispense counseling to gifted children. She provides details on the implementation of this highly original, promising, and cost-effective proposal.

In Chapter 4, Griggs examines the relationship between children's learning style preferences and counseling strategies. Learning style is defined as the conditions under which each person begins to concentrate, absorb, process, and retain new and difficult information and skills. Although learning style is highly individual, certain learning style features characterize certain kinds of gifted and talented children. For example, high intelligence type gifted learners as a group are highly motivated, internally controlled, persistent, and nonconforming.

Griggs explains one widely used and highly regarded approach to the measurement of learning style and provides detailed guidelines to counselors on how to interpret the scores. She cites findings of higher school achievement and more positive attitudes toward school when learning style and school environment match, and the opposite when they do not. Griggs suggests that counseling becomes more effective when counseling techniques are matched with the learning style preferences of gifted learners, and identifies counseling techniques that match particular learning style patterns. The chapter closes with a discussion of special problems that gifted children frequently focus on in counseling sessions, for example, peer issues or competition versus cooperation.

The critical influence of parents on the realization of potential giftedness is cited in every chapter of the book. Many authors strongly urge that parents receive substantial guidance so that their influence on the developing child will be positive and constructive. Chapters 5 and 6 are devoted to understanding how giftedness develops and special abilities actualized through the interaction of personality, family, third-party experiences, sociological and cultural influences, and the specific domain and level of giftedness. The two chapters complement each other in that Albert focuses on theoretical aspects of the gifted child's interaction with his/her parents and other adults, while Meckstroth offers practical guidance on the most frequently occuring challenges and problems of day-to-day parent-gifted child interactions.

The positive contribution of interested, involved parents and of other adults providing real-world experiences to the development and actualization of gifted abilities is widely recognized. In Chapter 5, Albert summarizes empirical data from his longitudinal study that provide a conceptual explanation of why and how intrafamilial and special extrafamilial relationships shape the development of young people destined to become eminent adults. In tracing the types of experiences that shape the lives of gifted youth, he differentiates between focal relationships and crystallizing experiences. Focal relationships are deeper and longer in duration and have broad influence on various aspects of the child's life, especially on personal-social development. Crystallizing experiences are more domain-specific, circumscribed in time and in situation, and have impact on one specific area of a child's life. Albert describes differing paths to the realization of potential in gifted youth in the different domains of giftedness. People in science-symbolic oriented careers report more crystallizing experiences in their early lives, while those in people-oriented careers remember more focal relationships.

The growing understanding of the benefits that gifted children and adolescents derive from sensitive parenting has received much attention in other chapters. In Chapter 6, Meckstroth proposes that parents provide teachers and counselors with information and support that will greatly benefit their gifted child. Meckstroth provides practical suggestions on strategies for conducting more effective parent-teacher conferences and parent discussion groups. She offers specific recommendations on how to conduct individual conferences or group discussions, provides detailed, practical advice on the organization and administration of parent groups, and recommends discussion topics and strategies for their meetings.

Meckstroth's chapter is unique in two ways. First, the author's basic respect for parents of gifted children and her deep understanding of their satisfactions and frustration are clearly reflected in the chapter. This refreshing attitude is in marked contrast to the dominant view that the parents of gifted learners are meddling, overinvolved, and annoying. Second, the content of the chapter and the style in which it is written convey the clear message that the author has herself followed the recommended content and strategies, and that they really work!

In Chapter 7, Milgram discusses career development and career education/counseling with particular reference to the gifted and talented. Career development is a lifelong process of crystallizing vocational identity. It involves learning about oneself, one's abilities, interests, attitudes, values, and skills in the vocational sphere. It also involves learning about and testing vocations in school and in a wide variety of other settings. Career education and guidance affect career development and should be part of the curriculum from preschool through high school. It should consist of a series of graded experiences, different at each age level, in which the individual acquires information about the world of work, becomes more self-aware, engages in exploratory vocational experiences, and develops decision-making skills. The responsibility for career education and guidance should be shared by regular classroom teachers, gifted education specialists, counselors, and parents.

Career development is not the same for all gifted and talented individuals. Just at gifted learners have unique needs in the academic sphere, they also require differentiated career education. Special career education for gifted and talented learners entails adjustments of curriculum content and teaching-counseling strategies in terms of the specific pattern of assets and concerns of each gifted learner.

Milgram presents a number of issues considered by many educators and researchers to play a significant role in the career development of gifted and talented youth. She questions the widely accepted view that the career interests and abilities of gifted individuals are multipotential. This view is contradicted by the demonstration of remarkable ability in a specific domain at an early age and by the early emergence of focused career interests.

The chapter concludes with comments on two promising directions for career education of gifted learners—distance education and experiential education. With regard to the first, a new development in the field of career education is the accumulation of extensive data bases available to users over a large geographical area by means of local modem or terminal connections to a mainframe computer. Computer-assisted strategies are particularly appropriate for career education in gifted learners. Since the gifted are frequently more independent, internally controlled, and self-motivated than their nongifted peers, it is likely that they will use such a long distance system effectively.

By the same token, experiential career education programs also make a unique contribution to the academic, personal-social, and career development of able learners. Since many gifted young people are highly motivated and independent, mentorships are probably particularly valuable experiences for them. It provides a continuing interaction with a respected and admired adult, thereby fostering self-esteem and self-confidence in the protege. The role modeling and support often found in mentoring relationships are especially important to gifted students.

Chapter 1
Counseling Gifted and Talented Children and Youth: Who, Where, What, and How?

Roberta M. Milgram

Most parent-teacher conferences are quite unremarkable but some will be remembered for a long time. One such memorable meeting took place between the father and the teacher of Albert Einstein. Although he became a world-famous scientist as an adult, Einstein had serious school problems as a child. The boy's teachers described him to his father as a dismal failure and conveyed a bleak forecast for his academic and vocational future. Fortunately, despite repeated failures in conventional school settings, Einstein's father continued to believe that his son had special abilities and eventually found a school that recognized the child's profound giftedness and unique learning style. Even if the story is apocryphal, as many claim, the message is clear. Some highly gifted adults did not appear to be so as children.

Another unusual parent-teacher conference was convened at the initiative of the teacher to discuss the school "problem" of a 12-year-old boy who was failing every subject. The teacher expected the meeting to be routine and was quite surprised when, before she had a chance to say anything, the father asked, "How much do you earn a month, Ms. Jones?" The teacher was flabbergasted and ignored the question, proceeding with her remarks about the boy. The father, however, was not to be deterred and asked the question again, and even a third time. Thinking to herself that she now understood where the boy's stubbornness came from, Ms. Jones realized that if she wanted this conference to take place at all, she had better answer the question, and proceeded to do so. The father immediately responded, "I thought so! My boy earns three times what you do each month, Ms. Jones, and

7

he says that there is nothing for him to learn in school." The incredulous teacher listened as the father described his son's gardening business. It had started with his mowing lawns in the neighborhood and had grown to a large enterprise yielding an income that could support a family. The boy was clearly not failing in some very important life areas.

In a third memorable conference the parents of a highly gifted third grader met with the teacher to discuss the child's complaint that she was bored in school. In this conference the situation was quite different. Both parent and teacher were well aware that the child was gifted and the focus of the conversation was on how to challenge the child intellectually so that she would not be bored. In fact, the child was not bored at school but had a different problem entirely.

Meetings like these take place in schools all over the world and reflect the commendable concern shared by parents and teachers in helping children achieve as much as they possibly can in school. Unfortunately, the probability that these particular meetings would help much was not great.

In the first two examples, Einstein and the child with the gardening business, positive results were unlikely because neither parent nor teacher was aware that the children under discussion were highly gifted, and had special educational needs stemming from their unique abilities. Both teacher and parent would have been astonished to have these children referred to as gifted. One reason these two children were not seen as gifted is that their abilities were not reflected in behaviors generally recognized as indications of giftedness, that is, school grades, and standardized tests of intelligence and academic achievement.

The third story illustrates another reason some gifted children do not actualize their potential. When a child is gifted by the conventional standard of high IQ and teachers and parents are fully aware of his/her special abilities, they may focus exclusively on providing intellectual challenges while other, sometimes more critical, needs go unrecognized. Adjustment difficulties in school or at home are frequently attributed to giftedness even though they really have no connection to it. For example, the child in the story presented above was unhappy in school at that particular time because she was not getting along well with several children in her class. She was reluctant to go to school each day and explained the hesitation by telling her parents that she was bored. The child herself probably did not realize the real source of her reluctance. Parents, teachers, and counselors found themselves dealing with the problem of academic boredom instead of what was really bothering the child. Incidents like this one occur rather frequently because adults, aware of the child's giftedness, expect the child to be bored in school and, therefore, focus on the giftedness/boredom problem. When dealing with gifted children, we are inclined to start off by seeing all problems as stemming from giftedness. Adults who acquire more knowledge about gifted children try first to understand and help in terms of the more general framework that one applies to nongifted children, and only when that approach fails, to consider the possible link between the problem and the child's giftedness.

Many readers might wonder why it is necessary to consider the counseling needs of gifted and talented children and youth at all. They believe that these fortunate children excel in school almost automatically, grow up with few adjustment problems, and achieve academic and vocational success as adults quite naturally. The three examples presented above demonstrate that children who are identified as highly intelligent and/or as having other capabilities highly valued in adult society do not automatically realize these potential abilities as adults. Two circumstances that contribute to lack of realization of abilities are (1) being unidentified and underserved in school like Einstein and our gardener, or (2) being identified and inadequately served like our "bored" little girl. Although estimates among authorities vary as to what proportion of children identified as gifted on the basis of their IQ scores do not realize their potential abilities when they become adults, there is agreement that failure to actualize one's abilities is a significant problem (Marland, 1972; Tannenbaum, 1983). The estimates, as distressing as they are, are probably a minimal estimate of the scope of the problem. Many highly gifted learners whose abilities are not reflected in IQ scores are unidentified during their school years, are not included in the estimates, and are even less likely to actualize their possibilities.

To sum up, there is an enormous need for counseling services and research about the counseling needs of gifted individuals, on the one hand, and the limited availability of such services and knowledge, on the other (Janos & Robinson, 1985; Myers & Pace, 1986; VanTassel-Baska, 1983).

This book is designed to give counselors, teachers, and parents (1) an understanding of giftedness as a phenomenon that includes a wide variety of special abilities, (2) specific information on the academic, career development, and personal-social needs of gifted and talented students, and (3) an introduction to methods and materials available to help meet these needs. The first chapter is divided into three parts. First, what is meant by gifted and talented learners? Second, what are the counseling needs of gifted and talented learners? Third, how and by whom are these needs to be met?

WHAT IS MEANT BY GIFTED AND TALENTED LEARNERS?

For many years the accepted definition of giftedness was that proposed by Terman (1925), that is, an IQ score of 140 or over as measured by the Stanford-Binet. In the 1950s the unidimensional definition of giftedness was expanded by Guilford (1956) to include creativity, and educators began to speak of the gifted and talented. In the 1970s Marland (1972), then United States Commissioner of Education, proposed a multifaceted definition of giftedness that included not only creativity but also leadership ability, and abilities in the performing and visual arts. The Marland (1972) definition represented an important theoretical advance and resulted in the development of a wide variety of multidimensional models of giftedness.

Despite the theoretical advances, most of the literature on counseling the gifted is limited to determining the needs of the high-IQ type gifted and considering ways to meet these needs. This is unfortunate, because a broader, more inclusive conception of giftedness leads to the understanding that children with different abilities require content and strategy of counseling that is differentiated in terms of the specific pattern of strengths of each child.

The 4×4 structure of giftedness model is a conceptual framework designed to organize what is known about giftedness so as to be useful to teachers, counselors, and parents, as they counsel the gifted. In the 4×4 model, giftedness is depicted as a multidimensional rather than a unidimensional phenomenon. It is designed to compare and contrast the different kinds of giftedness among children and within the same child, and to stress the understanding that giftedness occurs at distinct levels. On the basis of the model one can conclude that different expectations of accomplishment are to be expected in terms of the distinct pattern of abilities of each child. It directs attention to the need to tailor the content and strategies of counseling to groups of children gifted by one criterion and not by another, and facilitates planning for a specific gifted child according to his/her profile of assets.

In the 4×4 model, giftedness is depicted in terms of four categories, two having to do with aspects of intelligence (general intellectual ability and specific intellectual ability) and two with aspects of original thinking (general original/creative thinking and specific creative talent), and four ability levels (profoundly gifted, moderately gifted, mildly gifted, and nongifted). There are two other aspects to the model. First, there is the dimension of learning environment. Gifted and talented children and youth grow up in three interrelated learning environments—the home, the school, and the community. Second, giftedness is depicted

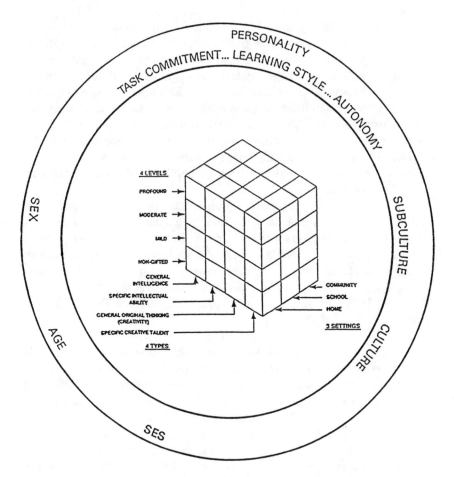

Figure 1.   Milgram: 4 × 4 Structure of Giftedness.

as embedded in a solid circle of individual differences associated with age, sex, socioeconomic status, culture, subculture, and personality characteristics (e.g., task commitment, learning style, and autonomy).

Four Categories of Giftedness

The first category, *general intellectual ability* or *overall general intelligence,* refers to the ability to think abstractly and to solve problems logically and systematically. This ability is measured in adults and children by performance on psychometric tests and is most frequently reported as IQ scores.

The second category, *specific intellectual ability,* refers to a clear and distinct intellectual ability in a given area, such as mathematics, foreign languages, music, or science. For example, a person in the mathematics category might demonstrate outstanding computational ability, knowledge of mathematical principles, and even deep understanding of mathematical concepts. In art giftedness is reflected in aesthetic appreciation and technical ability. Specific intellectual abilities are reflected in performance that may be highly competent, but not necessarily highly original. These abilities usually result in superior performance in specific school subjects as measured by scores on standardized achievement tests and school grades.

The third category, *general original/creative thinking,* is a process of problem solving in which unusual and high quality solutions are generated. Creative thinkers produce ideas that are imaginative, clever, elegant, or surprising. A wide variety of tests have been used to measure divergent thinking ability at ages ranging from preschool to adult (Kogan, 1983; Wallach, 1970; Milgram, 1983; Milgram & Arad, 1981; Milgram, Milgram, Rosenbloom, & Rabkin, 1978; Milgram, Moran, Sawyers, & Fu, 1987).

Original thinking people are different from others not only in the ideas they produce, but also in the way they perceive and define the world around them. They see things differently and notice things that others ignore. They probably store and retrieve information differently as well. As a consequence of these basic differences, they produce unique and imaginative solutions. This general ability has been referred to by Barron and Harrington (1981) as "raw creative ability" and distinguished from "effective creative ability," the fourth category of giftedness.

The fourth category, *specific creative talent,* refers to a clear and distinct domain-specific creative ability. Original thinking ability is applied to a specific sphere of human endeavor and is manifested in socially valuable, original products in areas such as science, mathematics, art, music, social leadership, business, or politics.

In many spheres, the realization of specific creative ability requires time to incubate and develop as a result of life experience. It is, therefore, more fully manifested in adults. It may, however, be evidenced long before adulthood in leisure-time, out-of-school activities. A number of researchers have developed biographical self-report questionnaires that tap leisure activities yielding scores that can be used to identify children and adolescents in this category of the 4×4 model (Anastasi & Schaefer, 1969; Holland, 1961; Milgram & Milgram, 1976; Schaefer, 1969; Terman, 1925; Wallach & Wing, 1969; Wing & Wallach, 1971).

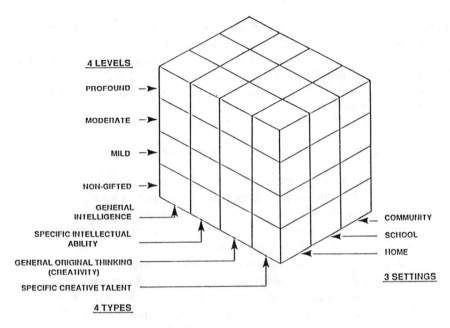

Figure 2.   Milgram: 4 × 4 Structure of Giftedness.

Levels of Giftedness

Gifted behavior may be found in children and adults at mild, moderate, and profound levels. These levels are hierarchical in organization and become increasingly infrequent in occurrence as one moves from non-gifted to profoundly gifted. Some researchers and educators differentiate between the profound and other levels of giftedness but they rarely distinguish between the mild and moderate levels. It is extremely rare for programs to differentiate among gifted learners by level. We sometimes find special programs or schools for profoundly gifted children, but almost never encounter practical consideration of the distinction between the mild and moderate levels of giftedness.

Failure to consider levels of giftedness is surprising when one considers the theoretical and practical importance attributed to the different levels of mental retardation (American Psychiatric Association, 1980). Parents and teachers are informed about the educational implications of each level in a clear and definitive manner. No one would suggest that mildly retarded individuals learn the same curriculum material, in the same way, and in the same setting as profoundly retarded.

By contrast, in conceptualizations of giftedness and in educational programming for gifted learners, the concept of levels has, for the most part, been ignored. This is unfortunate because levels of giftedness are similar to levels of retardation in that each reflects a distinct range of expectations with respect to short- and long-term accomplishments that are different from those of the other levels. In order to counsel gifted children effectively, it is essential to consider category and level for a particular child.

Learning Environments and Individual Differences

The realization of potential abilities is dependent on the complex interaction of environmental opportunities with cognitive abilities and personal-social characteristics. The 4 × 4 model reflects this understanding by citing three settings (school, home, and community) that affect and are affected by giftedness.

Few gifted adults mention their schools as important influences in the development of their abilities (Bloom, 1985). Some even cite school experiences as negative influences inhibiting the development of their abilities. This disturbing finding is probably a direct result of policies and practices in special education for gifted learners that fail to recognize the wide individual differences among gifted learners and therefore, fail to adopt curriculum materials and instructional strategies differentiated and individualized to meet the needs of each individual gifted child.

By contrast, gifted adults frequently cite the efforts of parents in stimulating and directing their developing talents (Bloom, 1985). The behavior and attitudes of parents and the quantity and quality of their interest in the gifted child as well as their interaction with him/her are important influences on the development of giftedness. On the basis of their studies of the families of gifted youth, Albert and Runco (1987) concluded that there are distinct patterns of family influences on different types and levels of giftedness.

Communities also influence the development of giftedness. Public policy decisions in communities determine the funding available for special education of gifted and opportunities for gifted learners to broaden the scope and depth of their educational experiences through interaction with community leaders and access to community institutions.

Individual differences associated with age, sex, socioeconomic status, culture, subculture, and especially personality characteristics, are also important in determining which abilities are realized and to what extent. The chapters that follow deal with each of these topics more specifically.

What are the Guidance and Counseling Needs of Gifted and Talented Learners?

Gifted children have the same guidance and counseling needs as all other children, plus a number of needs that stem from their remarkable abilities. Like other exceptional children whose development differs from the norm—for example, physically handicapped, intellectually retarded, hearing or vision problems—gifted learners cannot maximize their abilities in a regular school program unless it is adjusted for their specific exceptionality. The modification may take the form of special equipment, curriculum, instruction, administrative arrangement, or special services. The specific exceptional abilities of each gifted child requires distinctive guidance and counseling approaches and goals.

Some children may be exceptional in more than one way. Guidance and counseling must then be further modified to take into account the added requirements. Two chapters in this book deal with doubly exceptional gifted children. In Chapter 11, Daniels discusses the learning-disabled gifted; in Chapter 9, Zorman discusses the disadvantaged gifted.

The guidance and counseling needs of gifted children may be divided into three categories: the cognitive-academic, the personal-social, and the experiential.

Cognitive-academic needs. Gifted learners require knowledge about themselves and about their academic and career opportunities. They require complete and accurate information about options currently available within the school system, and details about the specific requirements for admissions, and positive versus negative features of universities and vocations that they might consider in the future. They need to understand the overall nature of giftedness in terms of the 4 (categories) × 4 (levels) model presented above. In addition, they need specific information about their own unique combination of abilities and the implications of these distinctive strengths for academic, personal, and career development.

Personal-social needs. Gifted children have special counseling needs in the personal-social sphere. Guidance should be directed to helping gifted children become aware of their special abilities on their feelings, attitudes, values, and interactions with their family, age peers, teachers, and other adults. Gifted children profit from the opportunity to explore their motivations and to examine their relationship to short- and long-term personal, academic, and professional goals.

Many teachers and counselors in the field believe that the personal-social adjustment of gifted learners is poor and that they have unusual needs for therapeutic counseling. The conviction that gifted children have many personal-social problems is usually based upon the limited personal experience of counselors and on introspective reports that frequently appear in the popular literature of gifted adults describing troubled childhood experiences. Moreover, even the professional counseling literature often focuses on difficulties in peer relationships, underachievement, perfectionism, depression, school dropout, delinquency, and even suicide (Myers & Pace, 1986).

Despite this widely held prejudice, gifted learners as a group are characterized by more positive personal-social characteristics and fewer life difficulties than their less gifted peers. This conclusion is based upon consistent research findings that have accumulated over a long period of time (Janos & Robinson, 1985; Tannenbaum, 1983; Terman, 1925; Terman & Oden, 1947, 1959). Only a small proportion of gifted children have psychological adjustment problems.

Despite the generally good psychological adjustment of gifted children, Janos and Robinson (1985) cite three instances in which giftedness may be associated with problems in personal-social adjustment. When the child's giftedness becomes the major focus of their relationship with parents, teachers, and other children, adjustment difficulties may obtain. Second, a variety of personal-social problems have been reported in children who are profoundly gifted—that is, characterized by very superior intellectual ability. Finally, gifted underachievers are likely to evidence special adjustment problems.

Experiential needs. Just as gifted children require special education in the formal school setting, they need special out-of-school experiences as well. Exposure to a wide variety of task-oriented, domain-specific, real-world experiences provide additional cognitive-academic knowledge and personal-social awareness, in general, and clarify career interests and values, specifically. These experiences may take place within the framework of one's immediate family, they may involve mentor or intern relationships with other adults in the community, or they may be leisure time activities that the child does entirely on his own.

HOW AND BY WHOM ARE THE COUNSELING NEEDS OF GIFTED CHILDREN TO BE MET?

The special needs of gifted and talented learners for academic enrichment/acceleration have received much attention in the literature. Comparatively little attention, however, has been devoted to their special counseling needs. Gifted children receive guidance and counseling from guidance counselors, regular classroom teachers, or parents. The training and experience of school counselors makes them the most appropriate source of counseling services. Unfortunately, the heavy workload of counselors in most schools makes it unlikely that they will be able to provide much support for gifted children. Teachers generally see their job as providing intellectual challenge for gifted learners and most would consider guidance and counseling beyond the scope of their competence and responsibility. Parents of gifted children are likely to be willing to devote considerable time and effort to provide information and advice. Unfortunately, they usually lack the required training and experience. Therefore, although all three groups are capable of providing counseling to gifted children, each group has reason for not doing so. How then can counseling services be provided to the gifted under such circumstances?

Innovative approaches to providing counseling services to gifted learners will have to be adopted. One way is to make school counseling more effective by making it more efficient; another is to focus on counseling services provided by parents and other adults outside of the school setting.

First, counseling within the school setting will be more efficient if counselors place major emphasis on group sessions in which regular classroom teachers are prepared to (a) differentiate the curriculum for gifted children, (b) individualize instructional strategies, and (c) provide counseling services to gifted learners. The rationale for this approach as well as exact topics for the sessions are discussed by Milgram (1989), Maker (1989), Dunn (1989), and Meckstroth (see Chapter 6). Although Meckstroth's chapter is directed specifically to parents, many of the same approaches and issues are appropriate for teacher groups.

Second, we must provide parents with the required counseling tools. Many teachers and counselors will view this suggestion with considerable skepticism. They see parents of gifted learners as overly ambitious for their children, overinvolved with them, and overprotective. They perceive them as part of the problem rather than part of the solution. This is unfortunate since, in fact, many parents have a significant and highly positive influence on the development and realization of potential abilities in their gifted children. Many highly successful gifted adults give high praise to their parents and cite their devotion and support as crucial to their career development (Bloom, 1985; Cox, Daniel, & Boston, 1985). In the light of the shortage of people to counsel gifted youngsters, it seems particularly wasteful not to harness the interest and energy of parents on behalf of their children and to help them acquire the knowledge and techniques they need.

Third, we must maximize the use of personal computers in the counseling process. Specific information about themselves and about community resources can be made easily available and computerized for personal use. Many gifted children are highly self-motivated and persistent and strongly prefer individual rather than group activities in and out of school. Computer-assisted counseling services make sense for gifted children because they are independent and often prefer to work and study alone. Computer-based counseling strategies are appropriate not only for high-IQ type gifted but also those high in original thinking ability and/or who have special abilities in mathematics, science, or music.

Groups of gifted children may be given brief explanations of the principles involved; thereafter each child considers the information independently. Many gifted learners will be able to use the information with no problem. On the other hand, some will seek further advice from adults. Such advice should be provided, but only when requested. The term *counsel* is defined in the dictionary as advice or guidance, especially *as solicited* from a knowledgeable person. With gifted children the emphasis must be on the *solicited.*

Another way to enhance the effectiveness of counseling is to match it with each individual's learning style. Considerable research has provided evidence that when instructional strategies and learning style are matched, academic achievement increases and attitudes toward school become more positive and that in mismatched situations the opposite results obtain (Dunn, 1987). In Chapter 4 Griggs describes the process of counseling highly intelligent learners for learning style and suggests that a match between the two leads to better results. A similar approach, matching counseling strategies with individual learning style, can be used with other gifted children as well. Counseling for learning style will benefit children characterized by the wide variety of combinations of abilities represented in the 4×4 model discussed above. Counselors can help gifted children, their teachers, and their parents understand the nature and importance of learning style-match and suggest ways that this information can be applied at home and at school.

Finally, special attention should be given to leisure activities. Leisure activities are defined as out-of-school hobbies and activities done for one's own enjoyment and by one's own choice, and not in order to fulfill school requirements or to earn grades or credits. Out-of-school or nonacademic does not mean necessarily nonintellectual (e.g., watching TV). Leisure activities may be highly intellectual projects not related to school (e.g., computer programming). Children who spend many hours reading, practicing an instrument, painting, or working in their "laboratories" are developing not only intellectual abilities but also task commitment, and other cognitive and personal-social attributes that positively affect life outcomes. The topic of leisure activities has been neglected in the professional literature. This is unfortunate because out-of-school activities probably play a key role in the development of talent.

The subject does not appear in recent authoritative sources (Horowitz & O'Brien; 1985; Tannenbaum, 1983; Sternberg & Davidson, 1986). Interestingly enough, Terman (1925), the pioneer investigator of giftedness, included out-of-school activities in the data that he gathered on the intellectually gifted children whom he followed throughout their lives.

Milgram (in press) has argued that leisure activities outside of school are more stable and valid indicators of giftedness than IQ scores. In a number of studies, high school and college students described their intrinsically motivated out-of-school activities (Holland, 1961; Holland & Austin, 1962; Holland & Nichols, 1964; Milgram & Milgram, 1976; Richards, Holland, & Lutz, 1967; Wallach & Wing, 1969; Wing & Wallach, 1971). These studies indicate that high school accomplishments resulting from out-of-school activities are associated with similar talented accomplishments in college. This finding is hardly surprising. It seems entirely reasonable that the best predictor of one's future interest and activity in a given realm is one's past attainments in that area. When it comes to academic achievement, past performance has been clearly demonstrated to be the best indicator of future achievement. The findings to date seem to indicate that a similar situation obtains in the realm of nonacademic talented accomplishment.

On the basis of these findings, one can conclude that gifted children should be exposed to a wide variety of leisure activities and encouraged to develop sustained activity in those that appeal to them. This advice is not to be misinterpreted as indicating that gifted children need more activities in formal settings. The intended emphasis is on freely chosen activities that each child does for his/her own pleasure.

Many people assume that giftedness is a stable characteristic: It is, that is, something that you are or are not as a child and will continue to be as an adult. They believe that if you are not gifted as a child, there is no chance of your becoming gifted as an adult. These widely held views, however, are not supported by research findings. Giftedness is better viewed as an emerging phenomenon. It is not something you are but rather something you do. Given proper nurturing experiences, older children, adolescents, and even adults may demonstrate gifted behavior even if they were not identified as gifted when they were children (Renzulli, 1978). Schools, families, and communities can contribute to the realization of giftedness by more effective teaching, counseling, and parenting.

REFERENCES

Anastasi, A., & Schaefer, C.E. (1969). Biographical correlates of artistic and literary creativity in adolescent girls. *Journal of Applied Psychology, 53*, 267–273.

Albert, R.S., & Runco, M.A. (1987). The possible personality dispositions of scientists and nonscientists. In D.N. Jackson & J.P. Rushton (Eds.), *Scientific excellence: Origins and assessment* (pp. 67–97). Beverly Hills: Sage.

American Psychiatric Association. (1980). *The diagnostic and statistical manual of mental disorders* (3rd ed.). Washington, DC: Author.

Barron, F., & Harrington, D.M. (1981). Creativity, intelligence and personality. *Annual Review of Psychology, 32,* 439–476.

Bloom, B.S. (1985). *Developing talent in young people.* New York: Ballantine.

Cox, J., Daniel, N., & Boston, B.O. (1985). *Educating able learners: Programs and promising practices.* Austin, TX: University of Texas Press.

Dunn, R. (1989). Individualizing instruction for mainstreamed gifted children. In R.M. Milgram (Ed.), *Teaching gifted and talented learners in regular classrooms* (pp. 63–111). Springfield, IL: Charles C. Thomas.

Dunn, R. (1987). Research in instructional environments: Implications for student achievement and attitudes. *Professional School Psychology, 2,* 43–52.

Guilford, J.P. (1956). The structure of intellect. *Psychological Bulletin, 53,* 267–293.

Holland, J.L. (1961). Creative and academic performance among talented adolescents. *Journal of Educational Psychology, 52,* 136–147.

Holland, J.L., & Austin, A.W. (1962). The prediction of the academic, artistic, scientific, and social achievement of undergraduates of superior scholastic aptitude. *Journal of Educational Psychology, 53,* 132–143.

Holland, J.L., & Nichols, R.C. (1964). Prediction of academic and extracurricular achievement in college. *Journal of Educational Psychology, 55,* 55–65.

Horowitz, F.D., & O'Brien, M. (Eds.). (1985). *The gifted and talented: Developmental perspectives.* Washington, DC: American Psychological Association.

Janos, P.M. & Robinson, N.M. (1985) Psychosocial development in intellectually gifted children. In F.D. Horowitz & M. O'Brien (Eds.), *The gifted and talented: Developmental perspectives* (pp. 149–195). Washington, DC: American Psychological Association.

Kogan, N. (1983). Stylistic variation in childhood and adolescence: Creativity, metaphor, and cognitive styles. In J.H. Flavell & E.M. Markham (Eds.), *Handbook of child psychology: Vol. 3. Cognitive development* (pp. 630–706). New York: Wiley.

Maker, C.J. (1989). Curriculum content for gifted students: Principles and practices. In R.M. Milgram (Ed.), *Teaching gifted and talented learners in regular classrooms* (pp. 33–61). Springfield, IL: Charles C. Thomas.

Marland, S.P., Jr. (1972). *Education of the gifted and talented: Report to the Congress of the United States by the U.S. Commissioner of Education.* Washington, DC: U.S. Government Printing Office.

Milgram, R.M. (1983). A validation of ideational fluency measures of original thinking in children. *Journal of Educational Psychology, 75,* 619–624.

Milgram, R.M. (1984). Creativity in gifted adolescents: A review. *Journal for the Education of the Gifted, 8,* 25–42.

Milgram, R.M. (Ed.). (1989). *Teaching gifted and talented learners in regular classrooms.* Springfield, IL: Charles C. Thomas.

Milgram, R.M. (1990). Creativity: An idea whose time has come and gone? In M.A. Runco & R.S. Albert (Eds.), *Theories of creativity.* Newbury Park, CA: Sage.

Milgram, R.M., & Arad, R. (1981). Ideational fluency as a predictor of original problem-solving. *Journal of Educational Psychology, 73,* 568-572.

Milgram, R.M., & Milgram, N.A. (1976). Creative thinking and creative performance in Israeli children. *Journal of Educational Psychology, 68,* 255-259.

Milgram, R.M., Milgram, N.A., Rosenbloom, G., & Rabkin, L. (1978). Quantity and quality of creative thinking in children and adolescents. *Child Development, 49,* 385-388.

Milgram, R.M., Moran, J.D., III, Sawyers, J.K., & Fu, V. (1987). Original thinking in Israeli preschool children. *School Psychology International, 8,* 54-58.

Myers, R.S., & Pace, T.M. (1986). Counseling gifted and talented students: Historical perspectives and contemporary issues. *Journal of Counseling and Development, 64,* 548-551.

Renzulli, J.S. (1978). What makes giftedness? Reexamining a definition. *Phi Delta Kappan, 60,* 180-261.

Richards, J.M., Jr., Holland, J.L., & Lutz, S.W. (1967). The predictions of student accomplishment in college. *Journal of Educational Psychology, 58,* 343-355.

Schaefer, C.E. (1969). The prediction of creative achievement from a biographical inventory. *Educational and Psychological Measurement, 29,* 431-437.

Sternberg, R.J., & Davidson, J.E. (1986). *Conceptions of giftedness.* New York: Cambridge.

Tannenbaum, A.J. (1983). *Gifted children: Psychological and Educational perspectives.* New York: Macmillan.

Terman, L.M. (1925). *Genetic studies of genius: Mental and physical traits of a thousand gifted children.* Stanford, CA: Stanford University Press.

Terman, L.M., & Oden, M.H. (1947). *Genetic studies of genius: Vol. 4. The gifted child grows up: Twenty-five years follow-up of a superior group.* Stanford, CA: Stanford University Press.

Terman, L.M., & Oden, M.H. (1959). *Genetic studies of genius: Vol. 4. The gifted child at mid-life: Thirty-five years follow-up of the superior child.* Stanford, CA: Stanford University Press.

Wallach, M.A. (1970). Creativity. In P.H. Mussen (Ed.), *Carmichael's manual of child psychology, Vol. 1* (3rd ed., pp. 1211-1272). New York: Wiley.

Wallach, M.A., & Wing, C.W., Jr. (1969). *The talented student: A validation of the creativity-intelligence distinction.* New York: Holt, Rinehart, & Winston.

Wing, C.W., Jr., & Wallach, M.A. (1971). *College admissions and the psychology of talent.* New York: Holt, Rinehart, & Winston.

VanTassel-Baska, J. (1983). *A practical guide to counseling the gifted in a school setting.* Reston, VA: The Council for Exceptional Children.

Chapter 2
Special Education Options For Gifted and Talented Learners

Roberta M. Milgram
Ellen B. Goldring

The goal of this chapter is to provide counselors and teachers with information on special education options used with gifted and talented learners and to compare their relative efficacy.

In the 1970s a pluralistic definition of giftedness was adopted by the United States Office of Education, and enacted into law by the Congress of the United States in the Gifted and Talented Children's Act of 1978. The definition reads as follows:

> The term gifted and talented children means children—and whenever applicable, youth—who are identified at the preschool, elementary, or secondary level as possessing demonstrated or potential abilities that give evidence of high performance capability in areas such as intellectual, creative, specific academic, or leadership ability, or in the performing and visual arts, and who by reason thereof, require services or activities not ordinarily provided by the school. (Sec. 902)

This definition firmly established gifted learners as "exceptional," that is, children whose physical, intellectual, or social-emotional development differs significantly from the norm. It also recognizes that gifted learners are similar to the other exceptional learners such as partially sighted, blind, deaf, learning disabled, and retarded children in that to maximize their potential achievement in school they require special education, that is, services or activities in addition to or in place of those generally offered by the school.

With the prestige of federal law behind it, this definition of giftedness was widely accepted. This broad view of giftedness was a clear step forward, as was the recognition that gifted and talented learners require additional educational activities or services in order to realize their full potential. The federally legislated, agreed-upon definition of giftedness led to a proliferation of legislation requiring states to provide special education for gifted and talented learners. By 1978, 42 states in the U.S. had either enacted legislation, or published regulations or guidelines based, for the most part, upon the U.S. Office of Education definition of giftedness (Karnes & Collins, 1978).

The exact nature of the services or activities to be provided for gifted and talented learners was not specified by law, but was left, instead, to the discretion of school administrators and school boards. Accordingly, a wide variety of administrative arrangements were developed to provide special education for gifted and talented learners (Fox & Washington, 1985). Policy makers and administrators, teachers and counselors were faced with the challenge of selecting one or more program options from among the plethora of those available to provide for the special needs of gifted and talented children.

The alternative administrative arrangements used in the education of gifted learners are often referred to in the professional literature as delivery systems. The term delivery systems is especially useful because it reflects the importance of distinguishing between issues related to what is taught (curriculum materials), how material is taught (the teaching-learning process), and issues relevant to where and in what organizational framework special education is provided for gifted and talented children (delivery systems). The concept of delivery systems helps us to bear in mind that special education for the gifted can take many forms. It can range from special schools where gifted children are educated in a completely segregated residential setting, to mainstreaming where special education is provided for gifted children entirely within the regular classroom. There is no necessary connection between a specific approach to curriculum and instruction and a particular delivery system. For example, one could provide radical acceleration in the regular classroom, the full-time special school, or by means of concurrent university enrollment (cf. Fox & Washington, 1985; Fox, 1979, 1981).

A recurrent theme of this book is that gifted learners differ widely in the type and level of their special abilities, in their level of motivation, learning styles, and other personal-social characteristics. When making decisions about special education options, counselors must consider each learner's cognitive abilities and personal-social profile. No one delivery system is the obvious choice as best. No one delivery system will assure that the needs of gifted children of all types and in all subjects are met effectively and efficiently. Only by using an individual approach is it possible to determine which of the available special education program options best meet the needs of a particular gifted or talented child.

Decisions about which delivery systems are implemented in a community are the result of the complex interaction of philosophical, social, and practical considerations. In the final analysis, however, decisions about where and in what framework a particular gifted child will receive special education will be influenced most by his/her own perception of the relative advantages and desirability of the special education opportunities that are available. These decisions are frequently influenced by the views of parents, regular classroom teachers, and counselors.

Counselors can help gifted learners, their parents, and teachers make wise educational choices by providing ongoing, systematic, specific, up-to-date information on the opportunities for special education available in the community. Counselors should build a resource collection of selected books, newspaper articles, and current periodicals on giftedness, as well as descriptive materials about program options. Parents of gifted and talented pupils are often willing to help with this project. In addition, counselors can plan meetings for parents and/or teachers devoted entirely to this topic. Another efficient and effective way to accomplish the task of providing information on delivery systems is to include discussion of the options available in a given community as part of an ongoing series of discussion groups conducted for parents and teachers such as those described by Meckstroth in Chapter 6 of the current volume. The focus on discussions of real-world alternatives recommended here is consonant with the counseling approach recommended by VanTassel-Baska in Chapter 3. She stresses the importance of recognizing "that gifted students respond better to stimuli that are offered in an intellectual framework that provides a context and a system of understanding rather than the piecemeal approach frequently typified by one-to-one counseling experiences in school."

The remainder of this chapter is divided into three sections. In the first, we list and define the 10 distinct delivery systems used in the United States and throughout the world. In the second section, we discuss the relative advantages and disadvantages of the various delivery systems and cite those delivery systems that offer exceptional promise or pose special problems. In the third section we conclude with comments on several innovative and especially promising special education options for gifted learners.

TEN DELIVERY SYSTEMS

Questions about delivery systems, that is, where and in what organizational framework special education will be provided for gifted learners are distinct concerns worthy of attention in their own right. Before focusing attention on the various delivery systems in greater detail, one caveat is in order. Issues relating to delivery systems are frequently confounded with controversies about definition of giftedness or acceleration versus enrichment as instructional or curriculum models. Special education can be provided for gifted learners of any type and level in any delivery system option. One encounters both product-oriented program goals of acceleration of progress through the curriculum and process-oriented goals of enriching and supplementing the learner's experiences in any one of the 10 delivery systems to be discussed below. One cannot state categorically which delivery system is best for which learners. The degree to which the needs of individual gifted learners are met in a given delivery system is determined by the specific requirements of the learner and the particular characteristics of the delivery system.

The 10 types of delivery systems most frequently used to provide special education for gifted and talented children are listed and defined below. The delivery systems can be divided into two major categories, replacement systems and supplementary systems. The six delivery systems in the first, replacement category, are those offered during the regular school day, that is in place of regular school hours for varying amounts of time. The four delivery systems in the second, supplementary category are offered in addition to regular school hours.

Replacement Systems

1. Enrichment or acceleration in the regular classroom. The regular classroom teacher and/or a teacher with special training in individualized instruction for the gifted provide for the individual needs of gifted children within the setting of the regular classroom. Independent Study is one of the major approaches used in this delivery system.

2. Special classes: Part-time/pull-out. Gifted students receive most of their instruction in heterogeneous classrooms and are "pulled-out" to study with other gifted children in a special class for a portion of the school day or week. The children may meet with the special education teacher in resource rooms in their own school building where they are provided with individual and/or small-group instruction, or they may travel by bus to the part-time special class held in a central location. Children may spend from one hour to a full day each week in the pull-out class.

3. Special classes. This is sometimes referred to as the satellite school-within-a-school approach. One or more classes within a regular school are designated for the exclusive purpose of providing special education for children of high overall general intellectual ability and scholastic achievement. These classes are generally full-time at the elementary school level and similar to special schools in philosophy and practice. They are generally characterized by selective admissions based mainly upon high intelligence test scores and grades. The degree of participation of gifted students with the regular school varies from almost total to nearly none, with the norm being participation in social events and nonacademic subjects. At the secondary school level special classes are frequently offered on a part-time basis. For example, advanced placement and fast-paced classes would fall into this category.

4. Full-time special schools. An entire school is designated for the exclusive purpose of providing special education for children of high general intellectual ability and scholastic achievement. These schools are usually characterized by selective admissions based mainly upon high intelligence test scores and grades. Some full-time special schools allow for continuous-progress and/or are nongraded. Gifted learners advance as they master curriculum content and skills, and traditional age-grade labels are not used.

5. Full-time specialized school. These schools are often referred to as *magnet schools.* They are designed to offer special opportunities for enrichment and/or acceleration to children of high ability in a specific academic discipline (e.g., mathematics, science, computer) or with special talents (e.g., music, drama, art). These are special, often single purpose, schools characterized by selective admissions based upon specific criteria.

6. Full-and part-time special schools: Residential. An entire residential school is designated for the exclusive purpose of providing special education for gifted and/or talented children. This is most commonly found on university campuses during the summer.

Supplementary systems

There are four types of delivery services that *supplement* regular school hours, used to provide special education to gifted and talented children.

1. Concurrent or dual university enrollment. Pupils who are profoundly gifted in a specific academic discipline, usually mathematics or science, are offered the opportunity for radical acceleration in that discipline by means of enrollment in one or more university courses. This system is referred to as dual or concurrent because the pupils are enrolled in the university part-time while still enrolled full-time in a regular or special class setting.

2. Classes sponsored by universities: Afternoon, weekend, summer, vacation periods. Classes designed to provide the opportunity for enrichment and/or acceleration for children of high overall general intellectual ability and scholastic achievement and/or for children of high ability in a specific academic discipline (e.g., mathematics, science, computer).

3. *Classes in public settings: Afternoon, weekend, summer, vacation periods.* Classes designed to provide the opportunity for enrichment and/or acceleration for children of high overall general intellectual ability and scholastic achievement and/or for children of high ability in a specific discipline. These classes often meet in public schools or other municipal facilities and are under the administrative responsibility of the local school district and/or the municipality.

4. *Internships and mentor programs.* This is a system of providing practical career and real world experience in a setting outside the classroom. Internships are, by definition, more limited in nature than mentor arrangements. Internships are domain-specific apprentice experiences in which the learner has the opportunity to receive guidance and supervision as he/she performs specific learning tasks. Mentorships, by contrast, are relationships between a young learner and a wise and trusted friend. It also involves real-world career experience, but is not limited to specific tasks, subject matter, or situations. The mentor-mentee relationship is more generalized and pervasive.

RELATIVE EFFICACY OF DELIVERY SYSTEMS

Since counselors will be advising both gifted students and their parents about delivery systems, it is important that they are familiar with the discussions regarding the efficacy of the delivery systems. There has been considerable legitimate debate regarding the relative merit of the various delivery systems. Overall empirical evidence comparing delivery systems is sparse. Two basic reasons may explain this lack of empirical study. First, there is a confounding of the definitions of the different delivery systems. For example, what one researcher calls mainstreaming, another researcher calls intraclass grouping. This problem is not merely one of semantics. When educators do not use consistent terminology it is difficult to know what program is being described. Second, there is difficulty in conducting research in this area. Many districts employ one delivery system and, therefore, there is no comparison group, other than gifted students who receive no treatment. For example, Kulik and Kulik (1984) conducted a metaanalysis on the acceleration and enrichment of gifted and talented students. They synthesized the results of 26 studies which compared accelerated gifted students with same-age controls and with older controls. It was not surprising when they found that "acceleration contributes to student achievement" only as far as same-age controls are concerned (p. 26). A similar result was found in regard to enrichment. It is totally unclear who the gifted students in the control groups were, why they did not receive acceleration and enrichment (perhaps they were not equally as gifted?) and if they were receiving any type of gifted education.

Given the unclear empirical evidence regarding the efficacy of the various delivery systems, the counselor must be knowledgeable about the advantages and disadvantages of the delivery systems offered in his/her local school community. In the next section we outline some of the crucial areas where counselors need to direct their attention when advising students, parents, and teachers.

Segregated versus integrated settings. There are contradictory opinions regarding the desirability of providing special education to gifted children in segregated settings, such as special schools or classes. Some educators maintain that the special needs of gifted students can best be met in special classes where the appropriate intellectual stimulation and challenges can be offered (Ward, 1975). Opponents of special classes claim that the isolation of gifted children from their nongifted peers can lead to negative effects such as a lack of emotional adjustment, loss of neighborhood friends, and a lower self-concept (Zilly, 1971).

The segregation-integration question was examined in a recent metaanalytic study (Goldring, 1987). Synthesizing the results of 23 empirical studies, the metaanalysis indicated that high IQ-type gifted students in special, homogeneous classes perform better than their gifted mainstreamed peers. However, this general conclusion must be viewed with care. First, the advantage for gifted students in special classes is greatest in science and social studies with the smallest advantage in writing and reading. Second, the gifted in special classes exhibited better attitudes toward school, but they did not indicate higher self-concepts, more creativity or more positive attitudes towards peers than gifted in regular classrooms. Third, the majority of empirical studies comparing gifted students in special classes and regular classes suffer from weak research designs. Hence considering the quality of the component studies, it is difficult to draw conclusions based upon the results of the metaanalytic analyses with certainty. Nevertheless, the metaanalytic findings provide some empirical evidence for the efficacy of segregated full-time special class as opposed to integrated delivery systems. Full-time special classes require minimal extra cost, since children are merely receiving their budget allotment in one setting versus another.

Many of the positive and negative attitudes about full-time special classes apply to full-time special schools and to specialized (magnet) schools as well. Many educators and community leaders are especially enthusiastic about specialized or magnet schools. Proponents of the specialized schools argue that, although highly selective, they are at the same time less elitist because the criteria for admission are generally psychometric plus real-life measures of achievement rather than psychometric measures of general intelligence alone. They also claim that magnet schools serve as a natural stimulus for the integration of children from advantaged and disadvantaged backgrounds who share a high-level special ability.

"Pull-out classes." The generally positive conclusions about full-time segregated delivery systems do not extend to part-time segregated classes, usually termed pull-out programs. According to the prestigious and authoritative Richardson Report (Cox, Daniel, & Boston, 1985), the delivery system most widely used is part-time special classes (pull-out). In discussing the advantages and disadvantages of pull-out programs, Cox, Daniel, and Boston (1985) refer to pull-out programs as "a part-time solution to a full-time problem," cite the false sense of accomplishment it can provide those who initiate and implement them, and conclude with the following statement: "While many believe that the pull-out program has served well, we think that it is a model whose time has come and gone." The regular classroom teacher often views the pull-out program as disruptive and thus may be antagonistic towards the gifted child. Counselors considering recommending participation in a pull-out program to a particular gifted child must continually consider the effect of it on the child's relationships with his/her regular classroom teacher and age peers.

The part-time special class (pull-out) is not only the least effective but it is also the most expensive delivery system. The cost of educating the gifted child in the regular classroom is not reduced and the cost of his special education in the part-time special class is added. It should be noted that in some instances, such as in sparsely populated areas within a large geographic region, pull-out programs may be a viable delivery system for education for the gifted.

Mainstreaming. Teaching gifted students in the regular classroom is an important delivery system. Mainstreaming or enrichment/acceleration in regular classrooms is the delivery system reported as the second most frequently used (Cox, Daniel, & Boston, 1985). One could interpret this finding as a very encouraging sign that the needs of gifted children are indeed being met within the framework of the regular classroom. Unfortunately, such is not the case. When the investigators wisely distinguished in their analysis according to whether a program option was merely "present" versus whether the district had a "substantial" program of the type described in each case, the findings were quite different. Enrichment in regular classrooms emerged as an infrequent rather than a frequently found program option. Only 16 percent of the districts reported having "substantial" programs of enrichment in regular classrooms as compared with the 62 percent that reported this program option being present at all.

This situation is unfortunate because enrichment within the regular classroom is a program option with many advantages (Milgram, 1989). This approach can provide for the needs of gifted and talented learners of all types, especially at the younger age levels. The within-regular-class approach is also the program option least likely to elicit hostility and opposition from parents, teachers, and school boards. Some of the advantages of providing for the needs of gifted learners within the framework of regular classrooms are as follows:

1. An impressive literature and body of materials has accumulated and is available to the teacher to be used in the process of differentiation of curriculum and individualization of teaching strategies.

2. The methods and materials used by teachers to enrich and/or accelerate the education of children by providing a differentiated curriculum and individualized learning experiences are immediately beneficial to other children in the classroom. The teacher who learns how to individualize instruction for the fast-learner is at the same time learning how to best deal with the problems of the slow learner. The provision of "learning centers" within classrooms will provide enrichment possibilities for all children, those identified as gifted and those not so identified. The expenditure of large sums for the special education of a small number of gifted children is frequently justified by saying that the methods and materials developed for teaching the gifted and talented learners will "radiate" to the rest of the school community and that ultimately many pupils will benefit from the developments funded. It is difficult to see how radiation can take place between the segregated schools for gifted learners and the remaining schools in a district. When special education for the gifted takes place in the integrated setting of the regular classroom, by contrast, "radiation" is immediate and almost automatic.

3. No special school or class can meet the needs of all the different types and levels of gifted and talented learners. Since gifted children are rarely gifted equally in all subjects, individualization of instruction offers special education exactly where it is required.

4. Some other children, not identified as gifted, may nevertheless share some of the interests and abilities of the child identified as gifted. When learning is individualized in the regular classroom, it is possible to plan individual, paired, and small-group instruction.

5. Some children are underserved because of where they live. More special education is being provided for children who live in the large

urban areas and environs than for those who live in rural areas in communities relatively far from the large urban areas. Enrichment in regular classrooms is one method of redressing this imbalance in opportunities.

6. Mainstreaming gifted students is independent of budget constraints, such as the availability of a specialist in gifted education in each school.

The effectiveness of mainstreaming gifted students is largely dependent upon the regular classroom teacher. Regular teachers must have inservice training and be given curriculum materials to teach the gifted student in the classroom. Carefully planned teaching strategies with clear goals must be emphasized in the mainstreamed class. Ebmeier, Dyche, Taylor, and Hall (1985) studied the impact of an inservice program where regular classroom teachers were trained to use curriculum materials for gifted education students. The results indicated that the gifted students taught by regular teachers achieved similar cognitive gains to those students taught by gifted specialists.

Supplementary systems. Other delivery systems which are relatively easy to administer are afternoon classes and concurrent university enrollment. Afternoon classes are deemed a popular, successful delivery system because they are easy to set up, easy to run, and they have no administrative conflict with the regular school system. One important advantage of classes sponsored by universities is that these programs operate under the academic supervision of the sponsoring university. Dual enrollment, that is, learning both in a regular school and a university simultaneously, offers unique challenges to gifted students, although its effectiveness depends upon coordination and cooperation between the two institutions. For example, the Richardson Report (Cox et al., 1985) cites problems of reconciling college credits with the high school diploma.

To sum up, mainstreaming is the delivery system that, although used very little at the current time, offers the most promise for the future. A certain limited degree of effectiveness has been demonstrated for full-time special schools and classes and specialized schools. The system that poses a special problem is the part-time special class (pull-out). Some of the advantages and disadvantages of the delivery systems discussed above are summarized in Table 2.1 (Kramer, 1980).

Numerous investigators have cited the paucity of empirical evidence on the outcomes and consequences of the various program options (Fox & Washington, 1985). The few studies that have been conducted have been limited to high-IQ type gifted learners and have been characterized by many methodological weaknesses. There is very little evidence verifying claims for the superiority of one delivery system over another in teaching gifted children of high overall intellectual ability. There is

Table 2.1. Advantages and Disadvantages of Delivery Systems*

Delivery System	Advantages	Disadvantages
Full-time *Replacement systems* (i.e., special classes)	-high level of academic achievement easier to maintain -provides intensive challenge and motivation opportunities -adaptable to needs of gifted and receptive to innovation	-requires taking students out of regular classrooms -accentuates distinction between gifted and nongifted -not possible to implement in all types of communities due to insufficient population base
Mainstreaming	-modifications built into child's normal learning environment -makes significant progress, within neighborhood school context -allows gifted programming to be used as vehicle for introducing new approaches for all children in class -highly accepted by others	-usually not sufficient for the extremely gifted -does not provide gifted with intellectual peer group -requires full system commitment to change, including training of teachers, principals, etc.
Supplementary systems (i.e., afternoon programs)	-creates intellectual peer group at least part of the time -requires virtually no institutional commitment or change -makes good use of outside community resources	-has little impact on daily learning experiences of gifted -dependent on outside agencies' little supervision of programs -requires parent financing: discriminates against economically disadvantaged

* Adapted from Kramer, A. (1980).

no evidence at all about which delivery system is the most effective for the other types of gifted learners. Accordingly, counselors would do well to use extreme caution in recommending replacement-type options that are conducted outside of the framework of the regular classroom. They should probably emphasize recommendations and referrals that emphasize supplementary-type options and mainstreaming.

PROMISING OPTIONS

We recommend the use of delivery systems that provide maximum opportunity for all children to be exposed to experiences in a wide variety of academic disciplines and spheres of talent. Children should be given the opportunity for continuous preparation and presentation of individual and group products in their areas of interest. The products will reflect both baseline interests, abilities, and motivation as well as growth and progress. Teachers in regular classrooms can provide a wide range of experiences by means of differentiation of curriculum, individualization of instruction, and creation of an overall creative atmosphere in the classroom. The rationale for this approach as well as specific guidelines for its implementation are described in detail by Milgram (1989). Innovative exemplars that reflect the recommended approach have been suggested in this volume (see Chapter 9) and elsewhere (Milgram, 1989). In these program options one or more teacher-consultants cooperate with the regular classroom teacher in meeting the challenge presented by gifted learners in their classrooms. The goal of both models is to provide all children with an early and an equal opportunity to systematically develop interests, abilities, and talents that diverge from the norm and require special attention in order to be fully realized.

One delivery system cited briefly above should be singled out for special attention—mentorships and internships. The mentor relationship is certainly, historically, the oldest of the delivery systems. The concept is based upon the relationship between Mentor and Telemachus, Odysseus' son, described by Homer in the Odyssey. The mentor–intern approach has been cited as particularly promising by Cox, Daniel, and Boston (1985). These authors distinguished between internships and mentorships. Internships are more circumscribed, domain-specific, career-oriented experiences and mentorships are more general, "functionally diffuse" relationships. The theoretical foundation and the practical operation of internship programs are described by Hirsch (1976) and of mentor programs by Runions (1980).

Many highly gifted adults attributed great importance to mentor influences (Albert & Runco, 1986, 1987; Bloom, 1985; Cox, Daniel, & Boston, 1985). Nevertheless, very little use has actually been made of the approach in the field. Gold (1979) cited the paucity of references to mentor programs in the literature of giftedness. He reported very few systematic efforts of school systems to use community mentors in their gifted education programs. One of the main reasons the approach, seen as so promising, is actually rarely used in practice is the administrative difficulty of implementing mentor programs (Gallegher, 1975).

Gray (1983) devised an interesting variation. He developed a unique approach to challenging gifted and talented learners through mentor-assisted projects conducted within the framework of regular classrooms. He organized a program in which preservice teachers received course credit and acquired valuable experience by serving as mentors for able learners in regular classrooms.

Realization of the goal of providing for the needs of gifted and talented learners with widely diverse interests and abilities within the framework of the regular classroom will require a major shift in policy and in budgetary priorities in most communities. Particular attention must be given to preservice and inservice training for counselors, regular classroom teachers, and teacher-consultants rather than to identification by means of psychometric procedures.

In a democratic society a prime concern is to provide equal education opportunity to all children. In light of the vast individual differences among children, offering the same education to all children does not provide equal educational opportunity. The challenge that faces school counselors is to be knowledgeable of the special education opportunities available in a specific school district and to help the children and their parents decide which of those available best meets their needs.

References

Albert, R.S., & Runco, M.A. (1986). The achievement of eminence: A model based on a longitudinal study of exceptionally gifted boys and their families. In R.J. Sternberg & J.E. Davidson (Eds.), *Conceptions of giftedness* (pp. 323-357). New York: Cambridge University Press.

Albert, R.S., & Runco, M.A. (1987). The possible different personality dispositions of scientists and nonscientists. In D. Jackson & J.P. Rushton (Eds.), *Scientific excellence: Origins and assessment* (pp. 67-97). Beverly Hills, CA: Sage Publications.

Bloom, B.S. (1985). *Developing talent in young people*. New York: Ballantine Books.

Cox, J., Daniel, N., & Boston, B.O. (1985). *Educating able learners: Programs and promising practices*. Austin, TX: University of Texas Press.

Ebmeier, H., Dyche B., Taylor, P., & Hall, M. (1985). An empirical comparison of two program models for elementary gifted education. *Gifted Child Quarterly, 29,* 15-19.

Fox, L.H. (1979). Programs for the gifted and talented: An overview. In A.H. Passow (Ed.), *The gifted and the talented: Their education and development* (pp. 104-126). Chicago: University of Chicago Press.

Fox, L.H. (1981). Instruction for the gifted: Some promising practices. *Journal for the Education of the Gifted, 4,* 246-254.

Fox, L.H., & Washington, J. (1985). Programs for the gifted and talented: Past, present, and future. In F.D. Horowitz & M. O'Brien (Eds.), *The gifted and talented: Developmental perspectives* (pp. 197-221). Washington, DC: American Psychological Association.

Gallegher, J.J. (1975). *Teaching the gifted child* (2nd ed.). Boston: Allyn and Bacon.

Gold, M.J. (1979). Teachers and mentors. In A.H. Passow (Ed.), *The gifted and the talented: Their education and development* (pp. 272-288). Chicago, IL: National Society for the Study of Education.

Goldring, E. (1987). *A meta-analysis of classroom organizational frameworks for gifted education students.* Paper presented at the annual meeting of the American Educational Research Association, Washington, DC.

Gray, W.A. (1983). *Challenging the gifted and talented through mentor-assisted enrichment projects.* Bloomington, IN: Phi Delta Kappa Educational Foundation.

Hirsch, P. (1976). Executive high school internships: A boon for the gifted and talented. *Teaching Exceptional Children, 9,* 22-23.

Karnes, F.A., & Collins, E.C. (1978). State definitions on the gifted and talented: A report and analysis. *Journal for the Education of The Gifted, 1,* 44-62.

Kramer, A. (1980). *Position paper of programming for gifted children.* Presented to the Israel Ministry of Education, Jerusalem.

Kulik, J.A., & Kulik, C.C. (1984). *Meta-analysis of evaluation findings on education of gifted and talented students.* Center for Research on Teaching and Learning, University of Michigan, Ann Arbor, MI.

Milgram, R.M. (Ed.). (1989). *Teaching gifted and talented learners in regular classrooms.* Springfield, IL: Charles C. Thomas.

Runions, T. (1980). The mentor academy program: Educating the gifted and talented for the 80's. *Gifted Child Quarterly, 24,* 152-157.

Ward, V.S. (1975). Program organization and implementation. In W.B. Barbe & J.S. Renzulli (Eds.), *The psychology and education of the gifted.* New York: Irvington.

Zilly, M.G. (1971). Reasons why the gifted adolescent underachieves and some of the implications of guidance and counseling to this problem. *Gifted Child Quarterly, 15,* 279-292.

Chapter 3
Teachers as Counselors for Gifted Students

Joyce VanTassel-Baska

Everyone involved in the special education of gifted children readily acknowledges their need for counseling. Nevertheless, it is rarely provided. Special needs populations like the gifted are not seen as prime candidates for mainstream counseling in our schools because of the strong emphasis on traditional "problem" students as a focus for counselor time.

In a recent survey of the attitudes of 200 parents of the gifted (VanTassel-Baska, 1987), only 9 percent reported receiving any counseling services from schools, while 68 percent rated the need for counseling services for their middle school-aged gifted children as the most critical school-related service they might receive.

The implications of this situation for the gifted are dire indeed, as they are for the majority of students in our schools. What it means is that no real counseling function is being provided for gifted students during their K-12 years in schools. It means that a gifted student who shows no severe outward manifestation of problem behavior will not receive counseling; a student whose academic program should be atypical will receive no assistance, and a student who wishes to consider college alternatives will be given a reference book.

Many individual counselors offer highly specialized services such as test taking, selecting a college, planning a program of study, and dealing with psychosocial concerns on a private basis. Since there is little expectation that either the schools or they as parents can provide such help, families who are financially able and live in a proximate geographic area to such services frequently use them. But what about the large number of gifted students in our public schools whose families cannot afford such services or who live in areas of the country where they are not available? What about these gifted students?

Much of the work in the education of the gifted has focused on differential characteristics and needs of the population. Affective differences as well as cognitive ones become the focal point for creating special counseling interventions which may be viewed as critical in three specific areas: psychosocial, academic, and career/life planning. Table 3.1 (Feldhusen, VanTassel-Baska, & Seeley, 1989) depicts the relationship between characteristics of a gifted population and the counseling approach necessary to address it.

In their authoritative and comprehensive summary of the literature on the psychosocial characteristics of gifted children, Janos and Robinson (1985) concluded that gifted children as a group possess more positive personal-social characteristics than their nongifted peers. Nevertheless, an individual gifted child that manifests such characteristics as those listed above to an intense degree is likely to suffer in various ways without appropriate counseling intervention. The nature of such suffering could manifest itself in (a) social isolation, either self-imposed or brought about by peer ostracism; (b) social accommodation, by creating a reversal or homogenization of the gifted characteristics, or (c) social acceptance-seeking by denying that the giftedness exists and finding ways to diminish its influence. Any of these conditions can result in a deleterious situation for a gifted child, with respect to himself

Table 3.1. Characteristics of gifted learners and related counseling approaches.

Characteristics	Counseling Provision
Cluster #1	
* ability to manipulate abstract symbol systems * retention rate * quickness to learn and master the environment	academic program planning that matches learner cognitive needs
Cluster #2	
* ability to do many things well (multipotentiality) * varied and diverse interests * internal locus of control (independence)	Life/career planning that presents atypical models
Cluster #3	
* heightened sensitivity * sense of justice * perfectionism	Psychosocial counseling that focuses on the preservation of affective differences

and his talent. Thus the nature of the gifted indicates a set of special counseling needs that extend well beyond those required for a more typical learner.

This chapter is divided into four sections. In the first section, the psychosocial needs of gifted learners and strategies for addressing them are described. In the second section, the question of who should counsel gifted children is discussed and in the third, specific teacher strategies for counseling the gifted are suggested. In the fourth section an innovative solution to the paucity of counseling services for gifted learners in the form of a partnership between school counselors and teachers of the gifted is presented.

PSYCHOSOCIAL NEEDS OF THE GIFTED AND STRATEGIES FOR ADDRESSING THEM

In our society, systematic exploration of feelings is limited to two areas of study: (a) literature and the arts and (b) various forms of psychotherapy. It is little wonder then that the gifted student is lacking counseling support, particularly as it relates to his feelings about himself, others, and the world around him. Some educators have argued that the gifted do not have differential counseling needs in the affective area but that the nature of their needs mirror those of more typical children. On the other hand, differential affective characteristics have been attributed to the gifted (Clarke, 1980; Piechowski, 1979; Silverman, 1983, 1987) and do, in my opinion, exist. It is a challenge to educators and parents of gifted children to work effectively with differences in the nature and degree of feelings that emerge. Table 3.2 (Feldhusen, VanTassel-Baska, & Seeley, 1989) presents a synthesis of five key social-emotional needs of the gifted that phenomenologically differ from those of more typical students. A strategy for addressing each of the five is also included for educators and parents to consider for implementation in a conducive setting.

Affective curricula have also been developed (Beville, 1983) which address key concerns such a perfectionism, tolerance, and social relationships. Delisle (1980) developed a prevention program which revolves around four key problems of the gifted:

Problem #1: Problems associated with realizing the nature and significance of intellectual differences and the accompanying feelings of inferiority and inadequacy.

Problem #2: Problems associated with social alienation or discomfort due to dissatisfaction with the frequency and merit of interpersonal relationships.

Table 3.2.

Social-Emotional Need	Strategies to Address Such Needs
* To understand the ways in which they are different from other children and the ways in which they are the same	* Use bibliotherapy techniques * Establish group discussion seminars * Hold individual dialogue sessions
* To appreciate and treasure their own individuality and the individual differences of others	* Promote biography study * Honor diverse talents through awards, performance sessions, special seminars, and symposia * Encourage contest and competitive entry
* To understand and develop social skills that allow them to cope adequately within relationships	* Do creative problem solving in dyads and small groups * Create role-playing scenarios * Devise appropriate simulation activities
* To develop an appreciation for their high-level sensitivity that manifest itself in humor, artistic endeavors, and intensified emotional experiences	* Encourage positive and expressive outlets for sensitivity such as: tutoring, volunteer work, art, music, and drama * Promote journal writing that captures feelings about key experiences
* To gain a realistic assessment of their ability and talents and how they can be nurtured * To develop an understanding of the distinction between "pursuit of excellence" and "pursuit of perfection"	* Provide for regular assessment procedures * Provide for grouping opportunities with others of similar abilities and interests * Create a "safe" environment to experiment with failure * Promote risk-taking behavior
* To learn the art and science of compromise	* Provide "cooperation games" * Work on goal-setting * Encourage the development of a philosophy of life

    Problem #3: Problems associated with a dull and meager school curriculum that provides little academic sustenance.

    Problem #4: Problems associated with locating and pursuing occupational and educational choices commensurate with the gifted child's interests and abilities (pp. 22–23).

    Delisle (1980) also presented activities designed to increase awareness of each problem area: discussion questions, books, films, cartoons, brainstorming activities, and quotations. An example of the activities follows:

- Communicate a series of goals that you expect to achieve and a series of goals that others expect you to achieve
- Compare these expectations;
- Rate the financial, societal, and emotional benefits of each expectation (Delisle 1980, p. 24).

Such resources as these can be useful in implementing a counseling program for the gifted.

WHO SHOULD COUNSEL THE GIFTED? PARENTS, COUNSELORS, TEACHERS, TEACHERS OF THE GIFTED

Parents. The nature of today's family—both parents working full-time with increasing frequency—obviates against the likelihood of parents performing a viable counseling role for the children without special help and encouragement. Parents are generally uninformed or misinformed about key issues with which their gifted children may need assistance. For example, fear of being different is a common complaint of early adolescence. How does a gifted student handle a type of difference that needs to be preserved at a stage of life when most adolescents are trying to obliterate such distinctions? Understanding rather than conforming parents are needed to ease the trauma, yet many parents of the gifted counsel their children to follow the social norms rather than to buck them.

Parents who are disadvantaged based on socioeconomic conditions may inadvertently doom their gifted children to a similar status in life. Gifted students who do not continue their education are much less likely to garner incomes later in life commensurate with their ability than their more educated peers (Crouse, 1979). Students who come from blue-collar homes are at risk for their educational futures partially because of seeing parents as role models, but also because of the parents' narrow sense of what is educationally necessary.

Parents frequently are early role models for their offspring, and such a situation breeds both positive and negative consequences. For professional parents, it may create a climate for children where the home becomes an educational center or at least an extension of school. It places a burden on such children to perform at the preconceived levels set by their parents, many times including a choice of careers. Thus students are preempted in making life choices at critical stages of development. For nonprofessional parents, parental role modeling may lower aspiration levels for gifted children unrealistically, keeping them from the pursuit of advanced degrees and concomitant professional careers. However, it can also allow the gifted child a certain freedom "to be" rather than "to perform," to play as a child rather than to be overscheduled for all sorts of enriching, private lessons.

Parents of gifted girls, regardless of SES status, are rarely cognizant of how their needs and aspirations will be played out differently from those of boys, and the special nurturing that is required to deal with such realities. The question for gifted girls is no longer: Shall I get married and raise a family or have a career? Rather it is more likely to be: How can I best organize my life to meet my needs for personal intimacy, children, *and* a career? Models are currently lacking to answer this latter question; thus clarification of personal expectations and an idea of concurrent or serial approaches to viewing the problem may be useful for parents to consider.

Counselors. We may realistically expect school counselors to provide some counseling to the gifted. It is unrealistic, however, to expect them to make this a major focus of their work. There are very good reasons for this. A counselor load in most school systems ranges from 300 to 500 students. To do a decent job with these numbers of students requires a yeoman effort. Working with the gifted under such circumstances is clearly perceived as an added responsibility with even more students to supervise. Another deterrent to gifted students receiving the required counseling services is the lack of counselors in elementary schools. In these settings, only teachers and occasionally a principal are available to perform the needed functions. The major problem, however, relates to a lack of understanding of the nature of the counseling needed by gifted students. This book, in general, and the current chapter, more specifically, are designed to contribute to understanding this problem and to suggest ways to cope with it.

Some general strategies that counselors could use to help meet many of the delineated social-emotional needs of the gifted might include:

1. The establishment of a counseling consortium within a school district or across districts on a cooperative basis that is made up of mental health specialists in the community, social workers, psychologists, and counselors. Such a consortium would be available to individual students and families as needed on a case basis. A hotline might be established for purposes of crisis intervention.

2. The establishment of parent education services that focus on the socioemotional and related counseling needs of their children. Speakers, group discussion, and case study problem solving comprise three viable approaches to organizing such efforts. Pure informational sessions could be included with sessions that are problem solving in nature.

The critical role of parents in the development of giftedness and its realizations has been highlighted in the literature (Albert, 1983; Albert

& Runco, 1986; Bloom, 1985). Several chapters in the current volume treat the topic in depth (see Chapters 5, 6, and 8, respectively). Many parents of gifted children need assistance in helping their children realize the opportunities they have as a result of their special abilities and interests. One major way that counselors can help gifted learners is by organizing parent support groups. Readers interested in a detailed discussion of how to organize and conduct parent groups are referred to Chapter 6 in this volume.

3. The establishment of student counseling seminars that deal with gifted students in a group context. Organized and run by a designated teacher or counselor, such sessions can be planned at least monthly and focus on the specific needs delineated earlier in this chapter. Using gifted students in the planning and implementation of such seminars heightens their effectiveness.

4. The establishment of in-service seminars for regular classroom teachers that offer information on the nature of giftedness, the cognitive and affective needs of gifted learners of different kinds, and discussion of strategies for meeting these needs within the framework of the regular classroom.

Typically, the role of the counselor at middle school and high school levels has deteriorated to performing routine functions such as scheduling, attendance, the follow-up referral cases, usually students who have challenged the system by truancy, maladaptive classroom behavior, and substance use. Thus the classical definition of a counselor as "one who guides" has been replaced by "one who responds to institutional demands."

School counselors may derive a good deal of satisfaction in helping gifted learners maximize their potential abilities. Within the limits of the situation that currently exists in most schools, counselors will probably be most successful in their efforts on behalf of gifted children by working with groups of children, parents, classroom teachers, and teachers who have the responsibility of providing supplementary or replacement types of special education to gifted learners. We have thus far discussed issues related to counseling gifted children and their parents. In the remainder of the chapter, we will deal with the ways in which counselors can best use the limited amount of time that they can realistically budget for helping gifted children by working with groups of regular classroom teachers and with teachers of the gifted.

SPECIFIC TEACHER STRATEGIES FOR COUNSELING THE GIFTED

In the psychosocial domain, teachers are in an excellent position to provide guidance to students in several areas of general concern. These guidance techniques may be seen as integral to other teaching and learning activities that are taking place in the classroom. They may be used profitably by either regular classroom teachers or teachers of the gifted.

Deliberately choosing books that have a gifted child as protagonist is an excellent way to begin to have students identifying some of their problems in others. Thus through discussion gifted students can come to new awareness about how to cope with such problems. One such example follows:

> Problem identified: Understanding differences
> Book: Lord of the Flies
> Key questions:
> "Why was Piggy ostracized by the group?
> "What might he have done to prevent such treatment?"
> "What happens to people who feel rejected, according to the author?
> "Can you think of a time when you have felt rejected? How did you respond or react? How might you have changed your behavior to obtain more favorable results?
> (Write individually and then discuss as a group)

An excellent teacher reference for this type of activity is a booklist from the National Council of Teachers of English entitled *The Gifted Child in Literature.*

The establishment of educational therapy techniques also constitutes a general approach that schools can use in addressing socioemotional issues. The strategies of bibliotherapy, biography, and journal writing all can serve dual purposes. They are valid curricular devices within programs for the gifted, but they are carefully structured to provide a context for students to discuss feelings, as well as ideas. Instructional strategies necessary to fulfilling this purpose, however, are those of discussion and debriefing after students have read, viewed, or heard particular presentations of material. Careful Socratic questioning can draw attention to feelings evoked by the materials, and stimulate and lead students into a deeper understanding of their own and others' feelings. Use of more structured literature-based programs like Junior Great Books and Philosophy for Children also carry the potential for adaption in these areas.

A second area of psychosocial development that teachers can help the gifted explore is their sense of perfectionism. By focusing on open-ended activities and leading students to engage in "safe" risk-taking behaviors, teachers can set a climate that encourages students to accept the realization that most situations in life do not require *one* right answer, thus rendering unimportant the standard often used by gifted students to rate themselves and others on the way to "perfection." An example of such an activity follows:

Pass out pictures (the same picture for every three students) that are impressionistic in style and ask students to respond to these vital stimuli according to the following paradigm:

1. What do you observe in the picture? (Make a list of what you see.)
2. What ideas does your picture convey?
3. What feelings does your picture evoke?
4. If you were to identify with an object in your picture, what would you identify with and why?
5. Now spend a few minutes synthesizing your observations, ideas, feelings, and reactions to your picture in whatever form you wish. You may choose to write a poem, draw a picture, create a descriptive story, and so on.

After each student has responded individually to these questions and activities, have groups of three students each discuss each other's perceptions of the pictures. The instructor then may ask individual students to share their pictures and their reactions to them. Follow-up may include whole group discussion of similarities and differences among the pictures. Such an activity can also introduce a unit of study on cultural or individual differences.

A third area of exploration with the gifted is forming meaningful relationships and developing friendships. For this area of psychosocial development, the use of bibliotherapy techniques may be the most useful. Books such as *The Bunny Who Wanted a Friend,* suitable for primary age students, is a good example of a key tool. Questions like the following can be used to elicit understanding of the strategies by which we gain friends:

1. What are all the reasons that the bunny did not have a friend?
2. What was wrong with his method of making friends?
3. What was his "secret" to finally finding a friend?
4. What if you were the bunny? How would you have tried to get a friend?
5. Why were the bunny and the bird friends at the end of the story? List all the reasons.

Teachers also can develop units that focus on some of these key topics. A sample list of possible unit topics follows:

Understanding others
Tolerance
Coping with being gifted
Sensitivity
Positive uses of Humor
Forming Relationships

Each unit should include various reading material that focuses on the topic, lists of discussion questions to be used with gifted students in small groups, and follow-up projects that might be done.

Teachers as facilitators of career exploration. The suggestions presented in this section can be implemented by counselors, by teachers of the gifted, or by regular classroom teachers. Teachers can incorporate these areas into their teaching and focus on them with gifted students. Writing experiences and questioning strategies in particular are relatively easy modifications for teachers to make that can have a great impact on students directly.

By the fifth and sixth grade, gifted students need assistance with academic planning, thinking through ideas they have about careers, and pursuing areas of interest to them. Again the role of teachers is critical in shaping appropriate options. According to a memo from prestigious colleges to secondary school principals, parents, and students, there are several areas of concern regarding the lack of preparation by bright students for college. These areas include:

1. Reading at an analytical and interpretative level
2. Writing of essays
3. Solid "discipline study"
4. Essay exam opportunities
5. Critical thought and inquiry

Academic advising implies knowing what direction colleges are recommending for students to be well prepared. Background in a foreign language, for example, is a key ingredient in a talented student's profile, and yet many counseling departments ignore its importance in building programs for talented learners. The following basic program constitutes a strong academic preparation for talented learners, according to the Consortium on Higher Education (CAHE):

1. English (3 years)
2. Mathematics (3 years)
3. History (2 years)
4. Science (1 year of lab science)

5. Foreign Language (3 years of one language)
6. The Arts (study of art/music)

Exposure to atypical career models is another area of need for the gifted. Silverman (1983) has generated some key prototypes that are worthy of discussion in the classroom:

1. Delay decision making
2. Serial or concurrent careers
3. Interests as avocations
4. Multiple options
5. Synthesizing interests from many fields
6. Real life experiences for explorations
7. Creating new or unusual careers
8. Explore life themes for career choice

One example from this list, that of delayed decision making, is important for gifted students to practice. Knowing that many important individuals in various fields did not make career decisions until the end of their undergraduate experience can be meaningful information to students struggling to make a career decision early. The following activities can be used by teachers to help such students grapple with the issues:

1. Read biographies of five important people in fields you are interested in. Track the development of their careers in terms of the issue of "timing."
2. Interview someone in your area(s) of interest. Research their early decision-making patterns.
3. "Shadow" a professional in a field of interest. Analyze the most important skills they have and relate them to the educational background they received. What is the correlation?
4. Survey a group of recent college graduates from your geographical area. Include questions related to when they decided on a career direction and whether they are still pursuing that direction. Report your results.

Each of the other career prototype issues for the gifted can be similarly explored by teachers structuring appropriate activities.

VanTassel-Baska (1981) outlined a series of six strands for teachers and counselors to focus on in career planning for gifted students. These strands from kindergarten to grade 12 highlight the following areas:

1. Biography reading and discussion.
2. Small group counseling on special issues and concerns (e.g., group dynamics, life planning, coping).
3. Mentor models and independent study.
4. Individual assessment of abilities, interests, and personality attributes.
5. Academic preparation for high school and college career exploration.
6. Internship opportunities

This scope and sequence of key elements in a gifted and talented career counseling program provide emphasis on the psychosocial needs and the need for planning and decision making among the gifted population.

A PARTNERSHIP: SCHOOL COUNSELORS AND TEACHERS OF THE GIFTED

Since school counselors, regular classroom teachers, and parents are often either unavailable or unskilled in relevant counseling issues for this population, one viable delivery system alternative for providing guidance to the gifted is the teacher of the gifted. In many settings, these individuals work with gifted children for varying amounts of time in the popular "pull-out" delivery system, and see the behavior of the gifted child from an objective stance and on an ongoing basis. They also have access to groups of gifted students at a given time. Frequently, these teachers are also skilled in the nature and needs of gifted children, both cognitive and affective. Thus it appears that the teacher of the gifted may be in the best position to provide the guidance so needed by the gifted student who generally spends most of his time in the regular classroom.

Teachers of the gifted as counselors for them presents a reasonable alternative to meeting many of the gifted students' counseling needs. A segment of time each week could be set aside to attend to specific issues as well as they arise in the context of the classroom—the gifted child, frustrated at having less than a perfect paper; another gifted child, disappointed about his peers' lack of enthusiasm for a project he has shared, and another's feeling of rejection at not being selected as the "best" student. These problems frequently can be quickly diagnosed by teachers of the gifted and given effective remedy in the same environment. In many instances such teacher interventions are quite successful.

It would be highly desirable and perhaps most desirable if regular classroom teachers could provide fully for the special cognitive and affective needs of gifted children in their classrooms. It is not impossible in the light of the advanced concepts of differentiation of curriculum and individualization of teaching materials and methods. We should certainly work continually toward that goal. On the other hand, it is unlikely to occur on a large scale in the immediate future. Accordingly, we will conclude this chapter with a discussion of what may be perhaps the best realistic compromise to consider in implementing counseling programs for the gifted, that is, a partnership of school counselors and teachers of the gifted. The following lists depict the strengths of each role that can be applied to the process of counseling the gifted:

School Counselors

1. Trained in general counseling and guidance techniques.
2. Sensitive to affective issues at various development stages.
3. Available to arrange mentorships, internships, special programs.
4. Trained to administer and interpret special tests and inventories.
5. Familiar with role-modeling techniques.
6. Capable of diagnosing problem areas in students' psychosocial development.

Teachers of the Gifted

1. Trained in effective intervention techniques with gifted learners.
2. Sensitivity to affective issues for the gifted.
3. Available to handle psychosocial issues on a daily basis in the classroom.
4. Trained to translate assessment information into program options.
5. Familiar with key gifted individuals who could serve as role models.
6. Capable of prescribing classroom activities that could assist in positive psychosocial development.

Each role is critical to implementing a successful counseling program for the population. A good general background in counseling and guidance provides a workable framework. Understanding the positive deviances of a gifted population provides the specific translation needed to make such programs effective. Responsibility for the overall counseling program then might be divided according to the following job descriptions:

Counselor for the Gifted (10% time)

1. Work with individual cases as referred
2. Provide small group counseling sessions across grade levels one every two weeks (1 hour each).
3. Establish mentorship-internship directories.
4. Develop a monthly lecture/discussion series on key career areas of interest to gifted students.
5. Sponsor a high school trip to selected colleges and universities for gifted/talented students.
6. Hold semiannual planning sessions for parents of the gifted.

Teacher of the Gifted (10% of instructional time)

1. Provide activities that promote positive psychosocial development among the gifted.
2. Implement an effective curriculum that focuses on the needs of the gifted.
3. Provide speakers in the classroom that are good role models for the gifted.
4. Prepare bibliographies that focus on the best of biography and autobiography and/or in fiction that focus on a gifted student as a protagonist.
5. Utilize small group and individual consultation as strategies to promote social and self understanding.
6. Use literature and art as tools to blend together cognitive and affective issues.

In this way, the responsibility is shared for meeting the counseling needs of the gifted, and the task does not become overwhelming to either counselors or teachers. Delineation of key activities will also prove useful in proceeding toward implementation.

CONCLUSION

It is probably important to comment that the nature of most of the strategies suggested are highly cost-effective but do require reorganizing instructional time and differential staffing of pupil services personnel. Such administrative changes may be met with initial resistance, but over time can and do prove themselves effective. Staff training coupled with the development of counseling curriculum units can help solidify the ideas and techniques. It is also important to note that these strategies should not be viewed as isolated alternatives but rather seen as inter-related in terms of a comprehensive counseling program for the gifted. In order to address the criticism that these strategies do not constitute clinical counseling strategies, it may be important to recognize that gifted students respond better to stimuli that are offered in an intellectual framework that provides a context and a system of understanding rather than the piecemeal approach frequently typified by one-to-one counseling experiences in school. Consequently, for this population, counseling programs must integrate affective issues into cognitive strategies in order to have the greatest impact on the client group. Literature and the arts can be as useful as psychotherapy in discerning identity and creating meaning for gifted individuals.

There are many problems associated with counseling the gifted in school settings. Since it is unlikely that schools can be easily changed, it remains for gifted educators to find workable approaches to this issue that accommodate to the current structure of schools and recognize the nature of the constraints within the structure. Modifying and adapting current practice is always easier than instituting a new job. Thus teachers and counselors can cooperatively structure new opportunities for affec-tive growth in the gifted, secure in the fact that such a program can be implemented without major trauma.

REFERENCES

Albert, R.S. (1983). Family positions and the attainment of eminence: A study of special family positions and special family experiences. In R.S. Albert (Ed.), *Genius and eminence: The social psychology of creativity and ex-ceptional achievement* (pp. 141–154). Oxford: Pergamon.

Albert, R.S., & Runco, M.A. (1986). The achievement of eminence: A model based on a longitudinal study of exceptionally gifted boys and their families. In R.J. Sternberg & J.E. Davidson (Eds.), *Conceptions of giftedness* (pp. 323–357). New York: Cambridge University Press.

Beville, K. (1983). *Affective curriculum for the gifted.* Aurora, CO: Aurora School District.

Bloom, B.S. (Ed.). (1985). *Developing talent in young people.* New York: Bal-lantine Books.

Clarke, B. (1980). *Growing up gifted.* Columbus, OH: Charles Merrill.

Crouse, J. (1979). The effects of academic ability. In C. Jencks et al. (Eds.), *The determinants of economic success in America: Who gets ahead?* (pp. 85–121). New York: Basic Books.

Feldhusen, J., VanTassel-Baska, J., & Seeley, K. (1989). *Excellence in educating the gifted.* Denver, CO: Love.

Janos, P.M., & Robinson, N. (1985). Psychosocial development in intellectually gifted children. In F.D. Horowitz & M. O'Brien (Eds.), *The gifted and talented: Developmental perspectives* (pp. 149-195). Hyattsville, MD: American Psychological Association.

Piechowski, M. (1979). The developmental potential of the gifted. In N. Colangelo & R. Zaffron (Eds.), *New directions in counseling the gifted* (pp. 25-57). Dubuque, IA: Kendall Hunt.

Silverman, L. (1983). Issues in affective development of the gifted. In J. VanTassel-Baska (Ed.), *A practical guide to counseling the gifted in a school setting* (pp. 6-21). Reston, VA: Council for Exceptional Children.

Silverman, L. (1987). What happens to gifted girls. In J. Maker (Ed.), *Defensible programs for the gifted: Critical issues in gifted education* (pp. 43-89). Rockville, MD: Aspen Systems.

VanTassel-Baska, J. (1981). A comprehensive model of career education for the gifted and talented. *Journal of Career Education, 7*(4), 325-331.

VanTassel-Baska, J. (1987). *Attitudes of parents of gifted.* Unpublished research report. Center for Development of Talent, Northwestern University, Chicago, IL.

Chapter 4
Counseling Gifted Children with Different Learning-Style Preferences

Shirley A. Griggs

Dunn and Dunn developed a theoretical model of learning style (1978) and recently Dunn (1989) applied it to individualizing instruction for mainstreamed gifted children. She cited impressive evidence demonstrating that higher academic achievement and more positive attitudes toward school result when the learning environment matches the individual student's learning style preference. The Dunn and Dunn (1978) conceptualization and the empirical findings supporting it provide a strong rationale for the position that the matching of counseling approaches and individual learning style will increase and enhance counselee learning, growth, and development.

Griggs (1984, 1985) collaborated with the Dunns in applying the learning style model to counseling. The fundamental thrust of learning styles-oriented counseling is eclectic. The counseling process begins with an assessment of individual needs and requirements for learning, including learning-style preferences, and identifies a variety of counseling approaches that are compatible with them. Those adopting the approach recognize the validity of a vast array of counseling theories, maintain that no single approach can meet the needs of all counselees, and focus upon selecting counseling interventions that match individual learning style. The learning style model of counseling should be introduced to practicing counselors after they are thoroughly knowledgeable concerning existing theories, techniques, and the basic tenets of counseling and human development.

Although the learning-style model is based on the premise of individual differences, research indicates that various special groups, including gifted children, are characterized by a core of learning style preferences that distinguishes them from their peers not identified as gifted (Griggs, 1984, 1985). Many gifted children will receive more help in coping with their special concerns in the social, personal, educational, and vocational spheres in a learning-style-oriented counseling process.

The overall purpose of this chapter is to provide school counselors with information that will enable them to recognize the learning styles of gifted children and to utilize counseling interventions that match them. The learning objectives are as follows:

1. To increase counselor effectiveness with gifted children through identification of their individual learning styles.
2. To provide counselors with a schema for matching counseling techniques with the learning style preferences of gifted youth.
3. To develop awareness among counselors regarding the special concerns of gifted youth.
4. To review the research that supports a learning-styles approach in counseling gifted children.

The chapter is divided into three sections. In the first section the basic Dunn and Dunn (1978) conceptualization of learning style and its measurement is briefly reviewed. In the second section learning-style-oriented counseling at both elementary and high school age levels is discussed. The third and major section of the chapter is devoted to the relationship between learning style preferences and specific concerns of gifted children.

IDENTIFYING INDIVIDUAL LEARNING STYLES

Learning style is the manner in which different elements from five basic stimuli affect a person's ability to perceive, interact with, and respond to the learning environment (Dunn & Dunn, 1978). The learning-style elements are as follows: (a) environmental stimuli (light, sound, temperature, design), (b) emotional stimuli (structure, persistence, motivation, responsibility), (c) sociological stimuli (pairs, peers, adults, self, group, varied), (d) physical stimuli (perceptual strengths, including auditory, visual, tactual, kinesthetic, mobility, intake, time of day—morning versus evening, late morning, and afternoon, and (e) psychological stimuli (global/analytic, impulsive/reflective, and cerebral dominance).

The instrument used to assess learning styles for youth in grades 3 through 12 is the Learning Style Inventory (LSI) (Dunn, Dunn, & Price, 1985). The LSI incorporates elements relating to the environmental, emotional, sociological, and physical preferences of the individual. It is based on a 104-item self-report questionnaire that was developed through content and factor analysis. The LSI uses a 5-point Likert scale for students in grades 5 through 12 and a 3-point Likert scale for students in grades 3 and 4, and can be completed in approximately 30 to 40 minutes.

In addition to the learning-style elements, three other psychological stimuli that affect learning style are included in the assessment of an individual's learning style. Zenhausern's (1978) Revised Dominance Scale is used to assess cerebral dominance, Sigel's (1967) Conceptual Style Test to identify global versus analytic styles, and Kagan's (1966) Matching Familiar Figures Test to identify impulsive versus reflective styles. A summary of the learning style preferences of learners is presented in the form of an individual learning style profile (see Dunn, 1989, Figure 1).

Interpretation of learning style areas is based upon identifying distinct preferences—that is, those elements in which the standard scores are below 40 (low preferences) or above 60 (high preferences). If scores are in the middle range (40–59), there is no strong preference for the element and accommodations do not have to be made in terms of the learning environment. Learning alone and peer-oriented and morning to evening are two elements on a continuum. In these cases, scores below 40 indicate preferences for learning alone or in the evening; scores above 60 suggest peer-oriented or morning learners. Table 4.1 illustrates the interpretation of the LSI for counseling purposes.

RELATING LEARNING STYLES TO EFFECTIVE COUNSELING

Human development theories provide the framework for counseling students through their individual learning styles. Erikson (1950) has identified nine developmental stages. At each stage the developing person is required to cope with a specific psychosocial crisis. The acquisition of relatively positive versus relatively negative personality traits reflects the degree of success with which an individual has met these challenges. The stages, together with the psychosocial crisis postulated by Erikson for each stage, are as follows:

1. Infancy   (0–2 yrs.)   Trust versus Mistrust
2. Toddlerhood   (2–4 yrs.)   Autonomy versus Shame
3. Early School Age   (5–7 yrs.)   Initiative versus Guilt
4. Middle School Age   (8–12 yrs.)   Industry versus Inferiority

Table 4.1.   Interpretation of the Learning Style Scales for Counselors.

Elements	Score 20–29	Score 30–39	Score 40–59	Score 60–69	Score 70–80
Sound during Counseling	Always needs quiet when learning, doing homework. Use of silence in counseling facilitates understanding.	Usually needs quiet when learning. Needs time for reflection in counseling.	Depending on the learning task, may prefer quiet or the presence of sound.	Some kind of sound (radio, recordings) enhances the learning process. Low tolerance for silence during counseling.	Consistently works in the presence of sound. Use of background music during counseling is suggested.
Light during Counseling	Always needs very low light. Eyes are sensitive and tire easily with florescent lighting.	Usually needs dim light to learn.	No strong preference for either low or high light.	Light area enhances the learning process.	Needs bright light and seeks out rooms with lots of windows when studying.
Temperature while Learning/ Counseling	Prefers a cool room and may find it difficult to tolerate heat.	Usually seeks out a cool environment.	No strong preferences for temperature extremes.	Usually seeks out a warm environment.	Prefers a warm room and may find it difficult to tolerate cold.
Design in Counseling	Prefers informal design, such as circular arrangement in a carpeted area for group counseling.	Usually likes informality and diversity in design.	Depending on the learning task, may prefer formal or informal arrangements.	Usually feels more comfortable in a formal setting.	Prefers formal design; tends to work consistently in the same area at a desk/hard chair.
Motivation for Learning and Counseling	Exhibits low motivation for learning and may demonstrate resistance in counseling.	Tends to procrastinate; evidences difficulty in beginning tasks.	Vascillates between high and low motivation depending on the approaches used in counseling.	Generally highly motivated for learning and counseling processes.	Consistently well-motivated; accomplishes learning tasks with enthusiasm.

Persistence during Counseling	Low level of persistence which may be evidenced by leaving counseling prematurely.	Somewhat limited time on-task; distractible.	Depending upon level of interest in counseling, may or may not persist until goals are achieved.	Generally commits self to counseling and endures until goals are achieved.	High level of persistence in counseling; works consistently to achieve goals.
Responsibility Evidenced in Counseling	Has to be reminded and constantly reinforced in counseling. Tends to blame others for own life circumstances.	Somewhat irresponsible, which may be evidenced in lateness or absence from sessions.	Vascillates between responsible and irresponsible behavior in counseling.	Generally follows through on commitment to counseling.	High level of responsibility in counseling; assumes responsibility for self and behavior.
High Versus Low Structure in Counseling	Responds to counseling approaches which utilize minimum structure and allow free expression (i.e., gestalt therapy).	Prefers counseling approaches which allow for minimum structure, i.e., client-centered counseling.	Prefers eclectic counseling approaches in which both active and passive techniques are utilized.	Prefers counseling approaches which define goals clearly and utilize structured techniques, i.e., behavioral counseling.	Strong need for structured counseling approaches and concreteness, i.e., trait-factor counseling.
Learning or Counseling Alone Versus Peers	Prefers to work things through alone; self-sufficient in many areas.	Generally prefers to resolve problems independently without peer counseling.	Depending on the situation, may seek help from peers or resolve problems alone.	Generally an effective peer group member.	Peer-group counseling is the strongly preferred mode. Change is most likely to occur as a result of group activities.
Individual Counseling	Not a good candidate for individual counseling. Likely to exhibit resistance in counseling.	If given a choice, would not seek out individual counseling.	Depending upon the counseling approaches used, change may occur in individual counseling.	Generally comfortable and motivated in individual counseling.	Individual counseling is the strongly preferred mode.

Table 4.1. (Continued)

Elements	Score 20–29	Score 30–39	Score 40–59	Score 60–69	Score 70–80
Variety in Counseling Sociological Structure	Generally uncomfortable with a variety of approaches; tends to favor a single mode of counseling.	Probably has a preference for a single counseling mode.	Depending upon the situation, may be open to a variety of counseling modalities.	Generally comfortable with diversity in counseling modes.	Prefers a combination of approaches in working through concerns, including alone, groups, and individual counseling.
Counseling Using Auditory Approaches	Tends to be "turned off" by talking approaches in counseling. Has difficulty listening and focusing on what is communicated.	Generally finds it difficult to participate in counseling if auditory approaches are used exclusively.	If the counselor is perceived as interesting and supportive, auditory approaches may be effective.	Generally auditory approaches in counseling are effective.	Responds well to auditory approaches; seem to have a tape recorder going and can recall conversations verbatim.
Counseling Using Tactual Approaches	Tends to avoid doing things tactual, such as writing, picture drawing, etc.	Generally there is limited interest in tactual approaches.	Does not have a strong preference for tactual approaches, but may find these approaches helpful on occasion.	Finds tactual approaches helpful when utilized during the counseling process.	Responds well to "hands on" approaches in counseling and the use of techniques such as puppetry, clay modeling, draw-a-picture, computer use.
Counseling Using Visual Approaches	Tends to be "turned off" by visual approaches in counseling such as bibliotherapy, or the use of pictures or films.	Generally finds it difficult to absorb visual content.	Depending upon the situation, visual approaches may enhance counseling.	Generally finds visual approaches helpful in counseling; i.e., the use of modeling through videotaping.	Responds well to visual approaches; seems to have a camera going and can recall faces, scenes, places.

Counseling Using Kinesthetic Approaches	Prefers counseling approaches that require body involvement such as role-playing and psychodrama.	Has a preference for action-oriented counseling approaches which involve body movement.	No strong feelings about kinesthetic approaches; discretion needs to be used.	Prefers not to engage in action-oriented counseling strategies.	Very uncomfortable with kinesthetic approaches in counseling.
Need for Intake during Counseling	Uses some kind of intake, such as food or drink, when working or learning.	Often uses intake while learning.	Occasionally will use intake and find it enhances the learning process.	Rarely utilizes food or drink while working.	Never has a need for intake while working.
Evening Versus Morning Energy Levels	Prefers morning hours for working, learning, and studying.	Generally prefers the morning for working on tasks.	Time of day or night is relatively unimportant.	Generally prefers the evening for working on tasks.	Prefers evening hours for working, learning and studying.
Late Morning Energy Level	High energy level in the late morning hours.	Generally prefers the late morning for working.	Time is not a critical element here.	There is somewhat of a lull in energy level around 11 a.m.	Sluggish and low energy level around noon.
Afternoon Energy Level	Afternoon is an excellent time to schedule counseling activities.	Energy level begins to increase during the afternoon hours.	Time of day is not important; energy level is relatively constant.	Energy level begins to drop during the afternoon hours.	Afternoon is a poor time to schedule counseling activities.
Mobility Needed in Counseling	Prefers action-oriented approaches in counseling, i.e., roleplaying, mime, art therapy.	Generally prefers action, high mobility approaches in counseling.	Responsive to either passive or active approaches in counseling with no strong preferences for either.	Generally prefers passive, low mobility, sedentary approaches in learning or counseling.	Low need for mobility in counseling with the ability to sit for relatively long periods of time.

5. Early Adolescence	(13–17 yrs.)	Group Identity versus Alienation
6. Later Adolescence	(18–22 yrs.)	Individual Identity versus Role Diffusion
7. Young Adulthood	(23–30 yrs.)	Intimacy versus Isolation
8. Middle Adulthood	(31–50 yrs.)	Generativity versus Stagnation
9. Later Adulthood	(51 yrs. –)	Integrity versus Despair

Learning Style-Oriented Counseling in Elementary Schools

Students enrolled in elementary schools are predominantly in the third or fourth stages of development—that is, the early and middle school age. During this period, the child learns the fundamental skills of the culture. There is increased emphasis on intellectual growth, competence, and a growing investment in work. The developmental tasks of this stage include (a) social cooperation, (b) self-evaluation, (c) skill learning, (d) team play, (e) learning appropriate sex roles, and (f) developing conscience, morality, and a set of values. Social cooperation is largely focused on the same-sex peer group and is characterized by movement from egocentric behavior to increasing sensitivity to group norms and pressures. While the early school-age child focuses primarily on the teacher for approval and acceptance, the middle-school child focuses on the peer group. This is a period of "best friends," private jokes, and secret codes. During this period, the child is engaged in self-evaluation—concerned with placement in the group and sensitive to labeling by teachers and peers. Skill learning involves the acquisition of intellectual, artistic, and athletic skills. The child learns the fundamentals of team play, including competition and learning to subordinate personal goals for group goals.

The psychosocial crises of elementary school children are initiative versus guilt, and industry versus inferiority. Initiative involves active inquiry and investigation of the environment; the child is curious about everything! If curiosity is stifled or the child is severely restricted in the area of expression, self-doubt and guilt develop. Industry is characterized by an eagerness for building skills and performing meaningful work. Each new skill acquired results in increased independence and self-esteem. Inferiority and feelings of inadequacy result from two sources: self and environment. Personally, the child may have physical, emotional, or mental limitations that prevent the acquisition of certain skills. Environmentally, children may be grouped and graded on the basis of how they compare to others. In extreme cases, counselors observe the reluctance, self-doubt, and withdrawal of the child who feels extremely inferior.

Education, the central process during the elementary school years, is responsible for the development of a personal sense of industry. Frequently, children are placed in situations where the probability of success is minimal: Adults set expectations or goals beyond reach. The school environment may be extremely competitive, resulting in failure for some students. Parents may reward success with acceptance, and failure with rejection. During this and all other stages it is essential that educators recognize individual differences: Some students for example, work well even in a noisy environment while others require absolute quiet; some require high degrees of structure, while others thrive on minimal structure; some prefer to learn independently, while others are motivated to learn through peer group interaction. It is important for educators to generate an educational environment that provides for these varied styles.

In deciding upon the counseling interventions that are most appropriate, the counselor should (a) analyze the learning style profile of the student, (b) consult Table 4.1 to interpret the profile in terms of preferences, and (c) select counseling interventions that are compatible with these learning style requirements. A range of counseling techniques that are especially useful at the elementary school level is presented in Table 4.2. Learning style characteristics most compatible with each technique are presented in the same table.

Learning Style-Oriented Counseling in Secondary Schools

Students enrolled in secondary schools are predominantly in the fifth stage of development in which the key feature is a search for identity. This stage is characterized by rapid physical changes, significant conceptual maturity, and heightened sensitivity to peer approval. The adolescent begins to think about the world in new ways, which have profound implications for counseling and learning. Conceptual development results in a more flexible, critical, and abstract view of the world so that counselors can utilize techniques that involve deep levels of cognitive processing.

The fundamental question for the adolescent is: "Who am I and where do I belong?" Group identity and a strong sense of belonging facilitate psychological growth and serve as integrating forces. Negative resolution of these issues results in alienation, loneliness, and isolation. Adolescence has been described as a period of intense stress and turmoil. The adolescent is torn between a need to be a conformist and behave and think like peers or parents and a need to develop individuality and uniqueness.

Table 4.2. Elementary School Counseling Techniques and Compatible Learning Style Preference Patterns.

Techniques	Description	Learning-Style Characteristics
Modeling	Observe the behavior of another person—live (counselor, friend, peer), or symbolic (videotape, films, books), or covert (imagine performing the desired behavior).	Visual perception; high need for structure.
Magic Circle	A technique for classroom use, where pupils and their teachers create an accepting climate in which they share their thoughts and feelings, develop confidence, solve problems, and learn to interact with each other effectively.	Informal, casual, relaxed design. Auditory approach predominantly. Both global and analytic approaches/preferences can be accommodated.
Art Therapy	The use of art activities (drawing, painting, clay modeling, collage construction) to provide emotional release and communicate nonverbally.	Tactual perceptual preference; low structure; accommodates a variety of sociological preferences (self, peer, adult).
Bibliotherapy	The student is given carefully selected material to read, based on age, emotional problems, and personality needs. Provides insight and understanding of self.	Visual perceptual preference; high structure, high motivation and responsibility, self sociological preference.
Block Play	The child uses a number of blocks to construct people, places, and things which she/he experiences and discusses the constructions with the counselor.	Kinesthetic perceptual preference; low structure; adult sociological preference.
Photographs	The student is asked to bring photographs of self, family, friends to a counseling session. This technique can be used to elicit personal crises or problems from specific developmental periods.	Visual and auditory perceptual preferences; adult sociological preference; moderate structure.

Puppetry	A technique of manipulating small-scale figures to create or re-enact situations, or events, for therapeutic counseling.	Kinesthetic and visual perceptual preferences; low structure; right brain dominant; accommodates varied sociological preferences (adults, peers).
Psychodrama	Small groups extemporaneously dramatize situations or past experiences to afford catharsis and social relearning for the participants and/or protagonist.	Kinesthetic; visual, auditory, tactual preferences; low structure; high motivation; peer sociological preferences; right-brain dominant.
Creative Writing	The student creates a real or imaginary story to share in individual or group counseling. The story should focus on feelings, situations, or concerns that the student is experiencing.	Tactual, auditory perceptual preferences; high motivation; high responsibility; accommodates varied sociological preferences.
Serial Drawing	The student creates a number of drawings, which successively tell a story that is shared visually and verbally in a counseling session.	Tactual, visual, and auditory perceptual preferences; right brain dominant.
Mime	In a group counseling setting, students portray some aspect of their character or dramatize a situation, through body language rather than words.	Peer sociological preference; visual perceptual strength; right brain dominant.
Charade Games	In a group counseling setting, students act out their feelings as they are related to specific theme areas (anger, failure, jealousy and guilt) while other group members try to interpret the message.	Peer sociological preferences; kinesthetic and visual perceptual strength; right brain dominant.
Mutual Storytelling Technique	The counselor creates a story that reflects a conflict situation that the student is experiencing. The student responds by resolving the conflict. The counselor then identifies other options that are more self-enhancing or effective and discusses these with the student.	Accommodates adult sociological preferences; right brain dominant; auditory perceptual strength; need for high structure.

Table 4.2. (Continued)

Techniques	Description	Learning-Style Characteristics
Music Therapy	Musical activity can be used to elicit such behaviors and feelings as: self-awareness, creativity, group solidarity. Techniques range from: a. Responding to the musical environment with pleasure. b. Learning music skills for successful group participation. c. Applying music skills in new situations.	Sensory awareness, particularly auditory; requires sound; high need for mobility.
Musical Improvisation	A creative and spontaneous technique for helping the counselee express a feeling through music, either vocal or instrumental.	Involves divergent thinking, low need for conformity; accommodates a variety of perceptual strengths; requires sound.
Game Therapy	Games can be used in counseling to: a. Serve as a projective assessment tool. b. Set up a situation in which anxiety about certain conditions can be confronted and worked through. c. "Rules of the game" can be an analogy to understanding societal norms. d. Allow for the counselee's playfulness and fantasy activity to emerge. e. Develop problem solving and coping behaviors in the client.	Right-brain dominant; high need for mobility; accommodates a variety of perceptual strengths; peer and group counseling preferences.

Selected learning style elements remain stable in individuals, such as time of day preferences and responsibility, while other elements such as perceptual strengths, appear to follow the growth curve. Price (1980) determined that preferences for tactual and kinesthetic modalities develop first, followed by visual modalities in later elementary school years, and lastly by auditory modalities in secondary school. Bandler and Grinder (1979) maintain that once the counselor has identified the counselee's favored representational system or perceptual strength and responded out of that system (auditory, visual, tactual, kinesthetic), feelings of trust and rapport increase. The development of auditory strengths during adolescence suggests that counselors can utilize a wide range of traditional, talking through counseling approaches, including reality therapy, client centered, cognitive, Adlerian, behavioral, and transactional analysis. For adolescents whose preferences are not auditory, a variety of interventions that accommodate visual, tactual, and kinesthetic preferences are outlined in Table 4.3.

COUNSELING GIFTED CHILDREN WITH DIFFERENT LEARNING-STYLE PREFERENCES

A number of researchers have emphasized the importance of personal characteristics, such as learning style, in determining the effectiveness of one counseling method versus another. Kivlighan, Hageseth, Tipton, and McGovern (1981) asserted:

> The literature on vocational counseling is replete with research in which no differences were found between various approaches in counseling. In most of the studies in which no differences between counseling methods were found, treatments were compared without regard to relevant personality variables of participants; the researchers implicitly made the uniformity assumption. (p. 319)

These investigators reported more desirable outcomes in group vocational counseling when treatment approaches and personality types (task-oriented versus people-oriented) were matched than when they were not. Similarly, Rosenthal (1977) studied the effectiveness of various counselor-training approaches on trainees with low versus high conceptual levels. He concluded that

> Comparing the results of one training method without considering trainee characteristics and learning style, as well as multiple assessment of skills, may lead to incomplete conclusions on the effectiveness of these methods. (p. 236)

Griggs, Price, Kopel, and Swaine (1984) studied the effects of group counseling on intellectually gifted sixth-grade students with different learning styles. Specifically, the study raised the following question: What are the effects of group counseling using career education interventions that are either compatible or incompatible with the learning

Table 4.3. Secondary School Counseling Techniques and Compatible Learning Style Preference Patterns.

Techniques	Description	Learning Style Characteristics
Systematic Desensitization	An anxiety-reduction strategy involving: Verbal set (overview of technique). Identification of emotion-provoking situations. Hierarchy construction. Coping responses. Imagery assessment. Scene presentation. Homework and follow-up.	Visual perception; analytical and deductive approach (left hemisphere).
Guided Imagery	The counselor asks counselees to relax, close their eyes, and create a mental picture of an event or experience. Clients share the imagery in an individual or group counseling session.	Visual, auditory perceptual preferences; right brain dominant; average need for structure; varied sociological preferences.
Autobiographical Writing	The student writes an autobiography, describing values, interests, goals, family, past events, etc., and shares it in a counseling session.	Tactual and auditory preferences; high structure; high responsibility.
Progressive Relaxation	In an individual or group counseling setting, the counselor directs students to tense and then relax all parts of the body progressively. Students are encouraged to apply this strategy in situations in which they feel anxious, tense, or nervous.	Accommodates either peer or adult sociological preferences; kinesthetic perceptual strength; need for high structure.
Metaphor, Parable, Allegory	Figurative language in which concepts are described symbolically or through stories or analogies.	Visual orientation; right brain dominant; global approach. May be utilized in individual, peer, or group counseling.
Free Writing	Counselees are instructed: "Conditions of tension, confusion, hostility, joy or excitement can be released through writing your feelings and thoughts freely. Keep a log of your writings to share in individual or group counseling."	Tactual perceptual strength; highly motivated and persistent; minimum need for structure.

style elements of: (a) low motivation and high need for structure versus (b) high motivation and low need for structure? The study was conducted with a pre and posttest experimental/control group design, using the Learning Style Inventory (Dunn, Dunn, & Price, 1985) to assess learning style and the Career Maturity Inventory (Crites, 1978) and the Occupational List Recall Test (Westbrook, 1972) as the dependent measures. A total of eight group counseling sessions were conducted with the same career education objectives but different counseling strategies. The results suggested that improvement in career awareness will be greater if students are matched to the type of counseling intervention that is compatible with their learning-style preferences for structure and motivation.

There are a number of special concerns that are frequently raised in counseling sessions with gifted learners. We suggest that counselors who learn (a) to identify the learning style and other personal-social characteristics of each child, and (b) to select counseling strategies that match them will be better able to help gifted learners deal with these concerns.

Learning Style Characteristics of Gifted Youth

Although the elements of individual learning styles of gifted students may vary, several recent studies revealed a pattern of core preferences among the gifted that distinguish them from their peers (Griggs, 1984). These investigations, as summarized in Table 4.4, suggest that gifted students are: independent (self) learners, internally controlled, persistent, perceptually strong, nonconforming, and highly motivated. Each of these preferences is discussed here, and implications for counseling these students are addressed.

Independent (self) learners. Gifted students are self-learners who require a high degree of independence and autonomy in learning. They prefer large doses of independent study and generally become bored with routine and rote memory tasks. These preferences may result in problems with authority, for these youth are frequently viewed as challenging, confrontational, and outspoken. The counselor's role as a consultant to teachers and parents is to support the student's independence and help adults deal effectively with student patterns of self-reliance. In the classroom, these students consistently prefer a self-learning modality to the other sociological stimuli of pairs, peers, groups, or adults. In terms of counseling, they generally prefer individual counseling centered on self-management and self-monitoring rather than group counseling.

Table 4.4.   Learning Style Preferences of Gifted and Talented Students.

Researchers, Date	Grade	Instruments	Findings
Stewart, 1981	4, 5, 6	Learning Style Inventory[a] Norwicki-Strickland Locus of Control	Gifted Are: Independent, internally controlled. Gifted Prefer: Independent study and discussions; no lectures.
Dunn & Price, 1980	4, 5, 6	Learning Style Inventory[b]	Gifted are: Persistent, nonconforming, perceptually strong. Gifted Prefer: Time to complete tasks, options, few/no lectures.
Wasson, 1980	4, 5, 6	Learning Style Inventory[a]	Gifted Prefer: Teaching games, independent study, peer teaching, programming. Gifted dislike: drill, recitations, lectures.
Griggs & Price, 1980	7, 8, 9	Learning Style Inventory[b]	Gifted are: Persistent, self-motivated, perceptually strong. Gifted Prefer: Learning alone, no lectures.
Kreitner, 1981	7–12	Learning Style Inventory[b] Swassing-Barbe Modality Index	Gifted are: Highly motivated, perceptually strong. Gifted prefer: Options, learning alone, no lectures.
Cross, 1982	9–12	Norwicki-Strickland Locus of Control	Gifted are: Self-motivated, internally controlled, self-directed, task committed.
Price, Dunn, Dunn & Griggs, 1981	4–12	Learning Style Inventory[b]	Gifted are: Self-motivated, persistent, perceptually strong and nonconforming. Gifted prefer: Options, formal design, no lectures, learning alone.

[a] Renzulli, J.S., & Smith, L.H. Learning Style Inventory. Mansfield Center CT.: Creative Learning Press, 1978.
[b] Dunn, R., Dunn, K., & Price, G.E. Learning Style Inventory, Lawrence, Kansas: Price Systems, 1975.

Internally controlled. Gifted students tend to be internally controlled or field-independent. They are usually aware of their own needs, feelings, and attributes, which they experience as distinct from those of others (Witkin, 1977). This distinction provides an internal frame of reference for dealing with other people and the environment in general. These students have a tendency to overcome the organization of the environment or restructure it. Generally, there is a pattern of relying more on self than externals, such as other people, chance, or luck. Field-independent children pursue active, experiential approaches to learning. This orientation has implications for counselors working with gifted students in such areas as decision making, career education, and moral development. For example, in the area of decision making, these students are more likely to generate options that are within their control and discount or fail to consider those options which involve heavy reliance on others or adherence to existing social practices or customs.

Persistent. Persistence is highly correlated with indefatigability, long attention span, and ability to sustain interest and involvement over a period of time. Gifted students usually thrive on projects that demand persistence. They welcome challenging and complex tasks. Renzulli (1980) observed that gifted persons are highly product-oriented. They attack a problem because they are attempting to produce a new and imaginative product. This suggests that the curriculum and the guidance program need to focus on high-level cognitive processing, reasoning, abstract thinking, and creative problem solving.

Perceptually strong. A number of counseling theorists recognize the importance of matching counselor style and type of counseling intervention to counselee style (Bandler & Grinder, 1979). The field of neurolinguistic programming (NLP) has developed around this concept (Harman & O'Neill, 1981). The NLP model stresses the importance of the counselor responding to the counselee's representational system, which may be auditory, visual, or tactile/kinesthetic. Research on the gifted reveals that they have well integrated perceptual strengths or a wide variety of representational systems (Dunn & Price, 1980; Griggs & Price, 1980; Kreitner, 1981: Price, Dunn, Dunn, & Griggs, 1981). Hence, a broad range of counseling techniques can be used with these students: predominantly auditory approaches such as rational emotive therapy and client-centered counseling; predominantly visual approaches such as guided imagery and puppetry; and predominantly tactile-kinesthetic approaches such as games, psychodrama, and serial drawing.

Nonconforming. Nonconformity is associated with dissimilarity, innovation, divergent thinking, and creativity. There is overlap in the constructs of conformity and field orientation. The field-independent person is a nonconformist, while, conversely, the field-dependent person is a conformist. Generally, gifted students tend toward nonconformity in terms of thought, attitudes, and behavior. Counselors need to recognize and support this uniqueness, which can take many forms.

Highly motivated. Highly motivated persons have a strong drive which propels them to action. They are capable of effecting changes within themselves with a minimum of counseling structure and counselor reinforcement. Gifted students are highly motivated in terms of academic achievement, self-growth and development, and learning. In helping these students change self-defeating behaviors (such as shyness, overweight, procrastination, or moodiness), the counselor will generally discover that counselee monitoring of change is more effective than counselor monitoring. Effective self-monitoring involves five important steps: discrimination of a response, recording of a response, charting of a response, display of data, and analysis of data (Thoresen & Mahoney, 1974). In overcoming shyness, for example, gifted students can monitor themselves by learning to discriminate between shy versus assertive responses, recording each incident related to these behaviors, developing a chart to record these behaviors over a period of time, displaying the data so that it acts as a reinforcer, and analyzing the data to determine patterns and circumstances that result in goal attainment.

In summary, research studies indicate that gifted students have a core of learning-style preferences that distinguish them as a group from other students. Findings that they are independent learners, internally controlled, persistent, perceptually strong, nonconforming, and highly motivated suggest that school counselors can use a broad range of techniques and strategies. These can focus on high-level cognitive processing, reasoning, abstract thinking, creative problem-solving and self-monitoring. However, it is important to recognize that assessment should extend beyond group differences, for within the gifted group there are broad differences as well as similarities in terms of learning-style preferences. Individual differences among the gifted suggest that counselors need to assess each youngster's learning-style preferences and devise interventions that are congruent with those specific preferences.

Special Concerns of Gifted Children

There are some common concerns among significant numbers of gifted children, which are related to their unique characteristics and the ways they are perceived by other youths and adults. These concerns frequently become the content of counseling sessions. In my work in supervising counselors of the gifted, I have identified theme areas that present special problems for the gifted, including (a) peer issues, (b) expectations of teachers and parents, (c) decision making, (d) competition versus cooperation, and (e) possible feelings of isolation, uncertainty, and anxiety.

Peer issues. Everyone has the need for affiliation with others but, during the stages of puberty and adolescence, unusually high importance is placed on peer friendship and acceptance. Most young people do not want to seem "different" from their peers; they seek a sameness in appearance, dress, codes of behavior, values, language, and expression. One gifted student made the following comment:

> I'm not a social outcast or anything, but sometimes I feel people my own age just don't understand me because I'm gifted. They tease me a lot. I wish my friends would accept giftedness as being a good thing. (Galbraith, 1983)

Gifted children sometimes find it hard to find acceptance among peers, because their goals and interests might be very different. Counselors can support gifted counselees by valuing their individuality and providing opportunities for the expression of feelings. These youngsters should be affirmed for striving to develop their uniqueness—part of the process of searching for an identity.

Expectations of teachers and parents. One of the hardest things for teachers and parents of gifted children to do is *not* to assume that emotional maturity will necessarily equal intellectual ability (Prichard, 1985). Frequently, gifted children are expected to excel in every area, and they complain that adults expect too much. Emotionally, gifted children need to express themselves as children, and counselors can facilitate this through the use of play therapy and games in counseling in which children can utilize their rich imaginations and fantasies.

Frequently, the school day is not organized to accommodate gifted youth and is typically divided into a number of periods of 30 to 50 minutes each. Exceptionally gifted children have intense powers of concentration and typically learn by total immersion (Tolan, 1985). Whatever subject claims their attention becomes an obsession until they feel that they have mastered it. They dislike repetition and drill, which comprise a sizable amount of time in regular classrooms. The counselor needs to function as an advocate of the gifted, stressing the importance of individual accommodation through directed and/or independent study.

Decision making. The process of decision making may be problematic for the gifted, because some excel in many areas. Frequently, gifted children are overextended in terms of sports, studies, hobbies, and pursuit of the arts. At the secondary school level, they tend to assume leadership positions in the extracurricular program and are frequently involved with student government, drama, journalism, music, and language clubs. They may have difficulty selecting courses at the secondary school level, due to broad interests and high aptitude in many disciplines. To some extent, the process of decision making involves identifying and delimiting options so that choices can be made from a smaller field. However, gifted youth frequently have difficulty with the focusing and delimiting process, so that decision making may be delayed. The role of the counselor is to help gifted youth engage in introspection in order to identify strong interests, aptitudes, and intellectual strengths so that options and choices are clearly identified and evaluated.

Competition versus cooperation. Gifted youth generally respond well to academic competition in the form of grades, honors, contests, awards, and scholarships. They frequently possess the motivation, persistence, and task commitment necessary to excel in the academic arena. However, of equal importance is learning to become an effective team member and to achieve excellence through cooperation with others. Gifted youth can become disenchanted in the process of working with a team when they perceive that the goal can be achieved more efficiently through their independent efforts. Counselors need to provide opportunities for group counseling of gifted and nongifted youth that bring about their working together to resolve crucial issues such as peer pressure, independence, dating, loss, and so on. The gifted can benefit from such group work, because the options and solutions generated in such problem-solving groups are traditionally more creative and analytic than those provided by a single individual.

Dealing with feelings. The emotional development of gifted youth is viewed by most school counselors as equal in importance to their cognitive development. Learning-style preferences for nonconformity and independent learning may result in feelings of isolation and loneliness. Gifted youth can benefit from counseling, aimed at helping them get in touch with their feelings and gaining insight into the differences between loneliness and solitude. Frequently, gifted youth engage in solitary activities (reading, problem solving, contemplation, etc.) to a greater extent than their nongifted peers, and such activities provide sources of satisfaction and fulfillment, if not judged as "atypical" or "unhealthy" by others.

Generally, the moral development of the gifted parallels cognitive development and there is concern regarding social and political issues during adolescence. Gifted youth are likely to be more disturbed by social injustices and the threat of nuclear war, because they have reached a higher stage of moral development than their peers. Rather than experiencing a sense of despondency and despair, youth need to be helped to gain a sense of empowerment in working for change. Through bibliotherapy, that is, reading about persons who have effected positive social change, and involvement in community service through volunteerism, the gifted can become involved in meaningful change.

CONCLUSION

Historically, the United States has recognized the importance of school counselors in the lives of gifted youth. In 1957, following concern over Soviet superiority with the launching of Sputnik, the federal government appropriated large sums of money in the National Defense Education Act to prepare school counselors, together with teachers of mathematics and science, to identify and educate the gifted. There should not have to be a national crisis to alert the public regarding the special needs and concerns of this population. Research findings indicate that gifted children have a core of learning-style preferences that distinguish them from their nongifted peers. However, the intragroup differences are greater than the intergroup differences. This mandates that we assess each child individually and select counseling interventions which respond to preferences. Counseling through individual learning styles can provide a powerful tool in helping each child to achieve maximum realization of potential, both academically and personally.

REFERENCES

Bandler, R., & Grinder, J. (1979). *Frogs into princes.* Moab, UT: Real People Press.

Crites, J.O. (1978). *Manual: Career Maturity Inventory.* Monterey, CA: CTB/McGraw-Hill.

Dunn, R. (1989). Individualizing instruction for mainstreamed gifted children. In R. Milgram (Ed.), *Teaching gifted and talented learners in regular classrooms* (pp. 63–111) Springfield, IL: Charles C. Thomas.

Dunn, R., & Dunn, K. (1978). *Teaching students through their individual learning styles: A practical approach.* Reston, VA: Reston.

Dunn, R., Dunn, K., & Price, G.E. (1985). *Manual: Learning Style Inventory.* Lawrence, KS: Price Systems.

Dunn, R., & Price, G.E. (1980). Identifying the learning style characteristics of gifted children. *Gifted Child Quarterly, 24,* 33–36.

Erikson, E.H. (1950). *Childhood and society.* New York: Norton.

Galbraith, J. (1983). *The gifted kids survival guide.* Minneapolis, MN: Free Spirit.

Griggs, S.A. (1984). Counseling the gifted and talented based on learning styles. *Exceptional Children, 50,* 429-432.

Griggs, S.A. (1985). *Counseling students through their individual learning styles.* Ann Arbor, MI: University of Michigan, ERIC/CAPS.

Griggs, S.A., & Price, G.E. (1980). A comparison between the learning styles of gifted versus average suburban junior high school students. *Roeper Review, 4,* 7-9.

Griggs, S.A., Price, G.E., Kopel, S., & Swaine, W. (1984). The effects of group counseling with sixth grade students using approaches that are compatible versus incompatible with selected learning style elements. *California Association for Counseling and Development Journal, 5,* 28-35.

Harman, R.L., & O'Neill, C. (1981). Neuro-linguistic programming for counselors. *Personnel and Guidance Journal, 59,* 449-453.

Kagan, J. (1966). Reflection-impulsivity: The generality and dynamics of conceptual tempo. *Journal of Abnormal Psychology, 71,* 17-24.

Kivlighan, J.R.D.M., Hageseth, J.A., Tipton, R.M., & McGovern, T.V. (1981). Effects of matching treatment approaches and personality types in group vocational counseling. *Journal of Counseling Psychology, 28,* 315-320.

Kreitner, K.R. (1981). *Modality strengths and learning styles of musically talented high school students.* Unpublished master of science thesis, Ohio State University, Columbus, OH.

Price, G.E. (1980). *Research using the learning style inventory.* Paper presented at the Second Annual Conference on Teaching Students through their Individual Learning Styles, New York.

Price, G.E., Dunn, K., Dunn, R., & Griggs, S.A. (1981). Studies in students' learning styles. *Roeper Review, 4,* 38-40.

Prichard, B. (1985). Parenting gifted children—the fun, the frustration. *G.C/T, 41,* 10-13.

Renzulli, J.S. (1980). What we don't know about programming for the gifted and talented. *Phi Delta Kappan, 61,* 601-602.

Rosenthal, N.R. (1977). A prescriptive approach for counselor training. *Journal of Counseling Psychology, 24,* 231-237.

Sigel, I.E. (1967). *Sigel Conceptual Style Test.* Princeton, NJ: Educational Testing Service.

Thoresen, C.E., & Mahoney, M.J. (1974). *Behavioral self control.* New York: Holt, Rinehart, & Winston.

Tolan, S.S. (1985). The exceptionally gifted child in school. *G.C/T, 41,* 10-13.

Westbrook, B.W. (1972). *Career Knowledge Test.* Chapel Hill, NC: Center for Occupational Information.

Witkin, H.A. (1977). Educational implications of cognitive style. *Review of Educational Research, 47,* 1-64.

Zenhausern, R. (1978). *Revised Dominance Scale.* Jamaica, NY: St. John's University, Department of Psychology.

Chapter 5
People, Processes, and Developmental Paths to Eminence: A Developmental-Interactional Model*

Robert S. Albert

Ezra Pound said that more writers fail from lack of character than from lack of intelligence. (Alfred Kazin, *New York Times*, 10/21/81)

For almost two decades I have been concerned with the life experiences of people who achieved eminence in their careers. I have studied family, personality, and educational variables that predict the achievement of eminence. I have focused on eminent individuals not because they are better people, but because within their careers, they are highly productive, creative, and influential (Albert, 1983a). In the current chapter I will discuss the types of experiences and interpersonal relationships necessary for the achievement of eminence and trace the developmental paths most likely to lead to eminence in the different domains of giftedness.

Knowledge about achieved eminence has been based, to a large extent, upon dramatic vignettes and clinical reports about famous individuals, rather than on the systematic study of such careers in the making. This chapter is based upon my research and that of others on how exceptional giftedness may be stimulated and facilitated during the first 10 to 15 years so that a gifted child may select and pursue a significant, satisfying, and productive career. Such careers are frequently the basis

* I wish to thank Dr. Roberta M. Milgram for her great patience, making completion of this chapter possible, and to Pitzer College and the Haynes Foundation for support through a summer social-science research grant.

of the achievement of eminence. Many of the concepts discussed in the chapter are based upon the findings of a major longitudinal developmental study of two groups of exceptionally gifted young men and their families (Albert, 1983a; Albert & Runco, 1986, 1987). Participants in the research project were first contacted in 1977 and 1978 when they were age 12. The special significance of this age will be discussed later. The areas of their giftedness were selected to represent two basically different domains (Gardner, 1983).

At the initial stages of the project we were also interested in how profoundly gifted children might differ from more moderately or mildly gifted children (Albert, 1969). This concern came from research (Cox, 1926; Gallegher & Lucito, 1961; Hildreth, 1954; Hollingworth, 1942) showing clear developmental and performance differences among subjects in the IQ range from below average to exceptionally high. There was, however, little empirical evidence about how such differences were related to family experiences, career choices, or career achievement. Therefore, one focus of our project was to observe over time the impact of critical family and parental variables and interactions on the development of giftedness. Readers interested in a more detailed discussion of the project are referred to Albert (1969, 1983a, 1983b) and Albert and Runco (1986, 1987).

The chapter is divided into four parts. In the first section some of the basic concepts related to the phenomenon of achieved eminence are presented. In the second section, a number of basic personality issues in career choice are discussed, specifically identity, ego ideals, and narcissism. The third section deals with the importance of focal relationships and crystallizing experiences (Walters & Gardner, 1986) and the fourth with discussion of the basic developmental paths to eminence through the interaction of personality, family, third-party experiences, and the specific domain of giftedness.

BASIC CONCEPTS

Eminence is a complex, heterogeneous, and infrequent phenomenon

Eminence is defined as a position of great distinction or superiority in achievement, position, rank, or character. Eminent individuals demonstrate outstanding performance, towering above all others, in their chosen fields. Achieved eminence is frequently related to profound giftedness. Children who achieve eminence as adults are characterized by a certain "specialness" (Albert, 1978; Bloom, 1985). This "specialness" refers to highly focused, intense, individualized, and perhaps stable perspectives and motivations. A child who is special in this way starts with some of the basic equipment for high creativity and achievement. Achieved eminence is a strikingly infrequent phenomenon. The search for explanation of this infrequency has been the focus of attention for many years beginning with the early efforts of Galton (1869, 1874) and continuing up to the more recent work of Rushton (in press) and Simonton (1987). This chapter continues the construction of a developmental-interactional model explaining this infrequency (Albert, 1969, 1983a, 1983b; Albert & Runco, 1986, 1987).

Although we tend to notice similarities among people more than differences, the differences may, in some instances, be more important. Even within the upper reaches of eminence, there is great heterogeneity (Cox, 1926; Howe, 1982; Jackson & Rushton, 1987; MacKinnon, 1963; Roe, 1952; Wispe, 1965). Although it is reasonable to expect profoundly gifted individuals to achieve eminence in their chosen fields, such is not always the case. One explanation is that eminence, or any type of achievement for that matter, requires more than a specific level of ability, but results from a particular, often idiosyncratic, mix of abilities, values, motivations, and experiences, some deliberate, some opportunistic.

Giftedness functions as an organizer within the individual's development, especially in interpersonal interactions

Giftedness, especially profound giftedness, can hardly go unobserved. Thus, giftedness from an early age serves directive and prescriptive functions in a child's exchanges with the environment. A situation in which the child is seen as capable, developmentally accelerated, and full of promise is both experience-producing and experience-directing.

Family, teachers, and mentors influence the development of achieved eminence

The family is the first and a highly important influence on the development of children who achieve eminence as adults. The family lays the basic groundwork, and sets the emotional and cognitive tenor for development. It determines the major themes and interests and directs the child toward the future. Families not only pass on broad genetic similarities, but they train broadly in terms of goals, values, history, and traditions. The family as an educational environment with its own values and aims has its earliest educational impact on the child's identity, self-esteem, and sense of competence.

As the child grows older, teachers and mentors will exercise more specific influences. To the degree that the child is characterized by interests and motivations that are highly focused, intense, and individualized, third-person efforts are likely to influence these special characteristics. Families of individuals who achieve eminence are often characterized by unusual experiences (Albert, 1971, 1983b; Berrington, 1983; Roe, 1952). For example, many such families experience early parental or sibling loss. The child destined for eminence is often an only child, or if not, then probably the oldest.

The developmental importance of age 12

Early adolescence appears to be a critical period in the achievement of eminence during which important cognitive changes, relationships, and performances occur and interact. By age 12 many important personality traits and values have become stable and more accurate predictors of later behavior. According to Piaget, this age is also critical in cognitive development with the appearance of formal operations, and the basic cognitive skills for abstract, future-oriented, hypothetical thinking. Hamilton (1983) integrated the findings from a wide range of empirical studies and summarized the developmental changes, biological and cognitive, that take place in early adolescence. These changes, according to Hamilton, give the preadolescent a degree of focused and selective attention not present before, and this, in turn, makes possible more cognitive control and self-pacing in behavior. She also points out that these changes are not simply seen in analytical thinking, but in daydreaming and imaginative thinking. This is an age at which a stronger sense of identity, positive or negative, appears, and with this, clearer ego ideals. The cognitive changes and the surging sense of identity contribute to the renewal of the egocentricity often characteristic of the period.

Personality development in early adolescence can be pervasive and frightening, unless accompanied by greater cognitive control and focus. It is here at the preadolescent early adolescence stage of development, in the meeting and synthesis of identity issues, strong emotions and new cognitive skills that a motivational-cognitive basis for the achievement of eminence begins.

Not only are these developments and new abilities important in their own right, but they underlie two very important experiences that often play a critical role in early identity formation and realistic career choice. These two experiences, to be discussed in detail later in the chapter, are focal relationships and crystallizing experiences. These are important because no matter how powerful the imagination, extraordinary the intelligence, or precocious the talent, they do not acquire validity until the youth uses them in ways that lead to real-life consequences. It is in such activities that the validity of talents, gifts, wishes, and aspirations are tested, and become more identifiable as characteristic of us in our own eyes and in those of others, that is, become part of our identity.

Achieved eminence requires "goodness-of fit"

Eminence is achieved when an individual's domain and level of giftedness, personality dispositions, motivations, interests, and education fit the demands of his/her chosen career. A congruent, synergic relationship among all of these dimensions is required in order for eminence to be achieved.

Not everyone with high ability automatically succeeds in his/her career. One of the most critical decisions underlying the achievement of eminence is the career decision itself. The concept of "goodness of fit" in the sphere of career choice leads to understanding the importance of experience-based selectivity in finding and pursuing appropriate relationships within formal and informal educational settings if one is to achieve a "good fitting" career. It explodes the myth that many eminent persons chance upon their careers. The truth of the matter is that such careers are often the result of much searching, experimentation, and thought (Albert, 1981).

No child, however bright and talented, knows the possibilities of careers that lay ahead. Decision making on careers is a chain of events guided by schema and feelings that only experience can bring forth, make explicit, and eventually validate. One observation that confirms this is that once a "good-fitting" decision is made, the individual usually becomes more involved, more deeply invested, energetic, committed, and more satisfied with their efforts in an existential sense. Parents and teachers have a critical role to play in the process by suggesting career possibilities to the child and by permitting and encouraging the child to experience these possibilities first-hand. An essential skill on the way to a "good-fitting" career is learning to read one's own experiences and feelings when engaged in new situations and activities.

BASIC PERSONALITY ISSUES INVOLVED IN
CAREER CHOICE: IDENTITY AND EGO IDEALS

Recently, Janos and Robinson (1985) summarized long-established performance characteristics of intellectually gifted youth. Among these are an abundance of energy, enthusiasm, physical and psychological vigor, and a capacity for investing energy and attention in hard work. These characteristics are the same ones that researchers have long attributed to creative individuals. But these characteristics are not related to a specific domain of creative activity, that is scientific or nonscientific, that a person will pursue nor are they related to the personality dimensions that distinguish between eminent achievement and lower levels of performance. We must look elsewhere for what attracts an eminent person to his/her career and what specific experiences stimulate and sustain hard work in it.

A number of writers have shown the great depth and complexity of the vocational process of identity construction, consolidation, and achievement (Gedo, 1983; Gruber, 1986; Holton, 1978). For the present, let us focus upon two major components of personality—identity and ego ideals—each of which experiences an acceleration in its development during early adolescence. Leaving aside the demand characteristics of specific talents in specific domains, personality and career choice first meet with real-life possibilities in the adolescent's formation of identity and ego ideals. Eventually career decisions express and consolidate personality, for better or worse.

A child's public performances and their consequences, that is, comparison by the child or by significant others, provide the framework for the personal and interpersonal meanings that these behaviors acquire (Heckhausen, 1967). Research shows that these meanings and evaluations stabilize around 8–9 years of age for males in the United States. From then on they are highly influential in the child's self-esteem and readiness for other comparisons. It is this readiness (or not) that makes up achievement motivation and it is the consequences of this motivation that determines the child's access into the family and culture systems of rewards and punishments, initially in learning situations. How these occur in the life of the child goes a long way in stabilizing identity and sense of competence. As formal and informal learning go, so starts and develops a child's preparations for and subsequent choice of career.

Careers are important in distinguishing among individuals. There are, however, only a finite number of jobs and careers available in any culture at any one time. Accordingly, individual differences both in career choices and performances are two highly personal means individuals have available for distinguishing among themselves. This brings us back to the issue of "goodness-of-fit" discussed above as one influential component of identity formation and later achievement.

The aspect of identity that Erikson (1968) has made us so aware of is how intimately it is related to the developmental lessons one has acquired and how well these meet other personal and social requirements.

Identity is a bodily and phenomenological sense of oneself in terms of learning these lessons or not (again the element of comparison) and acquiring a keen sense of sameness for oneself and for significant others over time: sameness and continuity. Needless to say, this sense of one's identifiable sameness is linked to doing and to the ongoing comparative judgments regarding the consequences. This is rarely smooth or without emotionality if for no reason than the developmental period in which it occurs. Erikson has made a strong case for adolescence being the developmental period in which many potentially creative children become actively creative in real life.

A second component of personality appearing during the same period with even more specific influence in career choices are the ego ideals. As Moore and Fine (1967, p. 93) define them, ego ideals consist of "the images of the self to which the individual aspires consciously and unconsciously, and against which he measures himself. They are based on identifications with parents and other early environmental figures, as they actually are, were in the past, or as they have been idealized." Ego ideals are the product of the process of identification and some performance. As such they have two sources, each with a validity of its own. One source, discussed more fully in the next section of this chapter, is focal relationships with important, usually older, persons. The other and, I believe, secondary source of ego ideals lies in how well one meets the expectations of and how close and similar one perceives himself and his performances to be to those of these exemplars. Somewhat similar to but not identical with identity, ego ideals evolve into aspirations and expectations. While a product of past relationships and experiences, they are more domain-specific and future-oriented.

There are no guarantees that ego ideals will be realistic or fitting with one's competencies. They may be too fantastic, yet like achievement motivation, they too are the products of comparisons. Making comparisons is one of the most critical developmental experiences in how people come to perceive themselves (identity) and view their future (ego ideals). It goes without saying that false images, erroneous judgments, misplaced efforts, and painful lessons can be incorporated in the process of acquiring ego ideals. Just how fraught, problematic, and ill-fitting this can be for young persons can be seen in the articles by Allen (1979), Fast (1975), Janos, Sanfillippo, and Robinson (1986), Keniston (1965), Miller (1981) and Ochberg (1986).

A good fit between person and career is indeed hard to achieve. In some ways there are so many components, previous experiences, and levels of meaning influencing the development and use of gifts, that it is easier to understand why and how the adolescent, no matter how gifted, may fail to achieve a "goodness-of-fit" among self, gifts, anticipations, and real-world careers. Having said this, we should not lose sight of the fact that some young people do achieve this fit and have satisfactory and important careers.

FOCAL RELATIONSHIPS AND CRYSTALLIZING EXPERIENCES

We now turn to the focal relationships and crystallizing experiences that contribute to the achievement of eminence. Before doing so, I want to stress that all interpersonal relationships derive a substantial part of their emotional power and significance on the basis of preceding relationships. A child's ability to seek and/or engage in significant relationships begins within the family, or its cultural counterpart, and transfers to outside persons. Without an understanding of these preceding relationships, it is impossible to understand the child's readiness and ability for new relationships or their significance for the child. How rapidly and smoothly a child enters into other significant relationships is related to the transferences of needs, emotions, and abilities.

Freud, Winnicott (1965, 1971), and other psychoanalytically oriented observers have described the family as the basic developmental springboard. Winnicott explains why it is that a child's potential as a human being, much less as a talent, cannot develop without other peoples' interventions. For Winnicott and many developmentalists, healthy development goes beyond mere survival, but makes possible the start of courage, playfulness, and early creativeness. The development of these capacities, however, does not require heroic parenting. Winnicott's "good enough" mother (or father) is one who is intuitively well calibrated to their infant's emotions, needs and, equally important, its capabilities—supporting, acknowledging, and allowing the child to have its own experiences, to learn to cope with them and, therefore, learn from them.

On the other hand, if there is any one trait that corrupts such development in a child, it is excessive narcissism—in the child and/or the parent(s). Perhaps nothing damages the parent–child or any significant relationship as subtly or as profoundly as either excessive, uncontrollable narcissism or continuous parental indifference and rejection which can mask hostility and an excessive, ill-controlled narcissism. This type of parent–child relationship stifles, if not corrupts, the young child's self-worth and initiative, causing it to focus too much energy and thought on the relationship and its ambivalence (Gottschalk, 1981; Miller, 1981; Montour, 1977). One of the most pervasive damages from such narcissism is that it prevents the development of depth in one's relationships; as a consequence it places an obstacle in the path of the child's personal and cognitive development. It makes trust and intimacy difficult and fraught with anxiety. This can often lead to lifelong difficulty in exploring one's feelings, competencies, and testing one's abilities in real-life situations. In the place of healthy, controlled, and task-focused explorations, opportunities may be countered with indifference, fear, low self-esteem, and chronic depression.

FOCAL RELATIONSHIPS

Often difficult, intensely convoluted early parent-child relations set the stage for and give impact to nonfamily focal relationships. Focal relationships are close, confirming relationships outside the immediate family that support, encourage, and stimulate the realization of potential abilities. They are specific in their setting, their timing, and their influences. They may compensate for early problematic family relationships or long-term deprivation and reduce the intensity and impact of anxiety and self-doubt, feelings that can hinder the development and expression of potential eminence. Although they cannot easily make up for them, they can modify some of the damage. The influence of focal relationships is limited by the fact that earlier experiences have developmental precedence; the longer they have occurred, the more deeply rooted they are in the child's makeup.

A focal relationship facilitates the realization of potential abilities in several ways: first, by giving the individual a sense of positive worth and security and a focus to their identity and goals; second, by placing explorations (internal and external) under greater attentional control rather than allowing them to occur, if they do, in the diffuse, scattered manner so characteristic of threatened and insecure people. Third, a focal relationship helps to verify the individual's existing interests and positive self-regard. To be liked, loved for oneself, is the first step to bravery regarding one's capacities (Clark, 1983). As Freud concluded from his own mother's deep love, such love is the foundation of lifelong self-confidence. Fourth, focal relationships may transfer their own benefits to subsequent relationships, thereby permitting an individual to move on developmentally. This is the nature of important relationships, and the power of transference. Five, these relationships allow an individual to fall in love with deeper feelings, hopes, and more personal ideas—the raw materials of creativity. In the literature, these intense, maturing third-party relationships are often described as shadowy in the lives and performances of famous leaders (e.g., Franklin Roosevelt and Louis Howes; Col. House and Woodrow Wilson; John Kennedy and his younger brother Bobby; or the young Freud with Wilhelm Fliess and, soon after, Breuer). Nor should we overlook the series of important teachers that Darwin and Freud had, people who were instrumental in assisting each eminent-to-be in breaking from the family mold to pursue highly personal interests and continue to develop. Among scientists, there are some similar relationships but with a major difference. The relationships often are much more domain-specific and task-oriented, less personalized, with less immediate impact on the young scientist's emotions and personality than the focal relationships attributed to nonscientists.

CRYSTALLIZING EXPERIENCES

If one wishes to understand the early interpersonal foundations of achieved eminence, one looks to those antecedent experiences that foster realistic self-esteem, a clear sense of one's interest and cognitive exploration. Among such antecedents are the crystallizing experiences as described by Walters and Gardner (1986) that stimulate and validate early talent. As Walters and Gardner (1986, p. 309) described it, a crystallizing experience is "the overt reaction of an individual to some quality or feature of a domain; the reaction yields an immediate but also a long-term change in that individual's concept of the domain, his performance in it, and his view of himself." They are quite clear in what they mean by a crystallizing experience. It is a time-limited, profoundly intense experience leading to a gifted youth's discovery of an unanticipated special gift. When such experiences occur, they alert and confirm for the talented (and eminent-to-be) youth their most salient interests and talents. Being so reality-based, these experiences can go a long way in dispelling self-doubts and give an intensely focused conception of what they might be and become.

Walters and Gardner (1986) believe that it is impossible to identify such experiences when they occur, but only in retrospect, that is, by the results. They reported that crystallizing experiences rarely occur as a result of formal teaching and cited numerous examples that demonstrate these learning experiences to be "intensely personal and private. . . . " One wonders if it is possible for another person to identify such experiences and help a young person understand and focus upon it while it is occurring.

FOCAL RELATIONSHIPS AND CRYSTALLIZING EXPERIENCES: SIMILARITIES AND DIFFERENCES

Focal relationships and crystallizing experiences are more or less independent types of learning experiences in the development of giftedness.

Focal relationships may, to some extent, provide the intellectual and emotional security for the crystallizing experience or come later as support for acknowledging and integrating the tremendous consequences of such a learning experience within subsequent development. The relationship between the two remains open for further research. One thing is clear, however, and that is that not all gifted children have either focal relationships or crystallizing experiences or the necessary antecedents for them.

Let me draw attention to some similarities and differences between focal relationships and crystallizing experiences. In common, both are reality-based and most likely to occur either during puberty or shortly thereafter. Each focuses or helps the individual to focus and acquire better cognitive control of learning experiences and thinking. In doing this, they each can assist the child to link, emotionally and cognitively, interests and aptitudes hitherto not focused upon, acceptable or only recently initiated. They are both private and public; the experiences take place in public and/or the presence of another. They are profoundly validating. The timing of occurrence is unpredictable in both instances, although I believe it is possible to assess a young person's *readiness* for either experience.

As for their differences, the most salient appear to be the following. First and most important are the differences in the domains in which youth demonstrate their giftedness. The mathematical-science-musically oriented children appear more likely to have crystallizing experiences than focal relationships, or at least these will have a greater saliency in their development. Each has its greatest influence in different parts of the gifted youth's make-up. Crystallizing experiences influence a fairly specific cognitive domain or talent, while the greatest impact of focal relationships lies in the area of personality dispositions, identity issues, and developing ego ideals. Crystallizing experiences are more specific, circumscribed in the time and situation in which they occur and in the number and roles of the participants. Focal relationships occur over longer periods of time, in a variety of interpersonal situations with a larger, but not infinite, number of persons. Furthermore, the roles that others play in the two experiences differ. Teachers, mentors, tutors, and sometimes friends often play important roles in crystallizing experiences (Zuckerman, 1983). The roles of significant others in focal relationships may include many others as well, for example, surrogate parents, close, intimate friends (usually older persons), individual or institutional patrons, therapists, admirers, and lovers. Focal relationships can be involved in a greater range of developmental issues and on deeper levels of experiences, and for longer, for example, Samuel Johnson (Bate, 1983), William James (Strout, 1983), and Beethoven (Solomon,

1977). Differences in crystallizing experiences and focal relationships cited above are reflected in their different impact on developing eminence. The impact of crystallizing experiences is more domain-specific and somewhat more isolated from other aspects of the youth's development than are focal relationships.

These powerful learning experiences—crystallizing experiences and focal relationships—frequently occur in the age period between 12 and 16 years, a period which brings with it impressionability, heightened receptiveness to troubling stimuli, both with and around oneself. When these sensitivities meet the cognitive developments of the period, a talented person has the drive and resources for transforming creative potential into real-life creative behavior (cf. Spark, 1987).

PATHS TO EMINENCE

All that has been said above is meant to lead to the presentation of two very distinctive developmental paths to eminence. They do not represent two ends of a continuum as much as they are the consequences of specific sets of relationships early and later, especially in adolescence, types of emotionality, types of identifications, and giftedness in specific domains. Each path utilizes either focal relationships or crystallizing experiences. And each path, I believe, has its own strengths and risks. Neither is an easy path nor a safe bet. I realize that there is a third developmental path implied by the above discussion—one derived from the working of a "good enough" family. Yet, my own observations tell me that such families, whether with gifted children or not, more often than not have "good-enough" children. There are children who fit Baumrind's (1971) competencies and Coopersmith's (1968) children of moderate to high self-esteem. These are children who may become effective to highly effective adults (MacKinnon, 1983) but probably will not achieve notable eminence. Furthermore, at this time, I frankly cannot visualize a third midpath merging the other two. I suspect that if there were such a path it would cancel out the power and focus of the other two to such an extent that little developmental drive and direction would come from it.

How do we know when development works well? Freud said when we can love and work; Erikson's answer is when we continue to grow and develop and learn age and culturally appropriate lessons. There are surely other answers, but I believe one sign is when, in spite of whatever the gifts, early stresses, confusions, frustrations to one's sense of identity, or levels and domains of abilities, they are synaptic, so well aligned that the expression of one is synergic to the use of the others. One does not really achieve eminence by simply wanting it, although this does contribute. Eminence is a by-product of how one develops and uses the tools and opportunities one has in life. Achievement of any degree of eminence is never linear, never a foregone conclusion at any one time.

We turn now to the two paths to eminence. One is a congruous path seen primarily in science-symbolic-oriented careers, and the other, an incongruous-conflicted path observed primarily in people-passion-oriented careers. Ironically, it seems that if an individual in either type of career has the opposite type of developmental path, she/he is less likely to achieve eminence than if paths and careers mesh appropriately. One path to eminence is made up of conflict, incongruencies between child and parents and often between the parents. Emotionally, the family and early development are a series of turbulent disagreements with either too little or too much parental control in determining what is wanted of the child and how it is to be attained. We mentioned earlier the danger of excessive narcissism. It can be at work in this type of family as well. It has shown itself in the exceedingly high ambitions and limited views of a gifted child in the histories of John S. Mills, Martin Luther, and in the case of one prodigy who failed, William Sidis. If anything, these examples demonstrate that often gifted children develop and succeed in spite of their parents.

The incongruent path is also made up of differences between the child and parents about career choice. I am struck by the number of famous writer and painters, especially in the 19th century, whose families, usually the father, had careers in mind that had little relation to the son's obvious talent. This type of intrafamily strife and dissonance is more likely to happen where the family's values are predominately those of conventional status and security.

From what has already been said, it is clear why this developmental path to eminence is fraught with a series of parent–child disengagements. Beginning as it does in conflict and disharmony, it probably never truly ends in close harmony or full acceptance. It is a path characterized by a high degree of risk for the child. Since the parents may be in conflict, one risk is for the gifted child to be seduced or co-opted by one parent, thereby engendering the rejection or hatred of the other. Needless to say, many such histories are characterized by a number of ambivalences, some of which become incorporated in the identity of the gifted child. Conflicts, ambivalences, rejections, extremes in control, and paradoxically, intrafamily relationships that may be too close, overly binding, and difficult to be freed of are frequently reported. The usual and necessary parent-child separations are often especially difficult. The child's progressive individuation is hampered or resented.

Because of these conditions within the family and between the parent(s) and gifted child, where these gifts are in the nonsciences and the child's temperament is more sensitive to internal and external stimuli ("thin-skinned"), the child has a great chance of being very interested in and sensitive to people and passionate relationships. All of these are powerful preconditions for seeking and establishing focal relationships of great intensity. Such relationships are likely to be sought out throughout a large part of the gifted person's active career for their noncognitive supports and rewards. They are more counterbalancing than reconciliations of early family issues. Focal relationships can rarely achieve this, but they can support and encourage the continued development of the child. In this manner, these relationships keep alive the child's cognitive growth by keeping it from being overly preoccupied or frustrated with the intrafamily turbulences and incongruities, allowing further explorations into self and gifts, even if at times this is a well-kept secret. There are two final remarks to make here. Focal relationships— and remember there is likely to be a series of them—often will be characterized by ambivalences, disappointments, and risks. It is a sense of need and disappointment that motivates them. These later-appearing relationships are often related to a particular period of crisis; once this is overcome, the lesson of survival learned anew, the relationship dissolves. One hopes it will be succeeded by a new focal relationship appropriate to the new developmental level and educational needs.

The second type of path to eminence is one of congruence. This is not necessarily a path of tranquillity. What characterizes it as much as anything is that the parent-child relationships are of moderation in their emotionality, in their career pressures, and in their overall involvements. This is not a matter of indifference, but more of temperament and prior family history. Although I think this path is more linked to science-symbol-oriented domains and careers, it can also be seen in the background of persons with other cognitive orientations. The congruent path to eminence can paradoxically appear in the career choices of those persons whose early turbulent, conflict-laden family life and socializations contribute to their extreme sensitivity to the needs and wishes of others, in childhood and later. Many come from homes in which, even as young children, they took care of the parent(s), managed the household, felt compelled to be good, quiet, and competent, often at great personal and developmental sacrifice. These experiences have led to a heightened, often driven, need of their own to meet the needs of others and to fit into their wishes. One example that probably reflects the congruent path is adult children of alcoholics. Such persons are very likely to find careers dedicated to working closely with persons in great pain and need, for example, nurses, social workers, teachers, and therapists in a variety of disciplines. But their apparent congruences are just that—more apparent than real once one learns of their early family history. What is congruent is their need to care for others, often at no little sacrifice of their own individuality and more fitting and satisfying use of their gifts.

Other persons who travel the more congruent path to eminence come from families that are more accepting of their development and talents, families with a high degree of agreement and low emotionality. If there are problems, they are sporadic rather than enduring, more of a here-now nature and more quickly resolvable (cf. Clark, 1983).

The temperances and congruencies are observable in a number of areas within significant family members' own personalities and their interrelationships with one another and their careers. Such families are also characterized by an unconflicted acceptance of the young child, and a recognition and early acceptance, if not encouragement, of this child's gifts. How different this is from the histories of many famous writers, social scientists, politicians, and humanistic philosophers! In such a family it is not likely or necessary for the gifted child to become embroiled in longstanding family clashes. Rather, these children move to their realization of giftedness and identity formation with relative ease.

Parental recognitions and encouragements are the backbone to this developmental ease. Along with this ease, there is often a steady, undramatic, unclogged series of age-appropriate separations and individuations between parents and child, so that interestingly the child often continues closeness with the family, and does not develop a personality or ego ideals too different or difficult for its family. This is not to imply that nonindividuation occurs in this child, but that it occurs in age-appropriate, family-tolerated increments and along recognizable dimensions. The guidelines of this individuation and self-acceptance are motivated by fitting into family rather than by exaggerated, contrafamily motives and values. In fact, these might hardly even be raised to the level of becoming explicit issues and goals, but remain as parts of a large assumptive mass.

One can see that the closeness that characterizes the congruent path is a product of several key processes within the family, not the least of which is the relative harmony between the parents and between them and their own goals and attainments. Also, without dramatic stress and recurrent conflicts within the family, the identifications occur more naturally and are based more on overt behavior than covert subtexts.

What I am describing is a family-child relationship that is comparatively low-key, agreeable to all, and mutually flattering—but one that is not necessarily flat or repressed, resigned, neutral, or deadening. What makes for this type of family and in turn makes it such a fitting developmental environment for this type of path to eminence is that the temperament, personalities, aspirations, and domains of aptitudes within it are congruent. We have already mentioned the similarity of talents and interests that are quite characteristic of families in general because of their genetics (Scarr, Webber, Weinberg, & Wittig, 1981) and ongoing socialization processes.

This particular congruent picture matches the nature of science-symbol-oriented gifts and establishes the grounds for their early recognitions, acceptances, and demonstration. The smooth transitions we see are both the basics and the manifestation of this congruence, making the area and degree of achievement far more contingent on the power of the child's gifts and the availability of appropriate careers than on the mediation of family life. This means that crystallizing experiences should play a much more critical role in the external validation of these gifts. The dramatic impact of these experiences on a young adolescent, with all the ripeness of that period, should furnish the drive to live out the developmental lessons learned from such a clear experience of one's gifts. The family's acceptances, harmony, or indifferences make up the contrasting background for a crystallizing experience and, if anything, sharpens its lessons.

Like the incongruent path to eminence, the congruent path also has its risks. With its moderate but comfortable closeness among members, its easy, ready acceptances, its broad tolerances and consistent affiliations, there is the risk that the gifted child will be too comfortable, too fitting in the family, and too identified with it. I almost want to say compromised, but this might be a value judgment. Be that as it may, the risk is that the gifted child may not be highly motivated to seek or meet challenges that can provide stimulation and rewards, nor be able to recognize careers other than those agreeable to the family's wishes and ego ideals and part of the family tradition. So, where the child traveling the incongruent path to eminence must struggle with, undergo, and overcome repeated emotionality, painful parental inconsistencies, ambivalent recognition of gifts and conflict within himself and his family, the child traveling the congruent path to eminence may rest too easily or too soon upon his early, accepted giftedness. When this does not happen, the congruence itself, directive and prescriptive as it may be, is a foundation and focus to great careers. I say this because the things we come to love and want often breed the very resources we need to find and nurture them.

REFERENCES

Albert, R.S. (1969). The concept of genius and its implications for the study of creativity and giftedness. *American Psychologist, 24,* 743-753.

Albert, R.S. (1971). Cognitive development and parental loss among the gifted, the exceptionally gifted and the creative. *Psychological Reports, 29,* 19-26.

Albert, R.S. (1978). Observations and suggestions regarding giftedness, familial influences and the achievement of eminence. *Gifted Child Quarterly, 22,* 201-222.

Albert, R.S. (1981). Special programs require special people. *The Roeper Review, 4,* 2-4.

Albert, R.S. (1983a). Toward a behavioral definition of genius. In R.S. Albert (Ed.), *Genius and eminence: The social psychology of creativity and exceptional achievement* (pp. 57-72). Oxford: Pergamon.

Albert, R.S. (1983b). Family positions and the attainment of eminence: A study of special family positions and special family experiences. In R.S. Albert (Ed.), *Genius and eminence: The social psychology of creativity and exceptional achievement* (pp. 141-154). Oxford: Pergamon.

Albert, R.S., & Runco, M.A. (1986). The achievement of eminence: A model based on a longitudinal study of exceptionally gifted boys and their families. In R.J. Sternberg & J.E. Davidson (Eds.), *Conceptions of giftedness* (pp. 323-357). New York: Cambridge University Press.

Albert, R.S., & Runco, M.A. (1987). The possible different personality dispositions of scientists and non-scientists. In D. Jackson & J.P. Rushton (Eds.), *Scientific excellence: Origins and assessment* (pp 67-97). Beverly Hills, CA: Sage.

Allen, D.W. (1979). Hidden stresses in success. *Psychiatry, 42,* 171-17.

Bate, J.W. (1978). *The achievement of Samuel Johnson.* Chicago, IL: University of Chicago Press.

Baumrind, D. (1971). Current patterns of parental authority. *Developmental Psychology Monograph, 4*(1), 1-103.

Berrington, H. (1983). Prime ministers and the search for love. In R. Albert (Ed.), *Genius and eminence: The social psychology of creativity and exceptional achievement* (pp. 358-373). New York: Pergamon.

Bloom, B.S. (Ed.). (1985). *Developing talent in young people.* New York: Ballantine.

Clark, R.M. (1983). *Family life and school achievement: Why poor Black children succeed or fail.* Chicago: University of Chicago Press.

Coopersmith, S. (1968). *The antecedents of self-esteem.* San Francisco: Freeman.

Cox, C.M. (1926). *Genetic studies of genius. Vol. 2: The early mental traits of three hundred geniuses.* Stanford: Stanford University Press.

Erikson, E.H. (1968). *Childhood and society* (2nd ed.). New York: Norton.

Fast, I. (1975). Aspects of work style and work difficulty in borderline personalities. *International Journal of Psychoanalysis, 56,* 397-403.

Galton, F. (1869). *Hereditary genius.* New York: Macmillan.

Galton, F. (1874). *English men of science: Their nature and nurture.* New York: Macmillan.

Gallagher, J.J., & Lucito, L.J. (1961). Intellectual patterns of gifted compared with average and retarded. *Exceptional Children, 27,* 479-482.

Gardner, H. (1983). *Frames of mind: The theory of multiple intelligences.* New York: Basic Books.

Gedo, J.E. (1983). *Portraits of the artist.* New York: Guilford.

Gottschalk, L.A. (1981). Psychoanalytic contributions to the generation of creativity in children. *Psychiatry, 44,* 210-229.

Gruber, H.E. (1986). The self-construction of the extra-ordinary. In R.J. Sternberg & J. Davidson (Eds.), *Conceptions of giftedness* (pp. 247-263). New York: Cambridge University Press.

Hamilton, J.A. (1983). Development of interest and enjoyment in adolescence. Part I. Attentional capacities. *Journal of Youth and Adolescence, 12,* 355-362.

Heckhausen, H. (1967). *The anatomy of achievement motivation.* New York: Academic Press.

Hildreth, G. (1954). Three gifted children: A developmental study. *Journal of Genetic Psychology, 85,* 239-262.

Hollingworth, L. (1942). *Children above 180 IQ Stanford Binet: Origins and Development.* Yonkers, NY: World Book.

Holton, G. (1978). *The scientific imagination: Case studies.* Cambridge: Cambridge University Press.

Howe, M.J. (1982). Biographical evidence and the development of outstanding individuals. *American Psychologist, 37,* 1071-1081.

Jackson, D.N., & Rushton, J.P. (Eds.). (1987). *Scientific excellence: Origins and assessment.* Beverly Hills: Sage.

Janos, P.M., & Robinson, N. (1985). Psychosocial development in intellectually gifted children. In F.D. Horowitz & M. O'Brien (Eds.), *The gifted and talented: Developmental perspectives* (pp. 149-195). Washington, DC: American Psychological Association.

Janos, P.M., Sanfilippo, S., & Robinson, N. (1986). "Underachievement" among markedly accelerated college students. *Journal of Youth and Adolescence, 15,* 303-313.

Keniston, K. (1965). *The uncommitted.* New York: Harcourt, Brace and World.

MacKinnon, D.W. (1963). Creativity and images of the self. In R.W. White (Ed.), *The study of lives* (pp. 250-278). New York: Atherton.

MacKinnon, D.W. (1983). The highly effective individual. In R.S. Albert (Ed.), *Genius and eminence: The social psychology of creativity and exceptional achievement* (pp. 114-127). Oxford: Pergamon.

Miller, A. (1981). *The drama of the gifted child: How narcissistic parents form and deform the emotional lives of their talented children.* New York: Basic Books.

Montour, K.M. (1977). William James Sidis: The broken twig. *American Psychologist, 32,* 265-279.

Moore, B.E., & Fine, B.D. (1967). *A glossary of psychoanalytic terms and concepts.* New York: American Psychoanalytic Association.

Ochberg, R.L. (1986). College drop-outs: The developmental logic of psychosocial moratoria. *Journal of Youth and Adolescence, 15,* 287-302.

Roe, A. (1952). *The making of a scientist.* New York: Dodd, Mead.

Rushton, J.P. (in press). Scientific creativity: An individual differences perspective. *Journal of Social and Biological Structures.*

Scarr, S., Webber, P.L., Weinberg, R.A., & Wiggig, M. (1981). Personality resemblance among adolescents and their parents in biologically related and adoptive families. *Journal of Personality and Social Psychology, 40,* 885-898.

Simonton, D.K. (1987). Developmental antecedents of achieved eminence. *Annals of Child Development, 4,* 131-169.

Solomon, M. (1977). *Beethoven.* New York: Schirmer.

Spark, M. (1987). *Mary Shelly: A biography.* New York: Dutton.

Strout, C. (1983). William James and the twice-born sick soul. In R.S. Albert (Ed.), *Genius and eminence: The social psychology of creativity and exceptional achievement* (pp. 374-385). Oxford: Pergamon.

Walters, J., & Gardner, H. (1986). The crystallizing experience: Discovering an intellectual gift. In R.J. Sternberg & J.E. Davidson (Eds.), *Conceptions of giftedness* (pp. 306-331). New York: Cambridge University Press.

Winnicott, D.W. (1965). *The maturational processes and the facilitating environment.* London: The Hogarth and the Institute of Psychoanalysis.

Winnicott, D.W. (1971). *Play and reality.* New York: Basic Books.

Wispe, L.G. (1965). Some solid and psychological correlates of eminence in psychology. *Journal of the History of the Behavioral Sciences, 7*(1), 88-98.

Zuckerman, H. (1983). Scientific elite: Nobel Laureates' mutual influences. In R.S. Albert (Ed.), *Genius and eminence: The social psychology of creativity and exceptional achievement* (pp. 249-252). Oxford: Pergamon.

Chapter 6
Guiding the Parents of Gifted Children: The Role of Counselors and Teachers

Elizabeth A. Meckstroth

Parents of gifted children can provide teachers and counselors with a wealth of information and support. If they are treated with consideration and respect they are likely to reciprocate by sharing some of the extraordinary visions and sensitivities that they have about their children. This information can help us meet the special needs of gifted children at school. Parents, teachers, and counselors should be partners in guiding the development of gifted children as many of them progress toward remarkable achievement. In the matrix made by gifted children, their parents, teachers, and counselors, every involved person can enjoy growth and success working as a member of a collaborative team to help gifted children realize their potential. Synergy develops as each person opens to receive the experience, sensitivity, intensity, abilities, and ideas of the other. Synergy refers to a situation in which the combined effect of several components is far greater than the simple sum of the effect of each component. By meeting with parents individually or in groups, counselors can serve as a catalyst to bring the synergy into the matrix.

This chapter is designed to help counselors and teachers achieve a working partnership with parents of gifted children. It is divided into two sections. The first section deals with parent conferences. The second section is designed to provide counselors with specific guidelines and practical suggestions for organizing guided discussion groups for parents of gifted children.

PARENT CONFERENCES

A parent conference is a formal meeting between a teacher or counselor and the parents of an individual gifted child. The goal of such a meeting

95

is to share information that will be of value to each in their ongoing efforts to help the gifted child realize his/her abilities more fully. In conferences, parents and teachers or counselors exchange information about a child's abilities, interests, and needs that will help each better appreciate the child's unique characteristics. Critical decisions that affect the life of a gifted child are made both at home and at school. The exchange of information in conferences can result in wiser decisions in both settings.

Parent conferences are not always highly valued by teachers and administrators. Occasionally teachers are given specific instructions on how to deter "parents' interference." Some teachers and counselors are trained to conduct parent conferences in ways to make parents feel as if they are being heard, to convey interest, but to avoid actually integrating the parents' ideas. Some teachers are instructed to appease parents by portraying concern, but in fact to practice complete autonomy and control. Counselors and teachers must recognize and acknowledge such training for what it is and replace it with more effective attitudes and techniques. Unfortunate attitudes and practices by teachers and counselors have resulted in many parents of gifted children reporting that they find the helping professions of very little help (Parent Perspective, 1974).

Parents and the Identification of Giftedness

Psychometric testing and teacher recommendations have clear limitations as methods of identifying gifted children. They tap only some components of a child's skills and characteristics. When the U.S. Office of Education conducted the School Staffing survey in 1969, 57 percent of school administrators responded that they had no gifted children in their schools (Marland, 1972). Contrary to popular prejudice, parents tend to be realistic predictors of their children's abilities and needs. Accordingly, parent conferences can be used to improve the validity of procedures used to.identify gifted learners. Several studies have indicated that teachers and other school personnel are generally a less reliable source of identifying gifted children than are the children's parents (Barbe, 1965; Jacobs, 1971). For example, Jacobs (1971) found that 76 percent of parents could correctly identify their gifted kindergarten children. By contrast, teachers identified only 4.3 percent of these gifted children. Jacobs' studies also showed that parents' concerns generally reflected the level of their child's ability. They were concerned about potential social maladjustment and insufficient educational stimulation to challenge and maintain the child's intellectual interests. Follow-up intelligence and achievement testing confirmed the accuracy of parents' perceptions in most cases.

Teacher observations and recommendations are very frequently used as an initial screening process to select children to participate in the psychometric testing programs designed to identify gifted learners. It is, therefore, critical that teachers be aware of their own possible bias in perceptions and come to recognize the value of parent participation in the process of identifying gifted learners. Studies by Pegnato and Birch (1959) found that teachers at the junior high level most often identified as gifted those children who are most like themselves, that is, cooperative, well-groomed children. The Pegnato and Birch study revealed that teachers identified only 45 percent of their students who were later found to be intellectually gifted on psychometric tests.

The results of Gogel's extensive survey (Gogel, McCumsey, & Hewitt, 1985) indicate that we may have confidence in most parents' appraisals. Gogel et al. found that 87 percent of parents questioned had recognized their child's giftedness before age six. Unfortunately, many of these parents may be labeled "pushy parents" by school personnel. One mother regretted that she was considered a "pushy parent" by the principal, but she wished that he would appreciate that she had a "pushy child!"

Despite the findings on the accuracy with which parents identify their children's giftedness, it is rare to find their opinions seriously considered in the process of identification. Many parents hesitate to initiate contact with the school and to request testing or individualized programming for their gifted children because of fear of negative repercussions from school personnel. In a support group for parents of gifted children, one father expressed his frustration in trying to cooperate with school personnel to achieve appropriate programming by saying, "They don't know, but they don't know that they don't know." The importance of receiving information from parents begins with identification, and extends through the entire involvement with the child.

Helping Parents Acknowledge Giftedness

In dealing with parents, counselors and teachers will encounter a vast range of information and emotional reactions to their child's giftedness. Some parents may be quite unaware of their child's giftedness, while others are overinvolved and overconcerned (Gowan & Bruch, 1971). In a family of high performers, a child who meets the parent's high expectations may not be seen as exceptional (Lester & Anderson, 1981). Sometimes a parent will plead, "If you don't label him gifted, then he may still have a chance to be normal." For parents like these, and those who feel insecure about acknowledging special abilities, the counselor and teacher may need to suggest some additional reading about the characteristics and needs of gifted children. Parents sometimes grieve for the loss of their "normal" child (Ross, 1964). They feel that as parents of a gifted child, more will be expected of them. They wonder if they can measure up. Since their child's abilities are now recognized and valued, they feel that the job of parenting must now be taken much more seriously.

There are cautions that need to be conveyed to parents when they learn that their child, because of his exceptional abilities, is going to participate in a special curriculum. Miller (1981) explains that parents of gifted children may focus on their child's accomplishments more than giving him support for how he feels and values himself. Miller warns that these parents may use children as a second chance to become what they, themselves, have missed. It does not escape astute children that they may be used and valued to make their parents look good. Willings (1985) found that gifted children who felt valued primarily for their accomplishments became unhappy adults and resented their parents. Parents need to be aware of this and consider their reactions to their children to insure that they do not inadvertently usurp their child's satisfaction.

When asked how their parents reacted when they were identified as gifted, 10-year-old Kevin revealed, "Oh, they were glad that they were— oh!, I mean that I was—gifted" (Kearney, 1986). In talking with a group of gifted children about the sources and causes of giftedness, and explaining the effects of environment and heredity, 8-year-old Jason reversed the flow of influence from parent to child: "I think that they (the parents) get it from us: First we're told that we're gifted and then the parents think that they're gifted too.'

Helping Parents Understand Giftedness

Children are greatly influenced by their parents' expectations. It is critical that school personnel cooperate with parents to identify each child's particular abilities. This process needs to include an individual conference with the parents. It is important that the tone of this meeting not be, "Congratulations, you have a gifted child. He can be anything he wants to be!" From such glorifications, parents may begin to perceive their gifted children as paragons of virtue (Cornell, 1984). These generalized statements are detrimental and perpetuate prevalent myths about gifted children. These popular attitudes may be summarized by, "Why do something for someone who has everything going his way?" When discussing giftedness with parents, it is critical that the focus be on their child's particular abilities and needs. The conference must focus on what giftedness means and what it does not mean. We should avoid a gifted–nongifted dichotomy and focus instead on the particular abilities, sensitivities, concerns, intensities, personality, temperament, and interests of the child. The goal is to appreciate the characteristics of that child's uniqueness, not just the ways he demonstrates achievement.

A prevailing caution for counselors to consider in interpreting giftedness to parents is that the label "gifted" does not apply to all abilities. There must be an interpretation of the identification criteria and findings. Too often, generalized superior expectations flow from a high score on a single achievement test. If the identification method was an achievement test such as the California Test of Basic Skills, the scores reflect achievement in the particular areas measured, not necessarily general intelligence. Often, an IQ score is extrapolated from these limited achievement scales. If this is the case, what this score does *not* represent must be emphasized.

If an IQ test such as the Wechsler Intelligence Scale for Children-Revised was administered, the score ranges of the particular abilities tested should be interpreted and explained to the parents. Extensive emotional damage has occurred when parents are told their child's general scores or IQ ranks in percentiles. One mother was told that her son tested in the top 1 percent. She said that was the beginning of a disaster for her son because she and her husband then imposed all the expectations of what a top 1 percent child should be. Parents may have their own stereotypic views that interfere with proper appreciation of their own child (Colangelo, 1979). Again, the specific components of subtests must be recognized, and the different ranges of scores explained. The interpretation must be in terms of particular abilities and needs.

Intellectual giftedness is a diverse and complex phenomenon. There is a range of abilities within the gifted group just as there is within the average and below average range of intelligence. Moreover, similar IQ does not indicate similar personality, interests, abilities, or temperament. A child with an IQ in the 160 range may be as different from other gifted children as he/she is from those children not identified as gifted. Rather than saying, "Your child is a gifted child," we need to explain the meaning and influence of the particular abilities identified.

In the current chapter, the emphasis is for the most part on working with parents of intellectually gifted learners. However, it is clear from the discussion above that it is advisable for counselors and teachers to be aware of the broad multidimensional definitions that have been adopted by most states in the United States to guide their programs of special education for gifted children. For a thorough discussion of the categories and levels of gifted behavior as we now understand them, readers are referred to the presentation of Milgram's 4 × 4 Structure of Giftedness model in an earlier chapter of this book.

What do parents of gifted children want for their children? 1,039 surveyed parents (Gogel et al., 1985) responded in three categories: In school they want appropriate education by creative and flexible teachers, leading to a productive, fulfilling career; on the personal level, they want their children to achieve self-acceptance, that is to have a positive self-image on the one hand, and to be accepted by their peers, on the other; from the community they want adequate funding for gifted programs and public acceptance of the need for these programs. Most counselors and teachers share these goals and objectives. When regular parent conferences provide the opportunity for parents, teachers, and counselors to share their goals and to cooperate in realizing them through school programming, gifted learners benefit greatly.

PARENT DISCUSSION GROUPS

Success at school will be greatly facilitated if parents are understanding and encouraging with their children at home (Sanborn, 1979). Parents are a primary influence in the development of their children. The relationship is the essence of the child's self-esteem. One effective way to inform and to encourage parents of gifted children is through guided discussion groups. Discussion among parents can offer rich insight about qualities of gifted children and guidance for their development. Counselors may indirectly support their gifted students by arranging and facilitating parent support groups.

Parent support groups become a more valuable experience if organized as a series of group discussions and if parents agree to attend the entire series. The series may consist of six to ten sessions meeting weekly or biweekly. It is recommended that sessions be scheduled for two hours, with the last half hour reserved for informal interaction, perhaps with refreshments. There is a definite advantage if both parents attend. Other involved people such as grandparents and babysitters may attend. It is recommended to limit the group size to seven to fifteen people.

It is recommended that the discussion groups be conducted by two people who act as coleaders. At least one of the leaders should be trained and experienced in facilitating group process. At least one coleader should have knowledge of the special needs of gifted children and their families. Even when one leader fills both roles, it is advisable to have a coleader in the group in order to meet the various group members' needs and personalities.

The series can be called something like "A Seminar on Bringing out the Best." Thus, the appeal is academic and positive. It is critical that there be no implication that this is a therapy or a counseling group. Most parents do not want to identify themselves as having problems and needing help. If possible, arrange a location on "neutral" territory so that association with the child's school setting does not restrict expression. A university or library location often lends an inquiring atmosphere.

Orientation Meeting

Prior to the seminar series, schedule a parents' orientation meeting. Notice of this meeting and the topic schedule for the series may be published in the local newspaper to involve interested persons. In this orientation, include general information about gifted children in order to help parents identify with other parents and to allow the group to meet the group leaders. This session can establish the purpose and need for the seminar. A suggested statement could be: "The purpose of this series is to help parents learn to be more encouraging to their children, and to facilitate their children's success at school and in their personal relationships."

The registration form might ask if child care during the meeting time is desired. Ask for the names and ages of children concerned. Concurrent child care might be arranged in a nearby area.

Facilitating Group Process: General Principles

Many counselors have received training and had experience in conducting support groups for parents. Most, however, have little knowledge of the particular challenges and problems presented by gifted children. The information and suggestions in the current section are designed to supplement that of trained counselors. It goes without saying that counselors without the requisite general training and experience should not undertake the task of organizing and conducting support groups for the parents of gifted children.

A succinct, basic manual of group process is the Leader's Manual for Systematic Training for Effective Parenting (Dinkmeyer & McKay, 1976). Here are some suggestions to enable group members to recognize their own strengths and abilities and to learn new insights and encouraging behaviors:

1. Turn questions to the group for answers. Build cohesion from sharing the same struggle! Encourage learning from each other. Build your information on the participants' responses.
2. Do not disparage anyone's contribution. Rather, ask how other people feel about the same issue.
3. Recognize progress of group members with statements such as, "You are gaining insight into the reasons for Lisa's getting poor grades."
4. Write statements made by participants on a wall chart or board to confirm and clarify their contributions.
5. Focus on the positive behavior of the children and the parents. This may be done by asking, "What did you learn? What might you try differently next time?
6. Recognize common themes. Point out similarities of group members' ideas and situations. Clarify. Develop principles from the group's statements.
7. If one group member develops a distracting emotional reaction, the coleader can ease the situation by taking the member away for private consultation.
8. Guide the group to focus on solutions. Use a decision-making process such as the Creative Problem-Solving Process:
   • *Define the problem and who owns the problem:* What would you like to be different; what is involved?
   • *Brainstorm alternatives:* What is important to me? In what ways might I make that happen? Go for quantity and make no evaluations at this point.
   • *Evaluate consequences:* How might this meet my criteria of needs? How might this work for me? How might this work against me? How would I feel then? Is it worth it?
   • *Find acceptance:* How might I integrate this change?
   • *Make a plan:* What will I do and by when?
   • *Do it!*
   • *Reevaluate at the following session:* What did I learn from this? How did it help? What might I do differently next time?
9. Keep in mind that parents will learn from your behavior.
10. Encourage parents to feel confident that they know much that is valuable.
11. Be aware of your body's messages: Maintain eye contact, open hands and body position. Draw in people by facing them and leaning forward. When appropriate, restrict participation by turning away from participant.
12. Recognize their feelings. Affirm their feelings. Help them label their feelings. Help them differentiate between their feelings and their behavior.

13. Be receptive to suggestions. Ask for feedback. Describe your own mistakes and disappointments so that you can demonstrate that these "failures" can be experiments and opportunities to learn that you may try in the future. Your co-leader can be cued to disagree with you and you can demonstrate constructive reconsideration.

14. Time spent on discussion of a particular topic or situation may need to be limited. You might suggest, "Let's limit our focus on Jane's power struggle to two more minutes because we need to include some other people's situations."

15. Close the session at the scheduled time. Parents of gifted children usually are eager to extend these group discussions.

16. Summarize the session to help members understand characteristics of giftedness and ways they can respond constructively.

17. At the end of each session, ask participants to write down one change in their behavior which they choose to make until the following session.

18. Allow time for informal interaction.

19. Begin each following session by asking members if they had any experiences since they last met in which they drew on the group experience and used any information or insights they had learned. Recognize and encourage any aspect of their experience that indicates changing their own behavior to encourage their children. Accept their mistakes and negative feelings.

Facilitating Group Process: Specific Topics

Those readers interested in a detailed and specific description of approaches found effective in organizing support groups for the parents of gifted children are referred to Webb, Meckstroth, and Tolan (1982). This book includes a session by session listing of topics and is, in effect, a complete step-by-step manual. The following specific topics are basic and will probably be included for discussion in most parent support groups. The topics are meant to be examples of those that might actually be selected. The list is not intended to be exhaustive.

The first session: Characteristics and identification. During the first session, establish a base for productive idea sharing. Introduce the concept that effective parenting practices that we learned from our own childhood experience, or from other sources, are not always effective in encouraging gifted children. Some of the ideas learned in childhood will be replaced in the course of this seminar. Some parents, "experts," and participants in our group may not agree with some of our ideas. Explain that this is not a therapy group, that members are competent and wish to progress by learning to be more effective in their relationships with their children. The group is not intended to deal with problems that require professional intervention.

There are some ground rules that need to be agreed upon during the first session. Stress the importance and necessity of confidentiality—not mentioning the names of participants outside the group and not introducing in group discussions the names of individuals not present. Ask the group to agree that anything expressed in the group is confidential. Another ground rule to establish is that members will not negatively criticize any statement. Instead, they may ask questions and try to better understand the thinking of other members. Ask the group for suggestions of further ground rules.

Other housekeeping topics might include raising the question of refreshments and, if wanted, how to provide them. Arrangements for cooperative child care can also be discussed.

Set the tone that you are there to learn from them too. Encourage each person to participate; explain that every person's contribution is valuable. Describe the disadvantages of one person monopolizing the time. Explain that each of us can be responsible only for our own behavior and reactions; we cannot control how another person acts. We can act in ways that help children become successful and happy.

Ask the participants to introduce themselves, tell a little bit about their life and children, and to talk about the behavior characteristics of their children that suggest that they might have exceptional abilities and sensitivities. The components of high intelligence should be discussed and clarified. The leader could briefly present the concepts of Structure of the Intellect (Guilford, 1967), the theory of multiple intelligences (Gardner, 1983), and the triarchic theory of intelligence (Sternberg, 1984). Explain the limitations of testing. The topic of "Interpreting Giftedness: General Principles" as presented in an earlier section of this chapter when discussing parent conferences should be discussed in the first group session. The levels of intellectual giftedness as reflected in the range of IQ scores and the relative frequency of occurrence must be understood. Describe the differences between talent, exceptional performance and achievement, and being high in overall intelligence. The distinction between potential and performance must be explored and understood.

Ask the group, "What does it feel like to be a gifted child?" This is to emphasize the importance of focusing on the emotional aspects of giftedness.

In this initial session, it is valuable to address the issue that giftedness does not go away. If parents have a gifted child, it is likely that at least one of them is a gifted grown-up. A frequent reaction to reading

Guiding the Gifted Child (Webb, Meckstroth, & Tolan, 1982) is "Now, I understand why I never fit in as a child. I always thought that there was something wrong with me, but I saw myself described on those pages." Acknowledgment of their giftedness is often a poignant experience for parents. This insight is also a way for leaders to understand some of the participants' emotional responses. Parents need to be offered the understanding that when they are dealing with their child, they might also be responding to the emotional reactions of their own growing up. Offer this consideration throughout the series. In closing, you could ask parents to closely observe their children to identify their exceptional characteristics.

Discipline

To begin the discussion of discipline, you might ask parents to describe methods that seem effective in disciplining their child. You might also ask them to tell about techniques that do not seem effective. Discipline, with many gifted children, requires approaches that are different from the conventional methods used with youngsters not identified as gifted. Gifted children inherently question and reason. They need to understand why they are asked to do anything. To simply say, "Do it because I say so!" is both ineffective and self-defeating.

The usual forms of punishment, especially those imposed without warning, do not generally work with gifted children. For them punishment is usually a destructive action that results in some form of retaliation. It puts parents in a power struggle in which they probably will lose in some way. As one 7-year-old explained, "I always have the last word." Although punishment probably does not affect intelligence, defined as one's overall ability to learn, it can decrease a child's *measured* intelligence. On the other hand, children from families that express encouragement, have stable structure, and reasonable, understood limits scored increasingly higher on IQ tests until age 8 (McCall, Applebaum, & Hogarty, 1978).

One effective discipline tool is to use the principles of decision-making processes discussed in an earlier section of this chapter with the children. See the section entitled "Facilitating Group Process: General Principles" for an explanation of the decision-making process. This section should be incorporated in the parent discussion groups. Parents need to be encouraged to see that they themselves have choices and are responsible for their own behavior at home. They can practice in the group sessions those behaviors that they would like to demonstrate in real life.

The goal for parents is to nurture a child who is secure, responsible, confident, and who feels that he or she is not a victim of circumstances, but can always choose from options. This is done partly by encouraging a child to develop self-control. A goal of discipline is to help the child see that she has control over her behavior; thus, she can choose the consequences of her behavior. The child needs to understand and agree that she will have advantages by cooperating. All rules, limits, and expectations should be mutually understood and agreed upon. This process includes agreeing on consequences—preferably ones that are not imposed, but instead are natural or logical responses to the child's behavior (Dreikurs & Soltz, 1964). Emphasis is on understanding the reasons for these rules. With this type of discipline, parents let the child experience responsibility. Children need to experience that their parents are responsible to carry out their own part of expectations and consequences too.

To promote positive behavior, parents need to recognize the specific behavior they want to develop. Rather than saying, "You're such a good girl," say, "When you help your sister tie her shoes, aren't you happy that you are such a helpful person?" Parents should recognize any slight increment of positive behavior that they want increased. They should focus on positive behavior and let the child know that he is important to them when he is managing himself in ways that work for him.

Children are encouraged if parents actually depend on their ideas and activities; use what they think and do. This conveys, "You matter to me. What you think and do matters to me." Ask the group to give examples of ways they can recognize and reward positive behavior.

One caution for parents of gifted children is not to think of them as small adults. Often, because gifted children have outstanding language and reasoning abilities, parents and teachers think that they should be free from error. This pressure may lead gifted children to lower their performance in the hopes that not so much will be expected of them. Parents sometimes forget that these children have not lived long enough to learn the social intricacies that may be appropriate. Ask the group to describe some ways that we inadvertently express, "You should know better," for example, "I told you once!"

If there seems to be a behavior problem, parents can first determine who owns the problem. If it is clearly the child's, parents need to explore what it is that the child is seeking. It could possibly be power, attention, revenge, or to get parents not to expect so much of him. A way to begin this discovery process is to talk to the child about how she feels about the situation. If you show her that you care about her and want to understand how she feels about the situation; if she feels that you are on her side, she will be more likely to consider alternative behaviors.

Until the next session, ask parents to try to interpret some of their child's motives for his behavior. In his mind, how does he figure, "What's in it for me?"

Underachievement Because of Lack of Motivation to Learn

Parents' concerns about gifted children often focus on underachievement. In this session, parents can learn about influences that may be contributing to underachievement and the "unmotivated" child. Underachievement is defined as a discrepancy between potential and actual level of academic achievement. There are many possible reasons for underachievement. One explanation refers to lack of motivation to learn. For example, underachievement associated with lack of motivation to achieve in academic settings is frequently seen in children from socioeconomically disadvantaged backgrounds. By the same token, because of their socialization, girls often underachieve, especially as they enter junior high school and beyond. Despite wide recognition of these two sources of underachievement, most of the literature until very recently has focused on underachievement that results from problematic interpersonal interactions, frequently between children and their parents. In this section on underachievement we will also limit our discussion to lack of motivation rooted in family conflict. However, it must be recognized that this is only a partial treatment of a complex topic.

Whitmore (1980) suggests some ways to understand the thinking of underachievers. Some of the characteristics of underachievers are:

• They are unmotivated to do assigned tasks.
• They have negative motivation, that is, not to try.
• They do not feel rewarded by school experience.
• They have not been challenged and rewarded.

Underachievers may be motivated by their own needs and rewards. These could include:

• They choose not to do because they think that not to do is more rewarding.
• They want to be independent.
• They gain power by refusing to comply and, thus, win a power struggle.
• They fear success that might result in higher expectations and more pressures.

- They feel that the rewards are not worth the effort.
- There is a poor match between the school program and the child's abilities or learning style, thus, there is little opportunity to perform brilliantly.
- Projects involve what they already know and have experienced in their mind.
- Physical energy is not appropriately released.
- Their mental focus is not channeled.
- The purpose of the assignment has little meaning to them.
- Peer acceptance is more important than achievement.
- They may want to punish their parents (Bricklin & Bricklin, 1967).

One way to narrow the gap between potential and performance begins by determining whose interest and needs are being met. What are the expectations of the different people? Some gifted children feel that their successes belong to their parents while their failures belong to them. Having a tentative career goal often is instrumental in instilling a sense of purpose. Thinking of himself being all the things that he would like to be in the future provides a focus that may invigorate gifted children. This preview may begin with believing in a cause that is important to him, like "save the seals" or "prevent child abuse." Gifted children may feel discouraged if they do not view their future as being more than a job. Other steps toward helping the child enjoy a sense of confidence and competence include:

- Allow the child choices with defined limits.
- Ask the child to suggest ways that she would like to learn.
- Relate the learning project to the child's interest.
- Break the project down into intermediate successes.
- Develop a relationship with a mentor who cares about the child; takes time to listen, not just teach; respects the child's questions; and shares meaning and success.
- Have the child ask himself, "In what ways will my decision help me and hurt me?"
- Find her a peer so that she can enjoy a cooperative experience.
- Cut out criticism.
- Focus on every increment of positive behavior!
- Be a model of self management and responsibility!

Ask the group to discuss the ways they can cooperate at home to motivate their children at school.

Overachievement

Some parents have negative attitudes toward their child's high achievement and consider it unjustified by the child's ability. Gifted children tend to live with a series of interests which they pursue intensely. Where does the idea of overachievement come from? One source is their knowledge of the child's test scores. Parents and teachers tend to expect students' performance to correspond to their test scores. Sometimes we do not consider that the child may have an intense interest in something. Moreover, group IQ scores represent only a small range of abilities. Some adult reactions to "overachievement" are:

- He should be satisfied with less!
- She has "pushy parents."
- He doesn't know his place.
- It's not as easy for her as she makes it seem.
- She's not as smart as she thinks she is.
- He gave up a lot to excel.

The message for the child is: "Other people don't expect me to be so good." From this experience, the child may not appreciate her competence or she may feel like she is an impostor (Clance, 1986). Were Thomas Edison, Winston Churchill, Abraham Lincoln, and Babe Ruth overachievers?

Ask the group to discuss an occasion when they were proud of something they did but felt put down by someone else. How did this happen? How did you feel? How did you wish they would have responded? Ask the group to describe how "overachievement" can be detrimental to the child, such as when an activity becomes the child's only identity; such as if he is unhappy; and if there is an emphasis on one activity to the exclusion of balancing physical, social, emotional, and intellectual development.

Perfectionism. The search for perfection can sometimes paralyze gifted children. Some children learn that to be accepted, they must perform perfectly. This may begin with a sense that they must make their parents proud of them. Some parents need to have perfect children. (Josh's birthday card was addressed to "The Future President of the U.S.") These children are then motivated to avoid failure. They feel, "Unless I'm outstanding, I'm not significant" (Alvino, 1986). Thus, the goal of the child's perfectionism is to earn care, love, and approval. Gifted children are particularly likely to feel that they are valued for what they can achieve. Even as adults, they may seek identity and stability in their accomplishments (Kerr, 1985). For these people, the fear of failure is tremendous; they may think of themselves as losers. Parents can be effective in reducing these self-defeating behaviors. Primarily, parents need to be aware of what their own behavior is teaching their children. How do they react to their own mistakes? They may encourage their child to have more courage to create by doing some of the following activities:

• Focus on the process, more than the product. Recognize the meaning, effort, and time a child has invested.
• Reward trying something different.
• Break the task down into small, attainable successes. Help him reduce his immediate expectations. This is especially hard for children with vivid imaginations!
• Read biographies of accomplished people that describe how persistence contributed to their success and how they always learned something from the experience.
• Help them to be task selective and not to overburden themselves.
• Help them to identify what is important and satisfying to them.
• Help them to differentiate between their feelings of self-worth and their performance.

Ask parents to be aware of how they react to their own mistakes and disappointments during the period until the next session. Ask parents to consider how much of their own identity and satisfaction they reap from their child's accomplishments.

Conveying understanding and courage. You might begin this topic by talking about Paul Torrance's research on teachers who made a difference (Torrance, 1981). In this work gifted adults report that they can usually identify someone who especially encouraged them. Ask the group, "Who encouraged you? What did this person do?" What were the specific ways that person acted toward you? In what specific ways did that person affect your life?" Have a group discussion to bring out specific behaviors.

Since gifted children meet few people who can understand their sensitivities and needs, parents must strive to make their home a secure place for their children. The following ways parents can develop an encouraging relationship with their child can be discussed in parent support discussion groups. Throughout this presentation, ask participants to describe situations illustrating some of the ideas:

1. Remember that a basic theme of your relationship is to *take your gifted child seriously.*

2. You can build trust and influence when he feels that you want to listen to him. Listen with:
   - Silence and slight head nods.
   - "Mm, uh huh, I see"; let him know you're there with him.
   - Paraphrase his thoughts; do not add your own ideas or experience.
   - Ask for clarification. "How do you mean? Tell me a little bit more about that."
3. Listen to understand, rather than to respond. Listen as if she has something important to give to you. Try to see and feel the situation her way. Allow her to own her feelings. "I sense that you're furious with your brother." Remember that accepting and understanding need not always mean agreeing.
4. Listen to the silence. What is not said may hold more significance than what flows easily. Gifted children may use:
   - Passive silence to avoid telling you who they are;
   - Mutinous silence to control some of their environment;
   - Silent submission to gain acceptance (Gerleman, 1986)
5. Be honest! Playing games may be a way to forfeit your positive influence.
6. Respond to his feelings. Affirm his feelings. Help him label his feelings. Gifted people tend to intellectualize their lives, to be rational. If he can identify his feelings, he can begin to plan what he can do about what his feelings are telling him. "I'm in a bad mood" might mean feeling inadequate because he has agreed to do more than he has time to do. With gentle questions you can focus on helping him assign priorities to his values and activities.
7. Pause a few seconds before responding. You let her know you are giving careful thought to what is being said. You also avoid interrupting and learn better.
8. Arrange private time together. It is important that you spend time alone with your child every day. It is preferable that this occur spontaneously. Sometimes your child will want your time when it is not convenient. If this happens, tell him that you really want to be with him when you can give him better attention, not at that moment. Ask if you can make an agreement to talk at a later time. When this time comes, or better, often during the day, give him your full attention. This usually involves going to him.
9. Be aware of your body's messages. Gifted people are very astute in perceiving the nuances of body language, such as a raised eyebrow.
10. If you are comfortable, reflect your child's body position. If she is sitting on the floor with her legs stretched out in front, you sit

on the floor with your legs stretched out. Try to keep your head level at her head height or lower. Face her and look at her eyes. (Unfortunately, some children associate being scolded with someone looking straight into their eyes.) Open your hands toward her or touch her. Lean forward slightly. Listen with your whole body, mind and spirit as if nothing else at that moment matters as much as her thoughts and feelings.

11. Keep in mind that the gifted child may have learned that expressing anger is childish—that she should understand the situation more reasonably. Receive the angry feelings, although their expression in behavior may need to be guided. To do this, you can ask how the behavior would help her, how it would hurt her. There are many ways to express anger which are not self defeating and do not hurt other people.

12. Understand that gifted children usually have a vivid imagination; sometimes they confuse what they imagine with what actually happens. Understand that what they imagine often is their reality, that they worry about what they think could happen.

13. Help them separate what they feel and imagine from their behavior. Gifted children at times think that they can make things happen by what they think. Sometimes, gifted children think that other people should already know what they think. It is important to convey that you do not know, but that you want to know.

14. To understand the reality of gifted children is to understand that they often take events and statements personally; they feel responsible for what happens. Again, rather than telling your child her thoughts are absurd, listen to her and ask her how she feels; take her seriously. Later, through questions, you may guide her thinking so that she may recognize that she may not have acted responsibly.

15. Join him in his mind and imagination; grant him in fantasy that which he cannot have in reality. For example, you might say, "You wish that you could live on the beach and go swimming every day." If you agree, add, "I wish you could too."

16. Be responsible for your communication. You may hear, "You don't care; why should I?" and a slammed door nine times. Keep on caring and showing that you care.

17. Help her understand and accept that some other people cannot or will not always understand or appreciate what she cares about.

18. Strive to give life to his ideas. Be aware of your positive-to-negative response ratio.

19. Be aware of ways that you may unintentionally convey the belief in her mind that you don't take her seriously and that you discount her ideas and feelings.

Ask the group to give examples of ways people sometimes convey, "I don't want to understand." Ask parents to pay attention to the ratio of their positive-to-negative responses toward their children until the next session.

Sibling relationships. When one child in a family is identified as gifted, the other children in the family will often automatically label themselves as nongifted. Although a large literature has accumulated over the years documenting the critical influence of the family, especially parents on the development and realization of gifted behavior, very little attention has been given to the effect that gifted children have on their families. In a recent study, Cornell (1984) raised the issue and conducted what is, to the best of my knowledge, one of the first empirical investigations of it. His results document the reciprocal nature of the family/the gifted child influence and are likely to generate additional research on this relationship.

Often it is the oldest child in the family that tends to be the high achiever, eager for adult approval. Parents usually expect more from their first child, and spend more time with that child than with their younger children. Thus, more of the parents' ego may be invested in the first child.

Each child seeks to find his special place in the family (Dreikurs & Soltz, 1964). Children in the same family compare themselves with other children in that household; they often measure their value by the amount of power, attention, and time that they receive from their parents. Gifted children inherently seem to require—and demand—more power, attention, and time from their parents. Gifted children are adept in drawing this parental attention, often in subtle ways. Their advanced language, reasoning abilities, and creativity often enable them to gain control. Thus, it may seem to the other children in the household that their gifted sibling has become the head of the house (Cornell, 1984). Rivalry ensues from siblings who are also vying for this parental focus.

Parents need to be aware of the ways they may relinquish control of the family decision-making process to the gifted child. An important caution is not to ask the older gifted child to "take care of" the younger child. This reinforces the roles of the capable and inept ones. One younger sister complained, "When I'm out with my sister, I feel like I'm on a leash!" The younger child's plea to parents is, "Don't let my sister take over!"

Parents should be aware that if one child is identified as gifted, they will tend to look for the same traits of giftedness in the other younger children. Remember, also, that usually less is expected from younger children. When the younger children do not match the first child's abilities, it is easy for parents to overlook the younger children's unique strengths.

Home is a place to recognize difficult-to-measure yet critically important qualities such as a cheerful personality, compassion, and helpfulness. It is essential for any child that parents not focus exclusively on the child's academic accomplishments. Alert parents appreciate and enjoy the presence of each child. Ask the group for examples of ways they can convey appreciation to each child for who he is rather than for his accomplishments.

Parents need to monitor their response to each child and ask themselves, "When does my child count? When is this child important to me?" If parents get involved only primarily when the children are fighting, perhaps they are teaching their children that they matter when they are quarreling, for that is when they get the attention. If parents do not become involved in squabble situations, they convey their belief that the children are capable of handling the situation themselves. A basic operational approach for parents is to refuse to become part of their children's competition, unless a child's safety is at risk. If they do get involved in their children's fights, they reinforce the negative behavior that drew their attention. Instead, parents should reward their children when they are cooperating. They must encourage sibling synergy and recognize that each child gets more by helping the other. Ask the group for specific ways they can promote sibling synergy. For discussion at the next session, ask parents to become aware of the situations in which they give power, attention, and time to each child.

Stress Management

Certainly some stress is required in order to activate the positive behaviors needed to meet life's goals. People do not know what they can do until they are challenged. Each accomplishment adds to the sense of competence. However, gifted children may be required to cope with some particularly stressful experiences, that is stressors associated with their giftedness that are above and beyond those experienced by their peers not identified as gifted. Ask the group to discuss some sources of stress in the lives of gifted children.

Here are some possibilities:

1. Because some gifted children learn without great effort, they may become accustomed to expect a relatively effortless existence.
2. We expect more from gifted children; they should not make mistakes. They should know better. We generalize from their intel-

lectual abilities to expect all-round excellence in unrelated non-intellectual spheres.

3. Emotional and intellectual growth do not keep pace with each other.

4. Differences from the norm create tensions. Gifted people tend to need to wait for others to catch up. Realizing that they see things and know things that others do not may be frightening and alienating (Saunders & Remsberg, 1985).

5. Gifted people wonder why things seem to bother them more than other people and may feel inadequate more often than most other children. They thus may view themselves as less able to cope, and talk about themselves more negatively (Whitmore, 1980).

6. Because gifted people are usually more curious and have more questions, they may think that they are less smart and know less than other people.

7. Gifted people are more sensitive and tend to take things personally (Saunders & Remsberg, 1985).

8. They are more intense and have a more acutely affected nervous system. They have trouble screening out; they are dealing with more. They are more likely to be overloaded.

9. Gifted people tend to be more aware of other people's incongruent verbal and body messages. Being aware of both, they may be more confused.

10. With their acute awareness and sensitivity, gifted people are usually more conscious of the whole situation, and may experience more stress from the ambiguity and dilemma of seeing all sides.

11. They accumulate information and meaning in a sort of geometric progression. They are coping with more possibilities, more meaning, more implications. They may seem to be working slower, but they are processing more information.

12. They deal with more alternatives; in their minds they are making more mistakes. They tend to be perfectionists and feel they are valued for their accomplishments. Stress is involved with change. In changing, we go from what used to be familiar to a new situation. With their keen imagination, gifted people are more frustrated because they want to actualize a greater number of options and cannot.

Ask the group to suggest ways to cope with this stress. Here are some suggestions:

1. Teach children to say "no" to too much involvement and risk of overburdening themselves that may interfere with accomplishing

what is meaningful and worthwhile. They may say, "yes" to the person and the idea, but "no" to the participation. Set priorities by evaluating the meaning, burdens, and benefits of their options.

2. Encourage the lifelong resource of listening to their own inner messages, trusting and responding to their own insights and intuition (Lovecky, 1986).
3. Help them have close personal friendships.
4. When appropriate, help the child to reduce his immediate expectations.
5. Help her set short-term goals.
6. Help him set meaningful, valuable long-term goals; a career focus; a purpose to live, with intermediate, attainable steps.
7. Encourage the child to be enthusiastic about her ideas and causes. Do not take away her dreams or tread on her imagination. Express reverence for her ideas!
8. Within well-defined limits, allow the child to be responsible for his behavior so that he is not conditioned to believe that he is a victim of circumstance.
9. Allow choices so that she experiences control over her life.
10. Help him be aware that he may be subject to misunderstanding by others.
11. Help her be aware of what she tells herself about herself and situations (self-talk). Help the child be aware that her self-talk can work for her or against her, for example,
    If I make a mistake, I'm no good.
    That was a dumb thing to do.
    Everybody should like me.
    Nobody likes me.
    What did I learn from this?
    I enjoyed doing that.
    I am responsible for my behavior.
12. Help the child be aware that he can change his self-talk. Like switching channels on a television, he can direct what he says to himself!
13. Share her enthusiasm and success. Define her behavior or attitude in a positive way. When another person reflects her success, she has a broader base of being OK. Your applause empowers!
14. Help him label his feelings so that he can define them and begin to work for a solution and control his behavior.
15. Help her distinguish between what she imagines and feels and actual behavior of herself and others.
16. Encourage physical exercise.

17. Encourage self-rehearsal: The mind is a place to try out new experiences: Mentally walk him through new experiences; anticipate consequences and explore options.
18. Guide her to think through what is feared before or after a situation. Explore available alternatives: Role play to experience confidence and understanding; replay tense situations at peaceful times; Ask: What might you have tried? or try?
    What do you think would happen?
    How would you feel then?
    What else might you try?

Ask the group to monitor the occasions that they feel stressful and how they cope with this stress during the time until the next session.

Parents as teachers. The message of this session should pervade the entire series. That is, "You teach what you are." Gifted people sometimes hear the inner voice; they are often astute and aware of the nuances and implications of our behaviors. It is essential that parents, teachers, and counselors take good care of themselves. They should live to reflect, "It's good to grow up." Without allowing the session to turn into a gripe session, it may be helpful to acknowledge how parenting gifted children may create some additional stresses on the parents. Some of these stresses could be:

1. Anger at school systems for not providing appropriate programming;
2. Exhaustion from responding to a high level of curiosity, verbal "invasion," and diverse interests;
3. Alienation from feeling uncomfortable telling friends what their child accomplishes and needs;
4. Financial strain from trying to provide opportunities to match their child's abilities and interests;
5. Resentment towards the child who consumes so much time and so many resources.

Parents, teacher, and counselors must keep in mind that just as children learn English by living in a house where English is spoken, so they learn our values, sense of responsibility, attitudes, dispositions, and appreciations for people. Encourage parents to:

- Live in the realm of solutions and use decision-making processes.
- Manage themselves to make time work for them, not against them.
- Spend time with people who inspire and give energy.
- Set personal daily and long-term goals that give a sense of progress.

- Choose activities they value.
- Invest time and care in themselves.

One of the major personal-social characteristics of gifted children is their autonomy. Some gifted children are not permitted to develop their own independence because of the overinvolvement of their parents in their everyday lives. Although this is often done for the good of the child, as defined by the parent, it can nevertheless be detrimental. Some children feel that they are their parents' report card. One way to minimize the possibility of overinvolvement on the part of the parent is to stress in the parent support group the value of parents developing their own abilities and interests. One can point out that being very busy developing one's own interests and talents serves two purposes for the gifted child. First of all, it provides a positive model of a learning, developing person worthy of emulation. Second, it results in the situation where the parent is too busy to do everything for the gifted child, thus giving the opportunity for her to develop independence. Ask the group to discuss ways that they maintain their energy and enthusiasm and how this benefits their children.

Synergy with the home and school. There are many ways that teachers and counselors can work with parents to facilitate the gifted child's education that will result in benefit to all concerned. In order to enlist cooperation, teachers should keep parents informed of their child's progress in his special program. Teachers should ask parents to keep them informed about any situations at home that might influence the child's school performance.

Parents are a valuable resource of skills and community contacts. Ask the parents to fill out a form indicating what skills and contacts they would be willing to share with other children in the school. In finding mentors for gifted children, use the available network of parents. If a child is doing an independent study, information from the parent resource file may be useful.

Parents might organize to provide a library of resources. Each parent could contribute one book or journal subscription to have available to the other parents and, just as important, to all the teachers in the school system. Available journals such as the *Gifted Children Monthly*, *G/C/T*, and *Challenge* are especially valuable where there is no separately organized gifted program.

Parents should join associations of parents of gifted children at the local and state level, if available. In the United States, at least one parent in the school system should become a member of the National Association for Gifted Children's Parent-Community group. Association will provide a sense of support and provide access to a large number of helpful materials, people, and events for parents of gifted children. Parents' involvement in the gifted child's education can be a significant positive force. In order for parents to contribute effectively to their child's education, they must have the cooperation and support of school personnel (Dettman & Colangelo, 1980).

Exceptional abilities emerge only in a receptive and nurturing environment. Unique qualities are either stifled or encouraged by responses in the child's world. Feldman's (1986) comments on prodigies also apply to gifted children with a broad range of abilities: "Since the circumstances favorable to such expression are rarely present, nature's gambit is to sacrifice an enormous amount of potential talent for the occasional sublime match of child to field that yields the prodigy." We probably do not begin to know what we are missing.

In being a person who makes an effort to bring out the best in someone else, each parent, teacher, and counselor is likely to express the best of himself. In seeking to reach beyond the boundaries of our limited experience, we can expand our lives more deeply and fully.

REFERENCES

Alvino, J.A. (1986). Presentation at the National Association for Gifted Children Annual Conference, Las Vegas, NV.

Barbe, W. (1965). *Psychology and education of the gifted.* New York: Appleton-Century-Crofts.

Bricklin, B., & Bricklin, P. (1967). *Bright child—poor grades, the psychology of underachievement.* New York: Delacourt.

Clance, P. (1986). *The impostor phenomenon.* New York: Bantam.

Colangelo, N. (1979). Myths and stereotypes of gifted children: Awareness for the classroom teacher. In N. Colangelo, C.M. Foxley, & D. Dustin (Eds.), *Multicultural non-sexist education: A human relations approach.* Dubuque, IA: Kendall/Hunt.

Cornell, D. (1984). *Families of gifted children.* Research in Clinical Psychology, No. 11. Ann Arbor, MI: University of Michigan Research Press.

Dettmann, D., & Colangelo, N. (1980). A functional model for counseling parents of gifted students. *Gifted Child Quarterly, 24,* 158–161.

Dinkmeyer, D., & McKay, G. (1976). *Systematic training for effective parenting leader's manual.* Circle Pines, MN: American Guidance Service.

Dreikurs, R., & Soltz, V. (1964). *Children: The challenge.* New York: Hawthorne Books.

Feldman, D.H. (1986). *Nature's gambit: Child prodigies and the development of human potential.* New York: Basic Books.

Gardner, H. (1983). *Frames of mind: The theory of multiple intelligences.* New York: Basic Books.

Gerleman, S. (1986). Presentation at the 38th Annual Reading/Language Arts Conference. Cardinal Stritch College, Milwaukee, WI.

Gogel, E.M., McCumsey, J., & Hewett, G. (1985, November/December). What parents are saying. *G/C/T*, pp. 7-9.

Gowan, J.C., & Bruch, C. (1971). *The academically talented students and guidance.* Boston: Houghton-Mifflin.

Guilford, J.P. (1967). *The nature of human intelligence.* New York: McGraw-Hill.

Jacobs, J. (1971). Effectiveness of teacher and parent identification of gifted children as a function of school level. *Psychology in the Schools, 8,* 140-142.

Kearney, K. (1986). Presentation at the Atlantic Association for Gifted Children and Adults Annual Conference, Fredricton, New Brunswick.

Kerr, B. (1985). *Smart girls, gifted women.* Columbus, OH: Ohio Psychology Publishing.

Lester, C., & Anderson, R. (1981). Counseling with families of gifted children: The school counselor's role. *The School Counselor, 29,* 147-151.

Lovecky, D. (1986). Can you hear the flowers singing? *Journal of Counseling and Development, 64,* 572-575.

Marland, S. (1972). *Education of the gifted and talented.* Washington, DC: U.S. Government Printing Office.

McCall, R.B., Applebaum, M.I., & Hogerty, P.S. (1978). Development changes in mental performance. *Monographs of the Society for Research in Child Development, 39*(3), 1-83.

Miller, A. (1981). *Prisoners of childhood.* New York: Basic Books.

Parent perspective. (1974, Summer). A mother and father of a gifted child find the helping professions helpless. *Gifted Child Quarterly,* pp. 110-111.

Pegnato, C., & Birch, J. (1959). Locating gifted children in junior high schools: A comparison of methods. *Exceptional Children, 25,* 300-304.

Ross, A.O. (1964). *The exceptional child in the family.* New York: Grune & Stratton.

Sanborn, M.P. (1979). Working with parents. In N. Colangelo & R.T. Zaffran (Eds.), *New voices in counseling the gifted.* Dubuque, IA: Kendall/Hunt.

Saunders, A., & Remsberg, B. (1985). *The stress-proof child.* New York: Henry Holt.

Sternberg, R. (1984). *Beyond IQ: A triarchic theory of human intelligence.* New York: Cambridge University Press.

Torrance, P. (1981). Predicting the creativity of elementary school children and the teachers who made a difference. *Gifted Child Quarterly, 23,* 56-62.

Webb, J.T., Meckstroth, E.A., & Tolan, S.S. (1982). *Guiding the gifted child.* Columbus, OH: Ohio Psychology.

Whitmore, J. (1980). *Giftedness, conflict, and underachievement.* Boston: Allyn and Bacon.

Willings, D. (1985). The specific needs of adults who are gifted. *Roeper Review, 8,* 35-38.

Chapter 7
Career Education For Gifted and Talented Learners

Roberta M. Milgram

Ray is a brilliant musicologist, educated at Harvard and making significant and highly original contributions to the literature in his field. Myrna is a professor at a major medical school, internationally acclaimed for her research in epidemiology. Sheri and Pat are designers of computer software, highly successful in their own company and recognized for their innovative work.

What do these people have in common? All traveled circuitous and frequently troubled routes to their chosen careers. All were given clear but inappropriate advice by high school counselors. Ray grew up in North Dakota and was discouraged from even applying to Harvard by his high school counselor. Myrna was encouraged to study social work, a profession deemed particularly suitable for a "girl" destined for the career of motherhood. Sheri and Pat were both nonconformist students. They preferred to work at times, in places, and in ways of their own choosing. As a result, their school grades were merely adequate and did not reflect the highly original and independent work of which they were capable. These gifted and talented individuals would have profited greatly from sensible and sensitive career counseling.

The goals of this chapter are (a) to provide counselors, teachers, and parents with understanding of the unique needs of gifted and talented learners in career development, and (b) to suggest ways to answer these needs.

One reason the abilities of Ray, Myrna, Sheri, and Pat were not recognized as remarkable was the limited and limiting IQ-oriented view of giftedness as developed by Terman (1925), and Terman and Oden (1947, 1959). This view dominated the thinking of psychologists and educators for many years. In the 1950s the definition of giftedness was expanded by Guilford (1967) to include creativity, and educators began to speak of the gifted and talented. Marland (1972), Assistant Secretary for Education in the U.S. Department of Health, Education, and Welfare in the 1970s, proposed a multifaceted definition of giftedness that was adopted by the United States Office of Education, and enacted into law by the Congress of the United States in the Gifted and Talented Children's Act of 1978. In addition to high intelligence, Marland's (1972) definition of giftedness included creativity, leadership, and abilities in the performing and visual arts. The definition represented an important educational advance because it defined giftedness broadly rather than in terms of IQ alone, and justified the provision of services to different kinds of gifted and talented children.

Marland also made intensive efforts to reform the entire American educational system by assigning top priority to career education in the school curriculum. He urged schools to focus on preparation for a life of work and acquisition of the skills to earn a livelihood. According to Marland (1972), "career education is not *a* major Office of Education priority . . . career education is *the* major objective of the Office of Education at this time and will remain so for the forseeable future."

Marland had a broad view of career education and thought that it should be part of the curriculum of all children during their school years, beginning in kindergarten. Marland's seminal ideas in the field of career education did not receive the same wide acceptance that his views on giftedness did. This is unfortunate because although great strides have been made in the clarification and expansion of the meaning of giftedness, little progress has been made in determining the special career education needs of gifted and talented learners and in providing for them.

In order to understand the unique needs of gifted and talented learners in career development, it is necessary to define a number of key concepts. Hoyt and Hebeler (1974) cite as outmoded the definition of work as "paid employment," career as "a succession of jobs or occupations," and leisure as "play." They define work as a conscious effort to produce benefit (money, satisfaction, or a visible product) for one's self and/or others, and career as all the work that we do during our lifetime.

Vocation is defined as one's primary work role and may be paid or unpaid, whereas occupation is one's primary paid work role. A person's vocation and occupation may be the same or different at any given point in time. For example, for a doctor, vocation and occupation usually overlap, but for a composer of classical music (vocation) who supports himself by working in a bank or elsewhere (occupation) they do not. One may have a vocation without an occupation. Leisure activities are defined as those that one pursues when not engaged in his or her vocation or occupation. Leisure is not play. One may spend leisure time doing activities that are ordinarily thought to be work.

For most children and adolescents the primary work role is that of student. The benefits produced include course credit, grades, and rewards from parents, teachers, and peers. Leisure activities for these young people are those that are not required by their work role. They are freely chosen and not done to receive any of the benefits cited above. The important role of leisure activities in the career development of gifted and talented individuals was discussed earlier (Chapter 1).

This chapter is divided into three sections. In the first section, the key concepts of career development, career education, and career guidance are delineated. In the second and third sections, career development and career education/guidance are discussed with particular reference to the gifted.

CAREER DEVELOPMENT, CAREER EDUCATION, AND CAREER GUIDANCE

Career development is a lifelong process of crystallizing a vocational identity. A wide variety of genetic and physical factors combine with personal-social, sociological, educational, economic, and cultural influences to shape each person's career. The cognitive and affective changes that occur in the process of career development can be modified in school settings by career education and career guidance. The definition of these two processes has been the focus of considerable controversy.

The term *career education* has been used in professional circles to refer to the position championed by some authorities, especially in school guidance and counseling, that the total effort of public education in the United States be directed to the acquisition of knowledge, skills, and attitudes that lead each individual to meaningful, productive, and satisfying work (Hoyt, 1980; Marland, 1972). Although this extreme approach was never widely accepted, more moderate forms of career education and guidance have evolved.

The most widely accepted goals of career education and guidance are to provide learners with the opportunity to (a) explore a variety of career alternatives, (b) consider in depth a smaller number of alternatives in terms of individual interests and abilities, (c) make career decisions, and (d) develop a life plan designed to realize these decisions.

Career education is a teaching/learning process with two aspects. The first stresses information about the world of work and the requirements and activities of specific jobs. The second stresses knowledge about one's own abilities, interests, attitudes, values toward work. Career education consists of formal and informal experiences designed to change the level of both aspects. Career education is a collaborative undertaking in that exploration of careers is done by teachers in regular classrooms, by counselors, by parents, and by others in the business, professional, or government community.

Career guidance focuses on using the information gathered in the process of career education in personal and individual planning and career decision making. Career guidance is the process of helping others to make wise decisions by coming to a better understanding of their own specific abilities and personal-social characteristics and the opportunities available at any one time.

We frequently assume (a) that the responsibility for career education rests with teachers, and for career guidance with counselors, and (b) that career education takes place in group settings, and career guidance in individual situations. However, career education and career guidance are not mutually exclusive. Both career guidance and career counseling may take place in individual or group situations. Both teachers and school counselors can help learners make wiser career decisions by providing career information and by conducting career guidance sessions with individuals or in small group settings. In many schools there are no or very few guidance counselors and it is regular classroom teachers who provide both career education and guidance. Guidance counselors may increase their efficiency and effectiveness by working with teachers, individually and in groups, to develop career education and guidance activities that take place in the classroom.

Career education and guidance should be part of the curriculum from preschool through high school. It should be different at each age level and hierarchical in nature. It should consist of a series of graded experiences in which the individual acquires information about the world of work, becomes more self-aware, explores vocational experiences, and develops decision-making skills. Special career education for gifted and talented learners requires adjustments of curriculum content and teaching-counseling strategies in terms of the specific pattern of assets and concerns of each gifted learner.

Career education in the elementary school is generally conducted in heterogeneous groups in regular classrooms. The focus is on information gathering. Students are exposed to a wide range of materials and experiences to clarify career interests and alternatives. During the junior high school years, exploration of careers becomes more specific. Learners acquire specific information about the activities and obligations associated with careers, the preparation required, and the personal, professional, and material implications of specific career choices. More attention is given to career guidance and counseling and to the identification of individual patterns of assets and weaknesses. It often takes place on an individual basis or in small homogeneous groups conducted outside of the regular classroom. Career education at this age level provides exposure on a rotating basis to specific, albeit still low-level, real-world work experiences.

In the high school years, with increasing age of learners and increasing differentiation of interests and abilities, schools should focus on small group or individual guidance and counseling. Efforts are directed to helping learners make decisions about vocational choice and the academic and experiential steps to implement these choices.

To sum up, parents, teachers, and counselors do not make decisions for children and youth, but rather provide the opportunities for those who seek their advice (a) to consider accurate and specific information about occupations, (b) to clarify their own abilities, interests, attitudes, and values, and (c) to decide upon short- and long-term goals and actions that lead to their realization.

CAREER DEVELOPMENT IN GIFTED AND TALENTED LEARNERS

Some people might question the need for career education for gifted and talented learners. When they grow up, gifted children seem to hold interesting and challenging jobs with high prestige and income and do well in their careers. Findings of longitudinal investigations of giftedness that spanned 25 and 35 years support the view that children identified as gifted on the basis of their IQ scores are, in general, more likely than their nongifted peers to attain academic and vocational success (Oden, 1968; Terman, 1947; Terman & Oden, 1959).

On the other hand, many children identified as gifted on the basis of IQ and/or achievement test scores do not become successful adults in terms of career achievements or professional and community leadership (McClelland, 1973; Tannenbaum, 1983; Terman & Oden, 1959; Wallach & Wing, 1969). Many highly intelligent children may not realize their potential without special education in general, and special career education, in particular.

According to the Marland Report (1972) "disturbingly, research has confirmed that many gifted children perform far below their intellectual potential. We are increasingly being stripped of the notion that a bright mind will make its own way." Some have estimated that as many as 15-30 per cent of high school dropouts are gifted and talented. Even these disturbing estimates may be an underestimate of the phenomenon because they are usually based upon consideration of high-IQ type gifted only. If we were to examine the career histories of other categories of gifted and talented learners, we would find even more instances of adults who failed to realize the promise of youth.

The distinct differences that obtain among gifted and talented learners in category and level of abilities have been described in the 4 × 4 model of the structure of giftedness presented earlier in this volume (Chapter 1) and elsewhere (Milgram, 1989). In this model, giftedness is conceptualized in terms of four categories, two having to do with aspects of intelligence (general intellectual ability and specific intellectual ability) and two with aspects of original thinking (general original/creative thinking and specific creative talent). Each of the four processes is manifested in the individual at one of four ability levels (profoundly gifted, moderately gifted, mildly gifted, and nongifted), hence, the name 4 × 4.

The 4 × 4 model has significant implications for career development, education, and guidance. The unique cognitive and/or personal-social characteristics of each kind and level of gifted child are reflected in their respective career development and accordingly, require qualitatively different approaches to career education and career guidance. For example, a learner who is profoundly gifted in music will require different career education and guidance from one who is mildly gifted in computer science.

In a recent position statement prepared for the Division of Career Development (DCD) and the Association for the Gifted (TAG), Delisle and Squires (1989) cite the increase in understanding of career development in gifted and talented youth and the providing of appropriate career education and guidance for them as high priority issues. They argue that since the gifted and talented contribute disproportionately to our society, career development programs on their behalf benefit them and society. Following the same line of reasoning, one might suggest that special attention be given to the clarification of values in career education for the gifted. The values by which these capable individuals assess achievement, self-worth, and self-esteem are important to all of us.

In a recent thought-provoking article, Howley (1989) examined the value systems of gifted university students. He distinguished between "careerists" who were "mercenary" in their goals and viewed their studies as boring but necessary to attain money and other similar goals, and "intellectuals" who regarded learning as an activity meaningful in itself. Many of today's gifted youth will be the decision makers and leaders in the future. The relative value that they place on self-fulfillment and self-development versus service and contribution to society will affect us all. Career education for gifted learners should include consideration of why people work, what kinds of satisfactions are associated with the different career options, and other topics related to ethics and values.

There is wide agreement that gifted learners require differentiated curriculum and individualized instruction (Dunn, 1989; Maker, 1989; Milgram, 1989). The same principles apply to career education and guidance for gifted learners in that their content should be qualitatively different, and the instructional/guidance strategies be individualized in terms of the pattern of assets of each learner.

We conclude this section with discussion of a number of issues considered by many educators and researchers to play a significant role in the career development of gifted and talented youth.

Multipotential versus unipotential. Authorities in gifted education invariably place multipotentiality—interest and abilities in a number of areas—as a critical factor in the career development of gifted and talented children and adolescents (Herr & Watanabe, 1979; Hoyt & Hebeler, 1974; Jepsen, 1979; Perrone, 1986; Van Tassel-Baska, 1983). They view gifted children as interested in many different vocational areas and having the requisite abilities to succeed in many of them. While nongifted children may not be able to pinpoint even one clear vocational interest, the gifted often have many. This "embarrassment of riches" makes it difficult for many gifted learners to make a commitment to a given career path and complicates the counseling process.

Some experts in the field, however, assert the opposite. They report that exceptionally gifted and talented children demonstrate early, intensive interest and activity in one career area. They persevere in this interest eventually achieving eminence in a single academic discipline or area of talent. A major source of evidence for this position are the self-reports of eminent adults and their parents (Bloom, 1985; Cox, Daniel, & Boston, 1985; Roe, 1952). The singleness of vocational interest reflected in those reports is in direct contrast to the widely held multidimensional view presented above.

Evidence for the unipotential position is found in Fox and Denham's report (1974) of children's highly crystallized interest in the investigative area on Holland's (1958) Vocational Preference Inventory (VPI). Unfortunately, their sample was highly select. All subjects were entrants in a math and science competition sponsored by a major university. It is, therefore, impossible to generalize from this sample and to attribute similar unidimensional career interest to randomly selected gifted children characterized by a wider range of career interests.

On the basis of her experience in the career education of gifted and talented adolescents Marshall (1981) noticed two distinct patterns of vocational development and cited their importance in guiding these children. She reported,

> The pattern I most often observed was one of indecision, displayed by students who possess a multiplicity of intense interests and high

aptitudes. The second pattern was quite opposite to the quandary of the multi-talented. Gifted and talented students displaying this latter decision-making pattern have sometimes been called early emergers, for they decide on a career preference at an early age, make commitments toward its pursuit long before leaving high school, and appear to follow this singular route throughout their total career development. The early emerger pattern is usually displayed by a much smaller number of gifted and talented students, but it is somewhat conspicuous in its persistent nature.

One explanation for the two distinct patterns may be found in the 4 × 4 model (Milgram, 1989). It seems reasonable to expect gifted learners at the profound level of one of the two specific categories—specific intellectual ability and specific creative talent—to be characterized by unidimensional vocational interests and abilities. By the same token, gifted and talented learners at the moderate and mild levels of the two general categories—general overall intelligence and creative thinking ability—may well be characterized by multipotential career interests. The reason the multipotential view is so widely held is because so many more gifted match that description and relatively few are unipotential. Both multipotential individuals and unipotential or early emergers require differential career education and counseling (Kerr, 1986).

Expectations. People that have contact with gifted children and adolescents in the school, home, and neighborhood become aware of their superior abilities and develop expectations about their current and future performance. Most people expect gifted children to achieve at a high level in school, earn high grades, receive school honors, gain acceptance to prestigious universities, and prepare for highly respected careers. They are subsequently expected to attain significant career accomplishments. For many children these expectations serve as a source of encouragement and strength. For others these positive expectations of parents, relatives, teachers, peers, and others constitute a continuing source of pressure to conform. The expectations of others, as well as those expectations that they have internalized, place significant limits on their career choices. The very expectation that they will contribute to the community and to the larger society may create conflicts for gifted children about what they consider an appropriate use of their time. In an earlier chapter Albert (Chapter 5), differentiated between two developmental paths to career eminence, one congruent-unconflicted and the other incongruent-conflicted. One major factor accounting for developmental conflict is the extent of match between the expectations of the parents and the career interests and abilities of the child. Accordingly, one goal of career counseling is to identify and clarify expectations of significant others.

Career as lifestyle. Gifted people frequently view career as one of the major means of expressing their special abilities and interests. They are also intensively aware of the implications of vocational choice for future lifestyle. For example, joining the "rat race" or "living in the fast lane" may be seen by some as an opportunity, and by others as a threat. From this perspective, work is far more than an income- and independence-producing endeavor, but rather an ongoing opportunity to realize potential talent.

In discussing career as lifestyle, issues of conflicting work-leisure values often emerge. For example, a person may be highly talented in computer science, but derive great personal satisfaction from outdoors activities such as rock-climbing, hiking, skiing, and other nature-oriented activities. A high school counselor performs a useful function when he/ she helps a young person to consider ways to combine these seemingly diametrically opposed career orientations. In discussions, one could propose possibilities that would satisfy both sets of needs and values. For example, a young person with these interests might consider setting up a private firm offering computer consultation from a log cabin in the wilderness, connected by modem to civilization.

Career as life style is part of career decision for all people, not only for gifted individuals. On the other hand, the implications of intense efforts to fulfill high aspirations and realize remarkable abilities may exacerbate these work-leisure conflicts, especially in gifted and talented individuals. Moreover, the awareness of values held by their family, friends, and society and the propensity to question those values (Colangelo & Parker, 1971; Sanborn & Niemiec, 1971; Webb, Meckstroth, & Tolan, 1982) make it especially important that work-lifestyle issues be routinely considered in counseling the gifted, even before problems in these areas appear.

Investment, commitment, and delayed gratification. Many career choices that gifted and talented individuals consider require intensive long-term personal commitment, considerable investment of time and money, and many years of academic preparation and acquisition of experience. Many careers to which gifted and talented individuals aspire entail long delays in receiving professional recognition and personal gratification. Individuals vary greatly on how able and willing they are to postpone receiving full recognition from society, including appropriate financial compensation for their work. Counselors can help gifted learners understand the short- and long-term interactive effects of specific vocational decisions, the requisite academic preparation, and the lifestyle associated with this preparation.

Career and autonomy. One of the most salient personality characteristics found in gifted learners of all ages is autonomy. The vocational choices of gifted individuals often require extensive and expensive higher education and protracted periods of training during which they may continue to be financially dependent upon their parents. This has proven to be a source of continuing conflict between gifted individuals and their parents. As a consequence, some gifted people have dropped out at an advanced stage of vocational preparation because they choose independence over career.

Career choice for gifted girls. Many gifted girls face additional career choice problems because their parents and teachers have high expectations for gifted girls in some respects, and lower expectations in others. As they grow up, gifted young women are led to expect that they will attain high academic and vocational accomplishments to the same degree as gifted boys. At the same time, they receive an opposite message, that may lead to lower vocational aspiration and accomplishment.

Fortunately, there is now a large literature devoted specifically to career development and counseling techniques for gifted girls. Kerr has written extensively on this topic (1985, 1986, 1988). The next chapter (cf. Chapter 8) is entirely devoted to this topic.

CAREER EDUCATION AND CAREER GUIDANCE FOR GIFTED AND TALENTED LEARNERS

Parents place high priority on career education for their children. When asked what they want for their children, 1,039 parents of gifted children said (a) that they want their children to achieve good personal-social adjustment, and (b) that they want good schools that provide their children with background and experiences leading to a productive and satisfying career (Gogel, McCumsey, & Hewett, 1985). These priorities are understandable in terms of the large amounts of time, money, and energy frequently invested by gifted learners and their parents in order to acquire the academic background and experience required for specific careers that they choose.

There has been a growing awareness of the special needs for the gifted and talented in the area of career education and guidance in professional circles as well (Colangelo & Zaffran, 1979; Hoyt & Huebler, 1974; Van Tassel-Baska, 1983). A number of comprehensive statements on career development in gifted and talented learners and career education designed to respond to these special needs have appeared in the professional literature. For example, the *Journal of Career Education* (Miller, 1981) or more recently the *Journal of Counseling and Develop-*

ment (Kerr & Miller, 1986) devoted special issues to the topic. Unfortunately, despite growing interest in the career development of gifted and talented youth, strategies and materials have not been developed to meet the needs.

Most school counselors agree with the opinion of parents of gifted learners cited above. They view one focus of their work as helping pupils to reach career decisions and to plan the course of action required to implement the decision. They would acknowledge that gifted and talented children and adolescents have special needs in the sphere of career education and counseling just as they do in other academic and nonacademic spheres. Unfortunately, in the real world most counselors are overburdened with other tasks and with nongifted children. When it comes to the gifted and talented, they frequently focus their efforts on the remediation of individual problems such as underachievement, perfectionism, and other adjustment difficulties. With counselor-student ratios ranging as high as 1:500 in many schools, it is unrealistic to hope that school counselors will provide career guidance for students in general, much less for gifted students, in particular.

Many regular classroom teachers agree that there is a strong need for career education and guidance and express willingness to help provide information and advice to their students and to relate the material they teach to the world of work (Myrick & Carrow, 1987). However, they do not feel that they have the knowledge and skills required to provide career education. It is likely that a similar situation obtains among teachers of gifted classes or among gifted education specialists. Accordingly, if we expect teachers to fulfill this function, we must provide preservice and in-service training experiences for them.

The skills required to offer career counseling include specialized background in career development, training in career counseling, and knowledge of materials available for career education. It is, therefore, imperative that school counselors with the requisite training and experience collaborate, or at least cooperate, with other school personnel in providing for the career development needs of gifted children.

In counseling gifted and talented learners about careers, a realistic, information-giving approach is most appreciated. These learners report greater satisfaction with counseling approaches that focus on the present and the future, on the real-world aspects of career choice and especially on the discussion of clear, accurate, and relevant information about careers. They do not react favorably to counseling sessions, individual or group, that are about past events in one's life, and focus on the exploration and ventilation of feelings.

Computers, some with the capability of connecting to large data bases outside the school, are already available in many schools. This makes it possible to establish an information service in each school that could not have been dreamed of a few years ago. For example, McDaniels (1988) described a computer assisted career guidance system developed in Virginia. Every person in Virginia has access to the Virginia Career Development System through a toll-free telephone line. The system is available to over 1,000 educational institutions ranging from middle schools to universities. Since gifted and talented children are frequently more independent, internally controlled, and self-motivated, it is likely that they would use such a system effectively.

Leisure activities in career development. In Chapter 1, Milgram stressed the critical role of out-of-school activities in the development of talent. She views out-of-school activities as an early indicator of career interest and urged teachers, counselors, and parents to give special attention to them. Gifted children should be exposed to a wide variety of leisure activities and encouraged to develop sustained activity in those that appeal to them. This advice is not to be misinterpreted as indicating that gifted children require more activities in formal settings, rather that they should have the chance to freely choose activities for their own pleasure. Productive leisure activities can serve as an early and continuing natural laboratory for career education.

Experiential career education: Mentorships, internships, apprenticeships. If career education is to be effective in helping learners become aware of their preferred lifestyle and formulate specific career goals, it must include reality testing. Without "hands-on" experiences, career education will be another intellectual and academic exercise, even if the curriculum topics are framed in the language of understanding self and career decision making. Experiential learning refers to "the learning that occurs when changes in judgements, feelings, knowledge, or skills result for a particular person from living through an event or events" (Chickering, 1976). Experiential learning occurs as a result of a person's activities both in and out of formal school situations (Bounous, 1986).

Many highly gifted adults cite the efforts of mentors in stimulating and directing their developing talents (Albert & Runco, 1987; Bloom, 1985; Cox, Daniel, & Boston, 1985; Goertzel, Goertzel, & Goertzel, 1978; Torrance, 1983, 1984). This has lead to a growing awareness of the value of mentorships, internships, and apprenticeships as approaches to career education with gifted and talented youth (Boston, 1976; Hirsch, 1976; Runions, 1980).

Experiential career education programs can make a unique contribution to academic, personal-social, and career development of able learners. Since many gifted young people are highly motivated and independent, mentorships are particularly valuable experiences for them. Mentoring can provide a continuing interaction with a respected and admired adult that fosters self-esteem and self-confidence in the protege.

The role modeling and support often found in mentoring relationships are especially important to gifted students. As a result of enrichment and acceleration, many gifted high school students finish curriculum requirements early. They then have the opportunity for exposure to real-world work experiences such as internships or mentorships that can result in integration of interests and abilities and in further clarification of career direction.

Many authorities have stressed the potential contribution of mentors to the realization of outstanding abilities in students ranging in age from preschool (see Chapter 10) to high school seniors (Kaufman, Harrel, Milam, Woolverton, & Miller, 1986). The value of female mentors to the career and personal-social development of female gifted learners was cited by Schwartz (Chapter 8) and by other researchers (Beck, 1989; Kaufmann et al., 1986). The Richardson report on gifted education (Cox, Daniel, & Boston, 1985) highlighted the experiential learning approach. In citing exemplary programs and promising practices in gifted education, reach-out type programs, internships, and mentorships received considerable attention. A large proportion of the best programs focus on career development, in general, and on mentor-type programs, in particular.

The literature on mentorships in gifted education consists principally of descriptions of successful programs. Texas A & M University's Career Education Model (Colson, 1980; Colson, Borman, & Nash, 1978) and Runion's (1980) Mentor Academy program, or the Purdue Mentor Program (Ellingson, Haeger, & Feldhusen, 1986) are representative samples of mentor programs for gifted learners. More recently, research efforts designed to attain a better understanding of the nature of mentor-protege relationships, the influence of mentorships on career development, and the academic, professional, and personal benefits that accrue to mentors and to proteges are appearing in the literature (Beck, 1989; Edlin & Haensly, 1985; Kaufmann et al., 1986).

Despite the growing interest in mentor programs and awareness of their potential educational value, there is a lack of clarity about what is meant by the terms employed in referring to these programs (Cox, Daniel, & Boston, 1985). For example, Torrance (1984) defined the term mentor loosely as "an older person in your (the protege's) occupational field or educational experience who 'took you under his/her wing." Cox, Daniel, and Boston (1985) suggested the following conceptual differentiation: intern, apprentice, or assistant is functionally specific—that is, the association is confined to a specific learning task. By contrast, the mentor relationship is functionally diffuse. It involves other areas in lives of both persons and is a privileged relationship.

Albert (Chapter 5) discussed the importance of mentor-type experiences in the development of eminence. He distinguished between focal relationships and crystallizing experiences. Focal relationships are deeper and longer in duration and have broad influence on various aspects of the child's life, especially on personal-social development. Crystallizing experiences (Walters & Gardner, 1986) are more domain-specific, circumscribed in time and in situation and have impact on one specific area of the child's life. Gifted adults in science careers are more likely to report crystallizing experiences in their development and those in the people-oriented careers, focal relationships. To sum up, mentoring is a promising approach that has much to contribute to career education of the gifted. However, the concept of mentoring has yet to be precisely defined in the literature of giftedness. If we are to understand the process, it is critical to specify the nature, duration, and elements of the process of mentoring, to define them operationally, and to examine them empirically.

Efforts have been reported to introduce mentor-based experiential learning experiences in various school settings. For example, Gray (1982) applied the term mentor to students of education cooperating with elementary and secondary school pupils on independent enrichment projects in the "mentor's" area of interest. Gray's idea of preservice teachers as mentors is an interesting variation. Cox (1984) reported a three-week experimental program in which university students "mentored" projects for gifted fifth, sixth, and seventh grades.

Preservice teachers and university students cannot ordinarily supply the kind of deep emotional and intellectual experiences discussed by Walters and Gardner (1986) or Albert (see Chapter 5). They can, however, provide a lower level experiential learning experience to a large number of learners. Learners at different levels of giftedness require different mentor experiences. The Gray (1982, 1983) and Cox (1984) type approaches are appropriate for mild and moderate levels of gifted ability and the Albert (see Chapter 5) or Walters and Gardner (1986) type mentorships most useful with highly or profoundly gifted young people. Almost all students can profit from experiential learning in the course of career education. I suggest, however, that the term mentorship be reserved for the special, intensive, one-to-one relationship between gifted students and older, wise, trusted friends with special expertise in the learner's sphere of giftedness.

In a recent position statement on career development for gifted and talented youth prepared for the Division on Career Development (DCD) and the Association for the Gifted (TAG), Delisle and Squires (1989) cite Kokaska and Brolin's (1985) stages of career development, career awareness, career exploration, career preparation, and career placement, follow-up, and continuing education. In their description of each stage, real-world career experience is suggested. The experiences begin with observing and talking to people in different jobs in early childhood, and progress through apprentice and mentor type experiences to actual career placement.

Despite the significant influence attributed to mentors in the literature and the desirability of initiating mentor programs in gifted education, relatively little use has actually been made of the approach in gifted education programs. Thus an approach seen as very promising is actually used very little in practice. One of the main reasons for this situation is the administrative difficulty of implementing mentor programs (Gallegher, 1975). The logistics of recruiting mentors, the extensive time and energy required to prepare students and mentors for the program, and the difficulty of making the required administrative arrangements all contribute to hesitation in initiating and implementing these programs. This is unfortunate in the light of the many benefits to be derived by both mentors and proteges.

We can only hope that, as knowledge continues to accumulate on the topic and as materials are developed, educators will be prepared to implement mentor-based career education for gifted learners.

REFERENCES

Albert, R.S., & Runco, M.A. (1987). The possible different personality dispositions of scientists and non-scientists. In D. Jackson & J.P. Rushton (Eds.), *Scientific excellence: Origins and assessments* (pp. 67-97), Beverly Hills, CA: Sage.

Beck, L. (1989). Mentorships: Benefits and effects on career development. *Gifted Child Quarterly, 33,* 22-28.

Bloom, B.S. (1985). *Developing talent in young people.* New York: Ballantine.

Boston, B.O. (1976). *The sorcerer's apprentice: A case study in the role of mentor.* Reston, VA: Council for Exceptional Children.

Bounous, R.M. (1986). Experiential learning programs: An organizational schema. *Journal of Career Development, 13*(1), 61-67.

Chickering, A.W. (1976). Developmental change as a major outcome. In M.T. Keeton, (Ed.), *Experiential learning: Rationale, characteristics, assessment* (pp. 62-107). San Francisco, CA: Jossey-Bass.

Colangelo, N., & Parker, M. (1971). Value differences among gifted adolescents. *Counseling and Values, 26,* 35-41.

Colangelo, N., & Zaffrann, R.T. (1979). *New voices in counseling the gifted.* Dubuque IA: Kendall/Hunt.

Colson, S. (1980). The evaluation of a community-based career education program for gifted and talented students as an administrative model for an alternative program. *Gifted Child Quarterly, 24,* 101-106.

Colson, S., Borman, C., & Nash, W.R. (1978). A unique learning opportunity for talented high school seniors, *Phi Delta Kappan, 59,* 542-543.

Cox, L. (1984). Adaptive mentoring. *G/C/T, 33,* 54-56.

Cox, J., Daniel, N., & Boston, B.O. (1985). *Educating able learners: Programs and promising practices.* Austin, TX: University of Texas Press.

Delisle, J., & Squires, S. (1989). Career development for gifted and talented youth: Position statement Division on Career Development (DCD) and The Association for the Gifted (TAG). *Journal for the Education of the Gifted, 13*(1), 97-101.

Dunn, R. (1989). Individualizing instruction for mainstreamed gifted children. In R.M. Milgram (Ed.), *Teaching gifted and talented learners in regular classrooms* (pp. 63-111). Springfield, IL: Charles C. Thomas.

Edlin, E.P., & Haensly, P.A. (1985). Gifts of mentorships. *Gifted Child Quarterly, 29,* 55-60.

Ellingson, M.K., Haeger, W.W., & Feldhusen, J.F. (1986). The Purdue Mentor Program. *G/C/T, 9*(2), 2-5.

Fox, L.H., & Denham, S.A. (1974). Values and career interests of mathematically and scientifically precocious youth. In J.C. Stanley, D.P. Keating, & L.H. Fox (Eds.), *Mathematical talent: Discovery, description, and development* (pp. 140-175). Baltimore, MD: Johns Hopkins University Press.

Gallegher, J.J. (1975). *Teaching the gifted child* (2nd ed.). Boston: Allyn and Bacon.

Gogel, E.M., McCumsey, J., & Hewett, G. (1985, November/December). What parents are saying. *G/C/T,* pp. 7-9.

Goertzel, M., Goertzel, V., & Goertzel, T. (1978). *300 eminent personalities.* San Francisco: Jossey-Bass.

Gray, W.A. (1982). Mentor-assisted enriched projects for the gifted and talented, *Educational Leadership, 40,* 16-21.

Gray, W.A. (1983). *Challenging the gifted and talented through mentor-assisted enrichment projects.* Bloomington, IN: Phi Delta Kappa Educational Foundation.

Guilford, J.P. (1967). *The Structure of Intellect, Psychological Bulletin, 53,* 267-293.

Herr, E.L., & Watanabe, A. (1979). Counseling the gifted about career development. In N. Colangelo & R.T. Zaffran (Eds.), *New voices in counseling the gifted.* Dubuque, IA: Kendall/Hunt.

Hirsch, S.P. (1976). Executive high school internships: A boon for the gifted and talented. *Teaching Exceptional Children, 9,* 22-23.

Holland, J.L. (1958). A personality inventory employing occupational titles. *Journal of Applied Psychology, 42,* 336-342.

Hoyt, K.B. (1980). Contrasts between the guidance and career education movements. In F.E. Burtnett (Ed.), *The school counselor's involvement in career education* (pp. 1-11). Falls Church, VA: American Personnel and Guidance Association.

Hoyt, K.B., & Hebeler, J.R. (Eds.). (1974). *Career education for gifted and talented students.* Salt Lake City, UT: Olympic.

Howley, C.B. (1989). Career education for able students. *Journal for the Education of the Gifted, 12*(3), 205-217.

Jepsen, D.A. (1979). Helping gifted adolescents with career exploration. In N. Colangelo & R.T. Zaffran (Eds.), *New voices in counseling the gifted* (pp. 277-283). Dubuque, IA: Kendall/Hunt.

Kaufmann, F.A., Harrel, G., Milam, C.P., Woolverton, N., & Miller, J. (1986). The nature, role, and influence of mentors in the lives of gifted adults. *Journal of Counseling and Development, 64*, 576-578.

Kerr, B.A. (1985). *Smart girls, gifted women.* Columbus, OH: Ohio Psychology Publishing.

Kerr, B.A. (1986). Career counseling for the gifted: Assessments and interventions. *Journal of Counseling and Development, 64*, 602-604.

Kerr, B.A. (1988). Career counseling for gifted girls and women. *Journal of Career Development, 14*(4), 259-268.

Kerr, B.A., & Miller, J.V. (Guest Eds.). (1986). Special issue: Counseling the gifted and talented. *Journal of Counseling and Development.*

Kokaska, C., Brolin, D. (1985). *Career education for handicapped individuals.* Columbus, OH: Merrill.

Maker, C.J. (1989). Curriculum content for gifted students: Principles and practices. In R.M. Milgram (Ed.), *Teaching gifted and talented learners in regular classrooms* (pp. 33-61). Springfield, IL: Charles C. Thomas.

Marland, S.P., Jr. (1972). Career education: 300 days later. *American Vocational Journal, 47*, 14-17.

Marshall, B.C. (1981). Career decision making patterns of gifted and talented adolescents: Implications for career education. *Journal of Career Education, 7*, 305-310.

McClelland, D.C. (1973). Testing for competence rather than for "intelligence." *American Psychologist, 28*, 1-14.

McDaniels, C. (1988). Virginia VIEW: 1979-1987. *Journal of Career Development, 14*(3), 169-176.

Milgram, R.M. (Ed.). (1989). *Teaching gifted and talented learners in regular classrooms.* Springfield, IL: Charles C. Thomas.

Miller, J.V. (Guest Ed.). (1981). Special issue on career education for gifted and talented. *Journal of Career Education, 7*(4).

Myrick, R.D., & Carrow, P.A. (1987). Teacher involvement in career education and advisement: Ready or not? *Journal of Career Development, 14*(2), 108-117.

Oden, M.H. (1968). The fulfillment of promise: 40-year follow-up of the Terman gifted group. *Genetic Psychology Monographs, 77*, 3-93.

Perrone, P.A. (1986). Guidance needs of gifted children, adolescents, and adults. *Journal of Counseling and Development, 64*, 564-566.

Roe, A. (1952). *The making of a scientist.* New York: Dodd, Mead.

Runions, T. (1980). The mentor academy program: Educating the gifted and talented for the 80's. *Gifted Child Quarterly, 24*, 152-157.

Sanborn, M.P., & Niemiec, C.J. (1971). Identifying values of superior high school students. *School Counselor, 18*, 237-245.

Tannenbaum, A.J. (1983). *Gifted children: Psychological and educational perspectives.* New York: Macmillan.

Terman, L.M. (1925). *Genetic studies of genius. Vol. 1 of Mental and physical traits of a thousand gifted children.* Stanford, CA: Stanford University Press.

Terman, L.M., & Oden, M.H. (1947). *Genetic studies of genius: Vol. 4. The gifted child grows up: Twenty-five years follow-up of a superior group.* Stanford, CA: Stanford University Press.

Terman, L.M., & Oden, M.H. (1959). *Genetic studies of genius: Vol. 4. The gifted child at mid-life: Thirty-five years follow-up of the superior child.* Stanford, CA: Stanford University Press.

Torrance, E.P. (1983). Role of mentors in creative achievement. *Creative Child and Adult Quarterly, 8,* 815-818.

Torrance, E.P. (1984). *Mentor relationships: How they aid creative achievement, endure, change, and die.* Buffalo, NY: Bearly Limited.

Van Tassel-Baska, J. (1983). *A practical guide to counseling the gifted in a school setting.* Reston, VA: Council for Exceptional Children.

Walters, J., & Gardner, H. (1986). The crystallizing experience: Discovering an intellectual gift. In R.J. Sternberg & J.E. Davidson (Eds.), *Conceptions of giftedness* (pp. 306-331). New York: Cambridge University Press.

Wallach, M.A., & Wing, C.W., Jr. (1969). *The talented student: A validation of the creativity-intelligence distinction.* New York: Holt, Rinehart, & Winston.

Webb, J.T., Meckstroth, E.A., & Tolan, S.S. (1982). *Guiding the gifted child.* Columbus, OH: Ohio Psychology Publishing.

Part II
Counseling Gifted and Talented Learners With Special Needs

In Part II, four kinds of gifted children and youth are examined. Each was overlooked in the past, but is currently receiving proper attention. The four are gifted girls (Chapter 8), disadvantaged gifted children (Chapter 9), learning-disabled gifted (Chapter 10), and gifted preschoolers (Chapter 11).

When gifted girls do not realize their full potential, both they and society are the losers for it. There have been many positive changes in attitudes toward women in the developed nations over the past few decades. Nevertheless, gifted girls are still underidentified and underserved. Although there is no compelling evidence for inherent gender differences in the intellectual abilities of men and women, fewer women than men demonstrate gifted behavior. Women are underrepresented in all high-status careers and in the upper echelons of political and social leadership. The reasons for the underdevelopment and underutilization of women's talents are to be found primarily in the realm of socialization.

In Chapter 8, Schwartz discusses a wide variety of issues relevant specifically to gifted girls. The reasons gifted girls fail to become gifted women may be divided into three categories: (a) attitudes and practices of parents, (b) attitudes and practices of teachers, and (c) personal-social characteristics of gifted girls. Schwartz views the sex-role stereotypes and sexist attitudes of parents and teachers as limiting the development of gifted girls. She also implicates an array of personality characteristics in gifted girls as barriers to their optimal development. She includes negative self-concept, low levels of aspiration and achievement motivation, fear of failure and fear of success, as well as sex-role conflict. She recommends specific strategies for parents and teachers to use with gifted girls to circumvent these barriers. She urges that instruction be individualized, nonsexist attitudes and behaviors be systematically reinforced, and strong efforts be made to provide positive role models. She concludes her chapter with a call for preservice and in-service teacher and counselor training programs that will assign high priority to assuring equal educational opportunity to gifted girls.

Disadvantaged gifted children have unique needs because of their different cultural background and different home and community environment. In Chapter 9, Zorman deals with the identification of gifted children from culturally diverse backgrounds, specifies the special problems of disadvantaged gifted children, and suggests ways to develop their abilities. She emphasizes (a) the necessity for utilizing indirect means of identification, and (b) the importance of exposing disadvantaged youngsters to many areas of interest and a wide variety of real-world experiences that provide opportunities to develop and demonstrate special abilities. She presents a model demonstration project developed by the Szold Institute for Research in the Behavioral Sciences in Jerusalem for identifying and nurturing potential among gifted disadvantaged learners.

There is growing recognition of the need to provide for the needs of gifted and talented children in the preschool years. In Chapter 10, Karnes and Johnson provide an up-to-date report of the status of gifted education at the preschool level. They describe the characteristics of these children, the specific problems they are likely to encounter, and approaches used to differentiate curriculum and to individualize instruction for them. Karnes and Johnson consider the competencies required by teachers of preschool gifted children and highlight the importance of fostering positive attitudes toward young gifted children in them. The authors suggest means of involving parents in providing the required enrichment and acceleration of their gifted preschool children.

There are very few full-time special education schools for gifted preschool children and most of these children are found in regular classrooms. Accordingly, Karnes and Johnson's detailed presentation of the problems and challenges of providing for preschool gifted children in regular classrooms is a major contribution to this field.

The possibility of a child being both learning-disabled and gifted is difficult for many people to understand. The two exceptionalities appear to be inherently contradictory, but may co-occur in the same children. In the last decade there has been increasing attention to children who are both learning-disabled and gifted. In Chapter 11, Daniels deals with the major relevant issues: (a) identification of these children through systematic diagnostic evaluation; (b) assessment of the cognitive and personal-social assets and deficits of the individual child by means of diagnostic teaching activities and other multidisciplinary diagnostic procedures; and (c) teaching and counselng these children.

In Chapter 12, the final chapter in Part II, Knapp presents eight fictional portraits of intelligent and creative children. The stories are not case studies of disturbed, gifted children. On the contrary, the children depicted are remarkably healthy, notwithstanding difficult environmental circumstances. All are drawn for 20th-century literature and were selected because of their diverse characteristics: They differ in age, ability patterns, interests, race, class, and national origin.

The stories provide a coherent view of the diverse experiences of each gifted child. The portraits focus on the overall pattern and meaning of the experiences and coping behavior of these children, not on isolated bits of information. These stories are remarkable, indeed unforgettable, and will supply teachers, counselors, and parents with insight into the intricate interactions of the intellectual abilities and personality traits of the child with the influences of family, school, and community. These interactions determine in the final analysis whether and in what ways gifted and talented children realize their gifts and talents.

Chapter 8
Guiding Gifted Girls

Lita Linzer Schwartz

"Until recently, that is until about five decades ago, the intellectual inferiority of girls was assumed, and public policy with regard to them fostered no expectation of intellectual performances on their part. Their social function was grounded in physique rather than in intellect, to produce the species, and to perform manual duties pertaining to and compatible with maternity" (Hollingworth, 1926, pp. 346-347). This statement is more than 60 years old, and girls' intellectual inferiority is no longer assumed as a guide for public policy. In today's world we find a number of different philosophical positions in addition to innate inferiority of women, that is, equality of males and females, superiority of women, or differential egalitarianism (Higham & Navarre, 1984). Persistent findings of greater homogeneity of intellect among females than males are likely to be attributed to "a manifestation of desire for conformity among gifted women in order to avoid being labeled as abnormal and the risk of social rejection" (Callahan, 1979, p. 409). It is, nevertheless, somewhat depressing to realize that the Hollingworth statement could have been written more recently, and that some of the prejudice expressed is still very much with us.

Although there have been many changes in attitudes toward women and toward their careers over the past few decades in most of the developed nations (Finn, Dulberg, & Reis, 1979), some traces of earlier encouragement of underachievement by girls persist. A shade of truth still lingers in Margaret Mead's statement of 50 years ago: "the boy is taught to achieve, the girl to prove that she doesn't achieve, will never achieve. The same threat hangs over the nonachieving boy and the achieving girl, the threat that he or she will never be chosen by a member of the opposite sex" (1935, p. 302). Even today, gifted girls may be confronted with ambivalent attitudes on the part of their parents, teachers, and counselors that parallel the confused self-image that some of the girls themselves have. Precisely because the gifted girl may perceive incoming "messages" as conflicting, it is necessary to provide guidance and counseling to her that may differ from that recommended for gifted learners, in general.

Gifted girls share with gifted boys in mainstreamed classrooms social and academic problems simply because they are different. In addition, personal problems of self-motivation, and external problems stemming from lack of challenge, lack of teacher, or curricular flexibility, and the ambivalence of a society that calls for excellence yet rejects "elitism" as reflected in special educational services for the gifted, affects boys and girls equally. An atmosphere in which intellectual activity, and even artistic talent, is valued primarily in monetary terms rather than for its own sake, further discourages gifted students of both sexes (Howley, 1987). However, in addition, the "Are you a girl or a 'grind' " question that has confronted gifted girls for decades is still very much with us. Admittedly, there is both greater recognition of and respect for their abilities today than was true many years ago. Nevertheless, the conflict between social peer pressures and academic or other talents persists, especially as the girls approach adolescence. It is for this reason that they require differentiated guidance and counseling.

It is important to help gifted girls, particularly adolescents, understand the prejudiced views that are held by many people. This understanding will help them anticipate and cope with the types of responses they are likely to encounter in the course of their education and career planning.

Most articles in the professional literature are directed to all gifted youngsters in either heterogeneous or homogeneous learning situations rather than to the unique problems and challenges faced by gifted girls in those settings. Furthermore, articles written several years ago may reflect situations and/or attitudes prevalent then but not now. As educators, we cannot affect that which is innate (genetic factors), but can and do affect, in varying degrees, the experiences and opportunities that gifted girls have. In order to respond in an appropriate manner to the needs of gifted girls, teachers and counselors should examine their own biases, and those of the people with whom we and gifted girls interact.

In this volume we have discussed a wide variety of issues relevant to counseling gifted learners in regular classrooms that apply to both boys and girls. Little if any attention has been devoted specifically to the unique problems of the gifted girl in regular classrooms. In this chapter, we highlight issues relevant more specifically to gifted girls.

Some gifted girls have personal-social problems unique to their gender that may become barriers to full realization of potential abilities. These problems often become the focus of discussions between counselors and gifted girls.

The remainder of this chapter is divided into three sections. In the first section, we clarify in greater detail the barriers to actualization of abilities cited above. In the second, we suggest ways that counselors and teachers can help gifted girls and their families circumvent these barriers. The third section focuses on preservice and in-service professional issues.

BARRIERS TO REALIZATION OF POTENTIAL OF GIFTED GIRLS

Parenting the Gifted Girl: Negative Self-Image and Low Level of Aspiration

Meckstroth and Albert dealt in depth with the problems and pleasures of the parent-gifted child relationship in separate chapters of this book. Albert's research focused specifically on gifted boys and their families. In this chapter the emphasis is on the interaction of gifted girls with their parents, especially as it affects academic and nonacademic performance in the regular classroom.

Negative self-image and inappropriately low level of aspiration is an all too common phenomenon among gifted girls. We are well aware that parents are the first shapers of a child's self-image. Accordingly, we need to ask parents whether they regard having a gifted daughter as a pleasure or a plague. Are they innatists? Ultrafeminists? Somewhere in between? Their responses may vary not only with their attitudes toward gender roles and giftedness, but with the age of the daughter. The ways in which parents behave with their gifted daughters may, for example, reinforce long-term vocational planning differently, as was found in a study of the parents of high creative and low creative women (Trollinger, 1983). If one or both parents had wanted a son, or resents the fact that the daughter may be academically brighter or artistically more talented than a son, this, too, has effects on the gifted girl.

The different expectations for males and females was demonstrated empirically "in a study of preschool youngsters' reactions to a drawing of a house in which they were asked how far from their own homes they could go. Most girls pointed out an area quite near to the house and stated that they complied with such boundaries. Boys, on the other hand, pointed out a much wider perimeter and generally exceeded it. This is only one example that suggests differential treatment by well-meaning fathers and mothers, but these expectations carry over into later life" (Lewis, 1985, p.130).

Blaubergs (1980) reviewed a number of studies that demonstrated sex-role stereotyping by parents in terms of behavior expected from babies and selection of toys for children. Until the gifted female student recognizes that parental expectations may differ from reality, she may be inhibited in expressing her own preferred activities. Later, school phobia or underachievement may stem from these perceptions and should be treated as a family problem rather than the girl's problem alone (Wendorf & Frey, 1985).

What order of priorities do the parents have? Is the daughter's academic standing of prime importance, or her social acceptance, or well-roundedness? Although, as Colangelo and Kelly (1983) have suggested, a gifted girl's peers are frequently other gifted students rather than the general student body, parents tend to be more concerned about peer rejection in the general sense than peer acceptance. They may also have some legitimate concerns about social and emotional maturity versus academic abilities, as well as involvement versus isolation, especially when a second-grader, for example, is doing high school math (Bennetts, 1980).

If the parents truly want their gifted daughter to be her own person, to be self-actualizing as she matures, then she must be allowed to express and follow her preferences (within the limits of safety). Parents also need to allow even the young gifted girl time alone in which she can pursue her special interests as they develop, set personal goals, evaluate her own performance, and dream her dreams. In Kerr's study (1985) of eminent and gifted women, she found that "time alone" was a key common element in their developing years. Parents often provide individualized or group instruction in art, music, drama, gymnastics, or other areas of talent, especially when their gifted daughter is mainstreamed. Parents must resist the temptation to overschedule their gifted daughters. These girls need private time and space in which to exercise fantasy, imagination, and intellect.

Despite the fact that approximately one marriage in two presently ends in divorce in the United States, girls, perhaps especially gifted girls, need support from their fathers for their achievement and career goals (Schwartz, 1980). If it is the so-called "masculine" world that the gifted girl seeks to enter, her initiation into it may be through experiences first shared with her father. In dual-career families, mothers, too, demonstrate that achievement and family life can be coordinated.

As the gifted girl continues through the school years in a regular classroom, she will come to recognize that boys may respect, but feel threatened by her abilities (Schwartz, 1987). Or she may feel valued for her "brain" or talent, but not as a whole person. This can be disconcerting, can cause her to become disinterested in academics or other areas of her giftedness, and can lead to an inappropriately negative self-image. Parents, teachers, and counselors can coordinate efforts to help her reorganize her priorities, rebuild her self-esteem, and establish a healthier and more balanced perspective.

Conversely, of course, there are girls (and boys) who are gifted in leadership, or academics, or sports, or the arts, and who have inflated self-images that similarly need to be put in perspective. Assuming that parents have not encouraged the attitude of being "better" than their peers, again a team effort of parents, teachers, and counselors is called for to help the gifted youngster recognize and strengthen weak areas while maintaining the strong ones.

Hollinger studied self-esteem and self-image in adolescent gifted girls (Hollinger, 1983, 1985a; Hollinger & Fleming, 1984). She has found, for example, "that possession of a self-image which includes expressive as well as instrumental traits is associated with higher social self-esteem than if the self-image includes instrumental traits only" (1983, p.160). This conclusion, underscored by additional research (Hollinger, 1985a, 1985b), suggests that counselors and others can point out that these traits can coexist rather than repressing one (expressive) in order to express the other (instrumental). Hollinger suggests that "given the apparent centrality of androgynous self perceptions to the experiencing of positive and social self esteem, facilitating a gifted young woman's exploration of her own self perceptions of instrumental and expressive attributes (particularly with respect to their congruence with her own perception of femininity) would appear to be a critical goal in counseling" (1985b, p.121).

Sexist attitudes in Teachers and Counselors: Attribution of Success and Failure

Usually the first school experiences for the gifted girl are in a heterogeneous group of age peers at the nursery school level. If the teacher has an image of little girls as playing in the "cooking corner," speaking quietly, and staying clean, the precocious girl may meet her first challenge. Not fitting the stereotype can evoke teacher criticisms (and most little ones crave teacher acceptance) that "turn off" her curiosity, creativity, and nonconformity. This possibility continues in kindergarten and the primary grades, but obviously varies considerably with the personal prejudices and flexibility of the teacher. Kirschenbaum (1982) offers a number of specific suggestions through which nursery school teachers can develop a nonsexist orientation for their preschoolers, thereby enabling little gifted girls as well as the other children to move toward varying goals that are not gender-stereotyped.

Some teachers have sexist ideas about differential abilities of boys and girls that attribute boys' successes to their abilities and skills, but girls' successes, when perceived, to luck or other external factors. This is particularly evident in cross-sexed tasks. "Since failure in a cross-sex-typed task is expected, the attribution for it is a stable one, i.e., lack of ability. Succeeding when success is unexpected does not change the expectations concerning future successes, but any failure when such failure is expected reinforces the expectations for continued failure" (Blaubergs, 1980, p.15).

Dealing with attributions for success and failure calls for helping the gifted girl or any child to develop internal locus of control. That simply means that she is aware that successes are due to her ability and/or efforts rather than luck or someone else's whim, and that lack of success—or failure, while sometimes attributable to factors beyond her control, may also be due to her own lack of effort (Schwartz, 1987). Developing internal locus of control begins in early childhood as the child is encouraged to make choices and then to take responsibility for the consequences, whether good or bad. For example, in a study of five 14-year-olds in rural schools in Kansas, Healy and Parish (1986) found that gifted girls, as well as gifted and nongifted boys, were less likely to experience stress as a result of rejection or expectations of perfection by others. This was attributed to their operating from internal locus of control. While building this internal locus, especially with a gifted child, it is important to make her aware that "to err is human," and that being gifted does not mean that she has to be perfect in every effort or at all times.

Fear of Failure and Fear of Success

Gifted girls who become perfectionistic, like their male peers, may suffer "fear of failure." More discussed however, is females' "fear of success," though this has been disputed (Hoffman, 1977; Horner, 1972; Kaslow & Schwartz, 1978). Both "fear of failure" that accompanies expectations, self- or externally based, of perfect performance and "fear of success" are inimical to the gifted girl's accomplishments in the classroom. In the former case, she becomes afraid to risk revealing lack of knowledge or skill, so refuses to venture into new areas or activities. If she doesn't try, obviously she can't fail, that is, be seen as less than perfect. If she doesn't try, however, she may also miss opportunities for learning, for achievement, for awards, for self-actualization (Hoffman, 1972; Whitmore, 1986). Again, teachers as well as parents have to be alert and make special efforts not to convey the message that to take risks is unwise or that girls simply don't have "what it takes" to work in a specific field.

Probably the most effective transmission of this message has been in the field of mathematics. Not only have girls been discouraged from taking advanced math (and science) courses because they presumably lack the ability to handle them well, but they have tended to score lower on SAT-Math tests than their male peers. They have been given the message so often and with such conviction that they believe it. They develop "math anxiety" even when they are quite capable of succeeding with the most challenging math courses. A recent report from staff at the Educational Testing Service, furthermore, suggests that girls must be actively encouraged in the middle school years (grades 4–8) to enroll in math, science, and computer science courses and to participate in activities in these fields or they will not select them in high school (Lockheed, Thorpe, Brooks-Gunn, Casserly, & McAloon, 1985). If gifted girls practice such avoidance in high school, they won't be prepared to take courses in college that will lead to employment in technical fields. This situation is changing. A recent article reported that 30 per cent of Bryn Mawr students—all of whom are perceived as being gifted females—are now majoring in the sciences (Collins, 1987).

"Fear of success" is tied more to nonacademic factors than is "fear of failure." Here, the gifted girl knows that she can achieve at a high level, but is afraid that this will make her unpopular with her peers, especially the boys, so holds back on giving the correct answer or hides the "A" or the "100%" on her paper. The outspoken gifted girl in a primary grade classroom begins to mute her voice as she moves into the upper grades and approaches adolescence. Continuing in main-streamed classes, moreover, promotes this pattern. It becomes a source of embarrassment rather than pride to have a teacher frequently turn to her, after others have answered a question incorrectly, for the right answer. Perhaps equally distressing to some gifted girls is their being used as tutors to others in the class. This not only emphasizes her being "ahead of" her peers, but also does little to strengthen or broaden her abilities. Although the girl may enjoy helping others (Johnson, 1986), and indeed should be encouraged to think of others as well as herself, there is a difference between volunteering and being exploited.

A colleague of the author, who had also been a schoolmate before the "feminist revolution," vividly recalls the counselor at our all girls' high school who would not allow her to apply for admission to a college of engineering. That was not a field for females, period! Today, of course, colleges of engineering are far more open to females, and the job market welcomes female engineers to demonstrate its commitment to affirmative action programs. An excellent example of a female's success in this field is the Dean of the College of Engineering at Pratt Institute (Brooklyn, NY). The colleague, incidentally, got around her problem by applying to a college of liberal arts and transferring to engineering after her initial acceptance.

Yet another example of "mis"-guiding gifted girls was seen in earlier forms of the Strong-Campbell Vocational Interest Inventory and similar vocational guidance measures. There was no scoring provision on the women's form for female doctors (or male nurses), lawyers, engineers, accountants (bookkeepers, however, were scored on the women's form), college professors, or other occupations inconsistent with traditional stereotypes. That has been changed in the most recent editions of these instruments. Such accommodation to antidiscrimination laws, however, has to be extended to the guidance counselors themselves.

Sex-role Conflict. Another problem common with gifted girls is the impending, though somewhat muted, conflict about future orientation—family and/or career? How does one manage to do both, if that is the choice, without becoming a "burned out super-woman"? Another major conflict confronting gifted girls is how to reconcile their academic interests and education with the areas of excellence traditionally seen by society as sex-role-appropriate for women. After all, some may ask, how much history or economics or physics can the gifted woman use in her role as wife and mother (Schwartz, 1980, p. 113)? This is a problem faced more often by gifted girls in communities that are traditional and perhaps isolated from metropolitan centers than for those in large cities where there tend to be more options for women. Yet even if the gifted girl is encouraged to pursue her interests *while in school,* it seems unrealistic, unfair, and inefficient to erect barriers to using her knowledge in the marketplace after graduation. In brief, having a future orientation that offers only intellectual/artistic frustration to the gifted girl is almost certain to inhibit her classroom performance.

Perrone (1986, p. 565) notes that "sometimes counselors' attitudes or values will lead them to raise issues of career and family conflicts with female students but not with male students. Counselors can assist students of both sexes most effectively by having them consider how they plan to combine work, family, and community involvement." They need to help them to set realistic goals, neither minimizing potential difficulties nor exaggerating abilities.

Underachievement

Another facet of giftedness for which teachers need to be prepared is underachievement by the gifted. Some gifted students lack motivation in one or more academic areas—to the great frustration of their teachers as well as their parents. For gifted girls, in particular, "rejection of an opportunity to participate in a more challenging academic program may be a choice made to avoid the psychological conflict created by social penalties experienced by students in such a program, or to allow more time for social activities" (Whitmore, 1986, p. 66). Not only does rejection of participation in special programs for the gifted create conflicts with parents, but it also poses special problems and challenges for the teacher. This is because the student is receiving her education in a traditional classroom exclusively and not taking full advantage of opportunities that are open to her. The child may be seen as "lazy," or rebellious, when in fact "the underachiever has learned to underachieve to avoid some discomforts or perceived penalties for effort" (Whitmore, 1986, p. 67). For girls, as has already been noted, the penalties tend to center around social rejection, especially beginning in preadolescence (Callahan, 1979; cf. Hollinger & Fleming, 1984). Unfortunately, there are few examples available for young gifted females of rewards for success of women in nontraditional endeavors or for demonstrating a high degree of competence in mixed-gender settings.

CIRCUMVENTING BARRIERS TO ACHIEVEMENT

What has already been said presents a somewhat dismal picture. Are there ways that the barriers to the realization of potential of gifted girls can be circumvented? There are, but the possibility of following different paths varies with the locality, the age of the gifted girls, and their number. What is financially feasible in New York City or San Francisco may not be in Park City, Utah, or Whitefield, New Hampshire. What is acceptable to the community similarly varies from place to place. However, all is not lost! There are alternatives that are not costly and that won't necessarily "ruffle anyone's feathers" as being elitist.

Reinforcement. The first guiding principle is that parents and teachers should reinforce attitudes and behaviors in gifted girls that contribute to realization of potential. Just as the teacher praises the learning-disabled, attention-deficient child for staying with a task for 15 minutes rather than five, so the gifted girl needs to be reinforced for doing her tasks well and/or quickly, or for exhibiting persistence in pursuing long-term goals. It costs nothing to build and maintain the positive self-image that she needs to continue achieving. Of course, the process of reinforcement will not occur automatically. Parents and counselors must seek opportunities to reinforce desirable behaviors and attitudes in gifted girls themselves, and to encourage parents and teachers to do the same.

Individualization. A second guiding principle is that gifted girls should be provided with the opportunity for independent study depending on grade level, subject matter, and individual interests. One of the major recurrent themes of this book and its companion volume (Milgram, 1989) is the need for differentiation and individualization in curriculum content and in the teaching-learning process. A large number of curriculum options using the concepts and instructional strategies of individualization in a wide variety of subject matter areas that meet the needs of gifted children in regular classrooms were presented and discussed by well-recognized authorities in the field (Milgram, 1989). We will not present this material again but suggest the need to adapt the approaches suggested in each content area to the specific needs of gifted girls.

For example, Anderson (1989) has highlighted the importance of reading in the lives of many gifted children. She did not, however, relate her approach specifically to gifted girls. The teacher can encourage, perhaps assign, the gifted girl to work with the school librarian on topics about female achievers. She can then share the results of her independent study with classmates. Such a project serves the dual purpose of supplementing textbooks that even now often neglect females in nontraditional as well as traditional roles, stimulating gifted girls to higher aspirations and encouraging her female peers to higher aspirations for themselves.

Another example of a situation in which a differential approach is required is with girls talented in the arts and/or music. Life is somewhat easier for the artistically gifted girl, as musical and artistic talent are expressive rather than instrumental in nature and thus fall within the female realm. Here, too, however, opportunities must be provided for their stimulation and expression. Whether the girl is encouraged to compose a "class song," perform at a school concert, act in school plays, exhibit her art products, or utilize these talents in support of academic projects, teachers need to be supportive and sometimes "pushy" in their encouragement. Opportunities for creativity must be provided with support for the lack of conformity that creativity often implies. Encouragement to enter competitions is important if the girl is to "make her mark" in the arts.

Role models. Another important alternative that costs nothing is to provide role models. It has been suggested that "gifted girls may not be less interested in the traditional female careers, but simply more interested than girls in general, in areas traditionally viewed as masculine, such as science, mathematics, and mechanical activities" (Fox & Zimmerman, 1985, p. 226). The principal point is to make the gifted girl aware of opportunities as well as continuing stereotypes (Callahan,

1979). Gifted girls are accustomed to seeing female teachers, but female engineers? Female physicians? Female scientists? Female college professors? Female business executives? Female clergy? Parents or teachers, if they are willing to make the effort, can seek out such women and ask them to meet or communicate with a gifted girl interested in their field.

> Counselors are in an especially advantageous position to help develop such relationships. First, they can provide information to potential mentors and proteges about the advantages of mentorships. Second, they can assist in identifying and matching individuals on the basis of teaching and learning styles, values, and interests. Third, they can establish and monitor mentorship programs in schools or professional organizations. Fourth, they can provide ongoing training in the mentorship process. Finally, in the case of gifted individuals, they can provide support groups for both mentors and students who have unique styles, needs, and interests. (Kaufmann, Harrel, Milan, Woolverton, & Miller, 1986, p. 577)

Edlind and Haensly (1985) similarly point out the mutual benefits to mentor and "mentee" of the relationship, as well as the advantages to the gifted student. If the location is too remote from even a community college to locate a suitable mentor, the teacher or counselor should guide the gifted girl to literature that she can read to find answers to her questions about a specific career or the difficulties she may meet en route to achieving her goals. Some starting points for this approach are to be found in Bachtold and Werner (1970) and Warner (1979).

Personal computers. The computer is an excellent tool for differentiating and individualizing instruction for gifted learners. The wide variety of ways that computers can be used for this purpose with gifted learners has been presented in detail by Bareford (1989). The computer has special value in programming for the gifted girl because it permits her to learn independently and without "jeopardizing" her position in the classroom. Unfortunately, many gifted girls share the "computer reluctance" that characterizes their less gifted peers. Mathematics anxiety, studied in many settings, is one of the more familiar problems. Allied to it is what we may call "computer reluctance," in which girls take less advantage of opportunities than boys do to become actively engaged in using computers as tools for problem solving, creative efforts, or even recreation. An interesting cautionary note was sounded by Lewis, citing an Educational Testing Service study: "In one U.S. high school, teen-age males were telling females they were stupid to discourage them from registering for after-school computer courses. The young men admitted they were harassing their female schoolmates deliberately so they could have more computer time" (1985, p. 131).

Despite these problems, counselors and teachers should encourage gifted girls to become computer-wise. A number of skills useful to the gifted girl are learned and reinforced when using the computer. "First, in learning to program a computer the programmer achieves the ultimate level of mastery over the machine, providing a powerful boost to self-esteem and confidence" (Hamlett, 1984, p. 253). Precision, a thorough understanding of the subject matter, and attention to detail are required to develop programs; creativity is encouraged with programs like "Print Shop," "MacPaint," and "Crossword Magic," among others; interactive simulation and decision-making games challenge the gifted girl's abilities to solve problems and to look ahead at possible outcomes; and if gifted in math and/or logical reasoning, puzzle programs using math will both challenge and teach her in these areas. Even using the word processing function of a computer has positive effects, since the drudgery of revision is removed. Thus, a potential author will feel freer to communicate her ideas, and may even find writing on the computer more enjoyable than writing in longhand or on a regular typewriter.

An increasing amount of educational software is available that can be used by the gifted girl as a source of independent study. Some of it is particularly useful because it can provide gifted girls experience with subject matter generally considered "masculine." One example given by Hamlett (1985) is a program called "Rocky's Boots," which leads a child from concepts of electricity and electronics to the construction of problem solving electronic machines.

Sex-segregated education. There is another alternative that is almost as controversial as specialized education for the gifted: sex-segregated education. Opportunities for leadership, encouragement to do well in math and the sciences, the chance to be "top" in a competition without anxiety about heterosexual relationships, and the beginnings of women's networks are all advantages to be gained in all-girl academic settings. One Bryn Mawr College senior, a major in physics who plans to do graduate work in oceanography, has said: "I do not think I would be doing physics today if I were not at a women's college. Women have so much less self-esteem that men that they tend to give up on difficult subjects like physics much sooner" (Collins, 1987, p. 1E). There is evidence that females who attend women's colleges are more likely to attend graduate school than those who have gone to coeducational colleges (Tidball, 1980). Graduates of Hunter College High School (N.Y.) who attended the school when it admitted only gifted girls reported the following benefits accruing from their special educational setting: "heightened intellectual and personal standards, superior teachers, diverse subject matter, increased political awareness and responsibility, greater personal assertiveness, and greater educational challenges. Additionally, the opportunity to openly compete without self-consciousness." (Walker & Freeland, 1986, p. 28; cf. Fishman, 1982; Mezzacappa, 1987). If there is opposition to, or an inability to provide, single-sex schools, teachers might organize sections that are single-sex where these advantages can be gained. Thus, at least some of the benefits might equally accrue to young gifted girls (see Vockell & Lobonc, 1981).

PROFESSIONAL ISSUES

The typical girl pupil, whether or not she is gifted, is usually expected to behave in a conformist manner. That is, she is relatively quiet rather than outspoken, speaks only when spoken to, does her assignments neatly and on time, and follows her teacher's instructions without a quibble. The girl who is assertive, who seeks challenges, who is individualistic, and who is high achieving may be perceived as atypical (i.e., "masculine") and possibly as less socially desirable by her teachers (Handel, 1982). The interactions of gifted girls with their teachers and counselors are sometimes problematic and, therefore, attention should be given to the topic in preservice and in-service professional education.

Several references have been made earlier to teachers and counselors of gifted girls and the ways in which they can help or hinder the girls' progress and self-image. Whether a first-grade teacher, or a specialist at the senior high school level, or a guidance counselor, these school figures need to be aware of whether they are practicing "benevolent abandonment" or "overstructuring" with respect to gifted girls in their charge. Sensitivity to the characteristics and needs of gifted girls (and gifted boys) should be developed in all prospective teachers and counselors in preservice and in-service programs.

Unfortunately, as of late 1986, only 21 of the 50 states had mandates for gifted/talented education, with only 14 states requiring certification for teachers of the gifted and talented. Only nine states had placed the education of the gifted/talented under P.L.94-142, with eight of them requiring IEPs (Individual Education Programs) for these students. Only 11 states require that all prospective teachers take at least an introductory course in special education (Dodd, 1987). Given these limitations in the education of classroom teachers, it is no wonder that regular classroom teachers frequently feel inept when confronted with gifted students. This situation makes it imperative to provide in-service training to regular classroom teachers so that they can more effectively interact with gifted students in general and gifted girls in particular.

In a study of teacher attitudes toward the academically gifted, Cramond and Martin (1987) found that both preservice and in-service teachers ranked nonstudious athletic-type adolescent students highest. "The brilliant-studious-nonathletic character, often the stereotype of the gifted student, was rated the lowest" (p. 17). They reasonably concluded that such findings, replicating of a study by Tannenbaum (1962), indicate a strong need for effective intervention strategies with both prospective and in-service teachers. Such programs have been described by Colon and Treffinger (1980), Ebmeier, Dyche, Taylor, and Hall (1985), Mulhern and Ward (1983), Robinson (1985), and Cropley and McLeod (1986).

Eccles, using a model that includes decision making, achievement, and attribution theories assumes that achievement-related choices, consciously or unconsciously arrived at, are shaped by: "(a) one's expectations for success on the various options considered, (b) the relation of perceived options both to one's short- and long-range goals and to one's core self-identity and basic psychological needs, (c) the individual's gender role schema, and (d) the potential cost of investing time in one activity rather than another" (1985, p. 267).

These factors are themselves influenced by parental and peer behaviors and expectations, cultural norms, and the individual's experiences. The interaction of such a conglomeration of factors cannot be easily and definitively illustrated as a predictive matrix, however. Rather, for each gifted girl, the priorities and weights assigned each factor vary, with the result that, as traditional Gestalt psychologists were wont to say, "The whole is greater than the sum of its parts." It therefore behooves the teacher and the counselor to know each advisee as well as possible, and to provide accurate information that will permit her to choose her options on the basis of facts rather than biases.

Of the 671 gifted females in the original sample of Terman's well-known longitudinal study, 430 responded to a follow-up questionnaire almost 50 years later (Sears & Barbee, 1977, p. 31). More of them went to college than their nongifted peers in an era when high school graduation was not yet even a norm for males; most married and had children; and 43 per cent were income workers. Whether or not the subjects married, had children, and/or had careers, however, Sears and Barbee found a high degree of life satisfaction among these middle-aged gifted women that they attributed to an ability to cope with whatever experiences living brought: "It may well be that the coping mechanisms that enable the gifted women to adapt flexibly to a variety of conditions, and in whatever condition to find good satisfactions, are related to the intelligence they bring to their life situations" (1977, p. 60). Hence, enhancing the gifted girl's ability to cope may be the greatest single service her counselors can provide. In order to do this they require knowledge about the cognitive and personal-social char acteristics of gifted girls.

CONCLUSION

In a recent article Feingold (1988) presented convincing data to support his argument that cognitive gender differences are disappearing. Accordingly, differences of achievement can be increasingly viewed as resulting from experience and opportunity. Guiding and counseling gifted girls in regular classrooms toward the goal of maximum realization of potential appears to depend more on people than on data. From the parents who, as primary socializing agents, contribute to the girl's self-image and value system in her most impressionable and formative stages to the counselors who advise her on the senior high school level and the teachers who interact with her in the years between, there is a need to nurture her abilities, her motivation to succeed, her openness to experiences and options, and her self-confidence. Lacking these qualities, the gifted girl will be inadequately prepared to make choices appropriate for her life. If the socializing agents steer her toward gender-stereotyped courses and careers, she may in time resent them for cheating her of other opportunities.

Much can be done to enhance the range of a gifted girl's options through supplementing the program in regular classrooms (see, for example, Dettmer, 1980). Local industry and nearby colleges can sponsor workshops and other special programs for junior and senior high school girls to expose them to different careers and to women who are achieving in nontraditional settings. After-school, weekend, and summer programs can similarly enrich the girl's storehouse of skills and information. These and other suggestions for precollege programs to expand the horizons of gifted and talented girls can be found in Ehrhart and Sandler (1987).

There is nothing wrong with a gifted girl finding fulfillment in family life, perhaps combined with volunteer work. However, in this day of high divorce rates, increasing options to choose the unmarried and/or childless life, and challenging opportunities in a wide array of fields, the gifted girl needs also to be prepared for economic independence as an adult. To attain that goal—economic independence—she needs to acquire a variety of skills that can be provided for in regular classrooms with the aid of willing teachers and counselors. Perhaps, most of all, the gifted girl needs to gain the self-confidence, as well as the information, to make informed decisions. She needs to feel comfortable avoiding stereotypical attitudes if her gifts and talents lead her to nontraditional roles. To achieve this psychological state, it is critical that those who surround and influence her similarly see beyond gender stereotypes and encourage her to activate her potential abilities, whether in the heterogeneous or "regular" classroom or elsewhere.

REFERENCES

Anderson, M.A. (1989). Assessing and providing for gifted children with special needs in reading and library skills. In R.M. Milgram (Ed.), *Teaching gifted and talented learners in regular classrooms* (pp. 179-203). Springfield, IL: Charles C. Thomas.

Bareford, K. (1989). Using computer application programs with gifted learners. In R.M. Milgram (Ed.), *Teaching gifted and talented learners in regular classrooms* (pp. 129-145). Springfield, IL: Charles C. Thomas.

Bachtold, L.M., & Werner, E.E. (1970). Personality profiles of gifted women. *American Psychologist, 25,* 234-243.

Bennetts, L. (1980, April 14). Organizing to overcome the pain of being different. *The New York Times,* Op-Ed page.

Blaubergs, M.S. (1980). Sex-role stereotyping and gifted girls. *Roeper Review, 2*(3), 13-15.

Callahan, C.M. (1979). The gifted and talented woman. In A.H. Passow (Ed.), *The gifted and the talented: Their education and development* (pp. 401-423). Chicago: National Society for the Study of Education. [78th Yearbook of the NSSE, Part I].

Colangelo, N., & Kelly, K.R. (1983). A study of student, parent, and teacher attitudes toward gifted programs and gifted students. *Gifted Child Quarterly, 27,* 107-110.

Collins, H. (1987, April 17). Small, but serious about science. *The Philadelphia Inquirer,* pp. 1-B, 2-B.

Colon, P.J., & Treffinger, D.J. (1980). Providing for the gifted in the regular classroom—am I really MAD? *Roeper Review, 3*(2), 18-21.

Cramond, B., & Martin, C.E. (1987). Inservice and preservice teachers' attitudes toward the academically brilliant. *Gifted Child Quarterly, 31,* 15-19.

Cropley, A., & McLeod, J. (1986). Preparing teachers of the gifted. *International Review of Education, 32,* 125-136.

Dettmer, P. (1980). The extended classroom: A gold mine for gifted students. *Journal for the Education of the Gifted, 3,* 133-137.

Dodd, D. (1987). Special without special education. *Journal for the Education of the Gifted, 10,* 65-77.

Ebmeier, H., Dyche, B., Taylor, P., & Hall, M. (1985). An empirical comparison of two program models for elementary gifted education. *Gifted Child Quarterly, 29,* 15-19.

Eccles, J.S. (1985). Why doesn't Jane run? Sex differences in educational and occupational patterns. In F.D. Horowitz & M. O'Brien (Eds.), *The gifted and talented: Developmental perspectives* (pp. 251-295). Washington, DC: American Psychological Association.

Edlind, E.P., & Haensly, P.A. (1985). Gifts of mentorships. *Gifted Child Quarterly, 29,* 55-60.

Ehrhart, J.K., & Sandler, B.R. (1987). *Looking for more than a few good women in traditionally male fields*. Washington, DC: Project on the Status and Education of Women, Association of American Colleges.

Feingold, A. (1988). Cognitive gender differences are disappearing. *American Psychologist, 43,* 95–103.

Finn, J.D., Dulberg, L., & Reis, J. (1979). Sex differences in educational attainment. *Harvard Educational Review, 4,* 477–503.

Fishman, K.D. (1982, January 18). The joyful elite. *New York,* pp. 43–48.

Fox, L.H., & Zimmerman, W. (1985). Gifted women. In J. Freeman (Ed.), *The psychology of gifted children: Perspectives on development and education* (pp. 219–243). New York: John Wiley & Sons.

Hamlett, C.L. (1984). Microcomputer activities for gifted elementary children: Alternatives to programming. *Teaching Exceptional Children, 16,* 253–257.

Handel, R.D. (1982). Teachers of gifted girls: Are there differences in classroom management? *Journal for the Education of the Gifted, 6*(2), 86–97.

Healy, T.G., & Parish, T.S. (1986). Parental reports of stress in gifted and nongifted elementary students. *Journal of Social Behavior and Personality, 1,* 593–598.

Higham, S.J., & Navarre, J. (1984). Gifted adolescent females require different treatment. *Journal for the Education of the Gifted, 8*(1), 43–58.

Hoffman, L.W. (1972). Early childhood experiences and women's achievement motives. *Journal of Social Issues, 28*(2), 129–155.

Hoffman, L. (1977). Fear of success in 1965 and 1974: A follow-up study. *Journal of Consulting and Clinical Psychology, 45,* 310–321.

Hollinger, C.L. (1983). Counseling the gifted and talented female adolescent: The relationship between social self-esteem and traits of instrumentality and expressiveness. *Gifted Child Quarterly, 27,* 157–161.

Hollinger, C.L. (1985a). The stability of self perceptions of instrumental and expressive traits and social self esteem among gifted and talented female adolescents. *Journal for the Education of the Gifted, 8*(1), 107–126.

Hollinger, C.L. (1985b). Understanding the female adolescent's self perceptions of ability. *Journal for the Education of the Gifted, 9*(1), 59–80.

Hollinger, C.L., & Fleming, E.S. (1984). Internal barriers to the realization of potential: Correlates and interrelationships among gifted and talented female adolescents. *Gifted Child Quarterly, 28,* 135–139.

Hollingworth, L.S. (1926). *Gifted children: Their nature and nurture.* New York: Macmillan.

Horner, M. (1972). The motive to avoid success and changing aspirations of college women. In J.M. Bardwick (Ed.), *Readings on the psychology of women.* New York: Harper & Row.

Howley, A. (1987). The symbolic role of eminence in the education of gifted students. *Journal for the Education of the Gifted, 10,* 115–124.

Johnson, J. (1986, March 12). High-achieving kids can't help but help others. *USA Today,* p. 1-D.

Kaslow, F.W., & Schwartz, L.L. (1978). Self-perceptions of the attractive, successful female professional. *Intellect, 106,* 313–315.

Kaufmann, F.A., Harrel, G., Milam, C.P., Woolverton, N., & Miller, J. (1986). The nature, role, and influence of mentors in the lives of gifted adults. *Journal of Counseling and Human Development, 64,* 576-578.

Kerr, B.A. (1985). *Smart girls, gifted women.* Columbus, OH: Ohio Psychology Publishing.

Kirschenbaum, R. (1980). Combating sexism in the preschool environment. *Roeper Review, 2*(3), 31-33.

Lewis, L.H. (1985). Old patterns: Changing the paradigm. *Educational Horizons, 63*(3), 129-132.

Lockheed, M.E., Thorpe, M., Brooks-Gunn, J., Casserly, P., & McAloon, A. (1985). *Sex and ethnic differences in middle school mathematics, science, and computer science: What do we know?* Princeton, NJ: Educational Testing Service.

Mead, M. (1935). Sex and achievement. *Forum, 94,* 302.

Mezzacappa, D. (1987, April 9). Girls like Girls just fine, citing school's advantages. *The Philadelphia Inquirer,* p. 14-B.

Milgram, R.D. (Ed.). (1989). *Teaching gifted and talented learners in regular classrooms.* Springfield, IL: Charles C. Thomas.

Mulhern, J.D., & Ward, M. (1983). A collaborative program for developing teachers of gifted and talented students. *Gifted Child Quarterly, 27,* 152-156.

Perrone, P. (1986). Guidance needs of gifted children, adolescents, and adults. *Journal of Counseling and Development, 64,* 564-566.

Robinson, A. (1985). Summer institute on the gifted: Meeting the needs of the regular classroom teacher. *Gifted Child Quarterly, 29,* 20-23.

Schwartz, L.L. (1980). Advocacy for the neglected gifted: Females. *Gifted Child Quarterly, 24,* 113-117.

Schwartz, L.L. (1987, April). *Gifted daughters.* Paper presented at the meeting of the Pennsylvania Association for Gifted Children, Philadelphia, PA.

Sears, P.S., & Barbee, A.H. (1977). Career and life satisfactions among Terman's gifted women. In J.C. Stanley, W.C. George, & C.H. Solano (Eds.), *The gifted and the creative: A fifty-year perspective* (pp. 28-65). Baltimore: Johns Hopkins University Press.

Tannenbaum, A.J. (1962). *Adolescent attitudes toward academic brilliance.* New York: Teachers College Press.

Tidball, M.E. (1980). Women's colleges and women achievers revisited. *Journal of Women in Culture and Society, 5,* 504-517.

Trollinger, L.M. (1983). Interests, activities and hobbies of high and low creative women musicians during childhood, adolescent and college years. *Gifted Child Quarterly, 27,* 94-97.

Vockell, E.L., & Lobonc, S. (1981). Sex-role stereotyping by high school females in science. *Journal of Research in Science Teaching, 18,* 209-219.

Walker, B.A., & Freeland, T. (1986, Fall). Gifted girls grow up. *Journal of NAWDAC,* pp. 26-32.

Warner, D.J. (1979, May). Women astronomers. *Natural History, 88*(5), 12-26.

Wendorf, D.J., & Frey, J., III. (1985). Family therapy with the intellectually gifted. *American Journal of Family Therapy, 13*(1), 31-38.

Whitmore, J.R. (1986). Understanding a lack of motivation to excel. *Gifted Child Quarterly, 30,* 66-69.

Chapter 9
Identification and Nurturance of Young Disadvantaged Gifted Children

Rachel Zorman

There is general agreement among researchers that giftedness in adults is usually some form of extraordinary performance or productivity in a publicly valued area (Tannenbaum, 1983). Therefore, giftedness in children is their *potential* to perform extraordinarily or to produce knowledge in some valued field. Baldwin's (1978) view that gifted disadvantaged children are those whose extraordinary potential may not be identified or nurtured due to external conditions is widely accepted. She cited the following external conditions:

1. *Cultural diversity* from the dominant culture in racial or ethnic background, language, or physical characteristics.
2. *Socioeconomic deprivation*—related to substandard housing, parental education, and jobs—that denies interaction with the dominant culture.
3. *Geographic isolation* from larger population centers.

Research on the characteristics of these children shows that they receive low scores on tests of general ability, such as the WISC-R (Mercer, 1978; Mercer & Lewis, 1978). In addition, they are characterized by external locus of control, that is, they lack self-discipline and need external supervision and direction (Baldwin, 1978). On the positive side, however, they often exhibit a certain "street-wiseness," a pragmatic problem-solving ability (Baldwin, 1978; Bernal, 1978) and their social skills are frequently well developed. Many gifted disadvantaged youngsters show sensitivity toward their peers, exhibit a sense of social responsibility and lead their peers in various activities (Baldwin, 1978; Bernal, 1978). Moreover, once they are exposed to the language of the dominant culture, as in the case of Spanish-speaking Chicano children, they are able to master it quite rapidly (Bernal, 1978).

The above view of the gifted disadvantaged clearly focuses on the lack of adequate exposure of children from minority groups to the experiences, skills, and concepts that the dominant culture values and promotes. However, if we look at the full range of environmental elements influencing the fulfillment of potential and consider the literature on the development of talent (Bloom, 1985; Goertzel & Goertzel, 1962; Goertzel, Goertzel, & Goertzel, 1978), we realize that within the dominant culture, as well, certain environmental elements may play an important role in recognizing the child's special aptitudes and abilities and nurturing them. For instance, a child in the dominant culture may possess a special ability to excel as a musician. However, if the child is not introduced to a musical instrument or to music composition, he or she may never discover that ability. Thus, the child may be handicapped not by cultural, socioeconomic, or geographical barriers, but by lack of exposure. Accordingly, children who come from dominant or minority background, with potential for extraordinary performance or productivity, who were not exposed to experiences, concepts, and skills in a variety of talent areas may be considered gifted-disadvantaged.

The remainder of the chapter is divided into two sections. In the first section, five major problems in identifying and nurturing the abilities of gifted-disadvantaged learners will be presented. In the second section, the demonstration program developed by the Szold Institute in Israel designed to cope with these problems will be discussed.

PROBLEMS IN IDENTIFYING AND NURTURING GIFTED-DISADVANTAGED CHILDREN

In this section we discuss the following five problems widely viewed as of critical importance in the identification and nurturance of the abilities of gifted-disadvantaged learners.

1. The elusiveness of potential.
2. The use of indirect means of identification.
3. The importance of exposure to various talent areas.
4. The context of the regular classroom in different neighborhoods.
5. The unique needs of the gifted disadvantaged.

The Elusiveness of Potential

It is quite difficult to tap the potential to perform extraordinarily in a certain talent area during childhood. The reason for this difficulty is that we cannot generally use commonly accepted criteria for excellence, such as scientific inventions and discoveries or virtuoso performance in the arts. Hence, we can only look for telltale signs of excellent performance in the future.

What are the signs of excellence that we can look for? From the review of biographies of gifted individuals who exhibited extraordinary performance in various areas of talent, we distinguish several fields in the arts and sciences where signs of excellence are noticeable from early childhood on (Bloom, 1985; Cox, 1926; Gardner, 1983; Goertzel & Goertzel, 1962; Goertzel, Goertzel, & Goertzel, 1978; Lehman, 1949, 1953; Roe, 1953; Robinson, Roedell, & Jackson, 1979). These include the following:

Natural and Physical Sciences. From early childhood, it is possible to find children who are astute observers of the world around them and constantly seek explanations for the occurrence of natural phenomena. They often investigate the patterns of various phenomena. For example, they may collect and classify various objects, such as rocks, insects, and plants. Also, they like to know "how things work"; that is, how complicated objects, such as watches, cars, radios, and televisions work.

Mathematics. It is possible to identify young children who interpret the world in mathematical terms. For instance, they count, add, multiply, and divide everything that they encounter. They also try to find lawfulness in the world surrounding them.

Music. Musical talent among young children is expressed, mainly, in their ability to perform on a musical instrument. This ability is comprised of good musical hearing, and an extraordinary sense for rhythm and for distinguishing the unique characteristics of tones.

Dance. The ability to dance among youngsters is reflected in a highly developed psychomotor coordination, in extraordinary skill for movement, and in a good sense for rhythm.

Whereas it is possible to notice the budding scientist, mathematician, musician, or dancer in early childhood, it is quite difficult to identify the budding philosopher, lawyer, or psychologist. A possible explanation for the difficulty in finding clear signs of talent in the humanities and the social sciences may lie in the reliance of these fields upon an accumulation of life experience and knowledge from various sources that is acquired through sheer living and learning.

It is important to note that even in those fields where signs of talent may be clearly recognized in childhood, it is not possible to claim with complete certainty that the identified potential will blossom. The fulfillment of promise depends on the child's persistence in a certain area of talent. Tannenbaum (1983) proposed five factors that interact to actualize childhood potential into full performance. These factors include:

1. *General ability,* consisting mainly of abstract reasoning ability as applied to different tasks and situations and measured by general intelligence tests.
2. *Special ability,* as denoted by certain aptitudes linked to specific domains of interest, such as science, arts, and the humanities.
3. *Nonintellective elements,* comprised of social, behavioral and emotional characteristics, such as achievement motivation, persistence behavior, self concept and self confidence.
4. *Environmental elements,* such as cultural influences and values, parental direction and encouragement, school and peer influences.
5. *Chance elements,* include unpredictable circumstances, such as being at the right place at the right time.

In summary, it is crucial not simply to discover signs of talent in childhood, but to nurture that talent to full bloom, attending to the needs of the individual child.

The Use of Indirect Means of Identification

It is clear from the above description of potential that the telltale signs of talent in childhood consist of observable behaviors that are comprised, in part, of general intellectual ability. However, they are also comprised of special abilities in specific fields, of nonintellective elements, such as interest and motivation and of environmental elements, such as parental direction and encouragement to engage in activities in music and dance.

In view of the nature of these signs of potential, how are they measured? The most commonly used measure of potential in childhood is the intelligence quotient (IQ) test. The IQ test gives us a picture of generalized precocity, generally based on abstract reasoning ability, logic, and language skills (Terman, 1925; Wechsler, 1974). Thus, it gives us information mainly about general intellectual skills in children.

What can the IQ score tell us? In a study of nearly 1500 high-IQ youngsters, the IQ score was shown to be related to general academic success at school and to general success in adult careers (Sears, 1979; Terman, 1925; Terman & Oden, 1947, 1959). It was impossible, however, to predict from childhood IQ in which specific talent domains these high-IQ children would excel. In reviewing the literature on highly productive adults in many talent domains, Guilford (1967), Renzulli

(1978), and Wallach (1976) assert that many gifted adults would not be identified as gifted during childhood by intelligence measures. Hence, childhood intelligence scores may be regarded, at best, as indirect, partial predictors of excellence in adulthood.

In the case of the gifted disadvantaged, the IQ measure presents even more serious problems. Children from different racial or ethnic backgrounds score lower than their counterparts from the dominant cultural groups on tests of general intelligence (Alvino, McDonnel, & Richert, 1981; Bernal, 1980; McKenzie, 1986; Mercer, 1978; Mercer & Lewis, 1978; Minkovich, Davis, & Bashi, 1977). On the basis of the findings that have accumulated, McKenzie (1986, p. 94) concluded that minorities and the disadvantaged have far less chance of participating in programs for gifted learners than do advantaged members of the majority culture. This is due to differences in cultural and family upbringing that affect concept acquisition and organization of abilities tapped by the IQ test and to lack of experience in taking such tests.

One solution suggested to deal with the above problem was to use a quota system for minorities by adjusting norms to each specific minority group (LeRose, 1978). Another solution was to restructure tests of intellectual ability so that items that discriminate against minorities are eliminated (Bruch, 1972). These solutions do not resolve the problem of the limited validity of intelligence tests for minority and socially disadvantaged groups.

Another type of solution is to combine input from various sources, such as tests, self-reports, parents, peers, and teachers concerning the children's economic and social conditions, intellectual performance, personality attributes, and talents (Bernal, 1980; Krantz, 1978; Mercer, 1978). This way of identification may provide a more holistic and multidimensional view of children, taking into consideration the lifestyle and values of the children's particular culture. However, if children are not given developmental opportunities that would allow them to demonstrate their talents in various fields, it would still be difficult to assess their ability to excel in these areas.

The Importance of Exposure to Different Talent Areas

Based on his research of socially and economically disadvantaged youth in Israel, Feuerstein (1979) contends that their lower performance on tests of intelligence is due to their lack of mediated learning experiences. These mediated learning experiences consist of help from others to structure, understand, and interpret people's interactions with the surrounding world. In addition, mediated learning experiences reinforce people's desire to learn, encouraging them to continue to learn on their own.

In light of the above view, one has to provide mediated learning experiences to those people who come from nonmediating environments, such as the socially and culturally disadvantaged, and measure the degree of cognitive modifiability that they consequently exhibit. For example, in order to measure potential intellectual ability, Feuerstein provides instruction on how to approach a test situation, and which tactics and general principles to use to solve problems similar to the ones appearing in the tests utilized to measure intellectual ability.

Feuerstein (1979) concentrated on designing mediated learning experiences for modifying general intellectual capacities. However, general intellectual ability represents but one of the factors that are important in the fulfillment of talent. As a result of the previous discussion on the elusiveness of potential, it seems that mediated exposure to specific domains of talent, such as science and mathematics, encouraging children to understand and interpret their interactions with the environment in scientific or mathematical terms may be crucial in giving their talents a headstart to blossom. Further, these mediated learning experiences may motivate them to persist in fulfilling their potential.

Equal opportunities for mediated learning experiences in various talent areas for both minority and dominant group children are required in order to maximize the realization of potential abilities in each group. In some instances the potential talent to excel of children from the dominant culture may lie dormant as well. They may also lack appropriate exposure to developmental experiences and skills in many fields.

The Context of the Regular Classroom in Different Types of Neighborhoods

Differing school environments and values stressed may depress or encourage the budding of potential (Passow, 1972). Gifted disadvantaged children who come from a home environment that is apathetic to their extraordinary potential may encounter a similar attitude in their de facto segregated neighborhood school. In such schools, teachers and administrators may understandably concentrate much of their efforts on compensatory programs geared to elevate the average achievement of the class. Therefore, their expectations of the students may not be high, creating a climate that does not encourage the emergence of extraordinary potential. Hence, there is a need to alter the doubly handicapping conditions for the gifted disadvantaged in de facto segregated schools.

The situation of gifted disadvantaged children in integrated schools may present difficulties of a different sort. The educational climate of these schools often promotes scholastic achievement. However, children with extraordinary potential who were not exposed to mediated learning experiences are obviously at a lower starting point than their advantaged counterparts. As a result, they have to invest much effort to close the gaps in competing with others for recognition. In addition, these children have to deal with the fact that they are often part of a minority in the class. Thus, their perception of acceptance or rejection by their classmates may also affect their motivation to invest efforts and to manifest their potential (Passow, 1972). This predicament, in turn, may reduce their sense of worth and their positive self-image. Consequently, they may not feel secure enough to develop their potential (Gallagher, 1973). In order to break this vicious cycle, it is important for teachers and counselors to attend to both affective and cognitive needs of these students in integrated classrooms where both advantaged and disadvantaged learners are found.

The Unique Needs of the Gifted Disadvantaged

The plight of the gifted disadvantaged in the regular classroom in both segregated and integrated schools highlights the importance of elaborating on the nature of the unique needs of these children. Frasier (1979), Colangelo and Zaffrann (1979), and Colangelo and Lafrenz (1981) focus on the special needs that these children have mainly due to their different cultural background and different home and community environment. Because of their background, these children face different problems and issues on social-personal, educational, and vocational fronts than gifted children from advantaged, majority background.

The special problems of gifted children from culturally diverse backgrounds include:

- Their need to establish their own identity as part of their cultural and/or ethnic group but also to adopt some of the majority culture's values and standards in order to realize their potential. Thus, they are constantly walking the tight rope between the cultures, trying to adjust to both.
- The task of coping with peer pressure not to conform and play the game according to the rules of the majority culture in order to succeed. This pressure may be felt quite strongly in adolescence, when peer opinion may be increasingly influential and may affect educational and career plans.

- Their lack of highly developed verbal and semantic skills. These skills are heavily emphasized in our school curriculum and are the basis for achievement in many academic areas.
- Their lack of capacity to reflect and introspect. The capacity to reason about new knowledge and to question how it fits with current ideas is essential in order to gain a much greater understanding of what is learned.

The gifted disadvantaged need a supportive environment of carefully designed learning experiences that facilitate the fulfillment of potential. These learning experiences should be based on the following principles:

- Introducing the gifted disadvantaged to many talent areas in order to discover where hidden talent lies.
- Making use of a variety of communication modes, such as visual and tactile, while gradually strengthening the verbal mode.
- Developing approach behaviors and thinking skills that are important for reaching high-level performance or producing knowledge in various fields.
- Enhancing the motivation to persist in developing one's potential talents to the fullest.

Gifted children from diverse cultural backgrounds particularly need to interact with adults who understand the values, standards, and norms of the students' families and of their peers. These adults should be able to apply this knowledge to assess how these values clash or integrate with the dominant culture's standards. As a result, they can help the children to assess their ability and talents realistically and to search for their individual identity and fulfillment of potential.

THE SZOLD MODEL FOR IDENTIFYING AND NURTURING POTENTIAL AMONG YOUNG GIFTED DISADVANTAGED LEARNERS IN REGULAR CLASSROOMS

It is clear from the above discussion on the problems of identification and nurturance of the gifted-disadvantaged that there are certain experiences, concepts, and skills that are important for a person to possess in order to begin to manifest potential for exceptional performance. Any testing procedure that attempts to assess potential for exceptional performance will not yield valid results when applied to individuals who have not had opportunities to acquire these experiences, concepts, and skills. However, these experiences, concepts, and skills can be transmitted in a properly designed learning environment. In the process of transmission, one can find children who are "turned on" to the experiences, who acquire certain concepts and skills fast, apply them to many situations, and persist in their interest.

The Szold Institute for Behavioral Research in Israel has developed a program for identifying and nurturing potential among gifted-disadvantaged learners in grades one to six. The program consists of two phases, exposure and selection, that will be described below. However, the reader should note that at this writing, only the first phase is being implemented on an experimental basis in grades one and two of three elementary schools. The implementation of the second phase is to follow.

The goals of the Szold program are as follows:

1. To nurture excellence among the gifted-disadvantaged by creating a supportive learning environment suited to their unique needs.
2. To develop more effective ways of identifying signs of excellence exhibited by elementary school children in various talent areas, such as the arts and sciences, especially among those children who did not receive appropriate developmental opportunities to be exposed to experiences, concepts, and skills in these fields.

The model is predicated on the principle that one may identify the gifted by observing and evaluating their interaction with a supportive learning environment consisting of a variety of enriching experiences, skills, and concepts in those areas of talent where clear signs of excellence can be discerned in childhood, that is, in the arts and sciences.

What is the particular nature of this interaction? The learning experiences formulated in the arts and the sciences are guided by the following research-based principles of learning summarized by Linn (1986):

- Students do not simply absorb new information that is presented to them. Rather, they react to it in terms of an intuitive individual world view that they construct in the course of personal observations and experiences.
- Different cultural groups have differing world views. For instance, a child from a culture that mainly relies on nonmechanistic explanations for various natural phenomena may ignore information that stresses the scientific mechanisms that govern these phenomena.
- Differences in world views among children may be also caused by lack of appropriate access to informal learning experiences.
- Students' beliefs about themselves also affect how they respond to instruction. For instance, students who believe they lack competence

in drawing may be hesitant to engage in any other form of artistic activity.
- Students who are taught to understand their learning process by such means as questioning how new knowledge fits into their existing world view, examining the relationship of one idea to another, and interpreting errors as stepping stones for future problem solving, understand new concepts and acquire knowledge better than those who do not.

In view of these principles, the role of the teacher in our program is to identify the different intuitive world views of the students with regard to central concepts taught and help them integrate new knowledge and reconstruct their world views accordingly. All the while, it is also important for the teacher to strengthen the students' beliefs in their ability to cope with new concepts and knowledge, thus enhancing their sense of worth and encouraging them to persist in their interests.

We proceed to apply the above principles to the content areas of arts and sciences in the following manner:

Science activities. The science activities are designed with the following objectives in mind:

- Encouraging children to ask questions about various phenomena. The development of a questioning attitude may help children to begin to experience what scientific investigation is all about.
- Promoting understanding of scientific thinking processes, such as how to define a problem, how to analyze it, how to hypothesize various solutions to it, and how to examine these solutions by gathering data, evaluating it, and reaching conclusions.
- Integrating basic scientific concepts into their world view. These concepts include the nature of material objects, criteria for classification of objects, and the nature of interaction of substances and phenomena.
- Enhancing understanding of the applications and relevance of scientific concepts and skills to other domains. For example, we can discuss the implications of scientific inventions, such as machines and electronics to our daily lives.
- Getting to know the world of the scientist.

The science activities consist of active inductive exploration of phenomena. This exploration involves experiences utilizing the following tools:

- Different sorts of substances.

• Instruments that increase the range of our natural senses, such as binoculars and microscopes.
• The creation of unusual environments, such as experiencing weightlessness or being in a dark room.

The science curriculum improvement study (Karplus & Thier, 1969) has shown that these kinds of explorations, stressing concrete experiences with familiar and unfamiliar elements, stimulate motivation and interest among students and develop their questioning attitudes. Moreover, these explorations may also help the teacher to identify the students' intuitive world views.

Following the initial exploration, the children are introduced to the central scientific concepts that are being taught. They proceed to examine the validity of the concepts deductively by designing scientific experiments to test them in a variety of situations. This type of examination helps students understand their own learning process better and consequently integrate new knowledge concerning scientific thought processes and concepts into their world view. Also, it helps them understand how scientific processes are performed by others.

An example of a series of sample activities illustrating exploration, introduction of scientific concepts, and testing their validity focuses on variation and measurement. These activities include asking children to count how many peas are in a pod. After each child counts a few pea pods, the group records the number of peas in each pod in a histogram on the board. The group is then introduced to the concepts of variation, distribution, range, and average. Afterwards, the children are asked to make predictions concerning the number of peas they may find in any pod. They try out these concepts by studying variations in height and weight among the children in the group and making predictions concerning the height and weight of a new child that may come into the group.

In the above activities, the children engage in a low-threat, interest-provoking series of investigative experiences that provide opportunities for success and enhance their feelings of competence in science. They learn to observe phenomena carefully, to gather data, to record and analyze it, to reach conclusions and apply them. Also, they integrate basic concepts of statistics into their world view and begin to comprehend their usefulness for daily life. In addition, they enhance their social skills by interacting with other children to gather, record, and analyze data, and they develop verbal skills by reporting their findings verbally.

Art activities. We are beginning the art activities of the program in the domain of the plastic arts. The plastic art activities are designed with the following objectives in mind:

- Developing the technical skills that are necessary to excel in the arts, such as drawing, sketching, and sculpting.
- Promoting understanding of the nature of various creative media, in order to explore the possibilities offered by them to express ideas to the fullest.
- Enabling students to deal with artistic problems, such as creating a certain mood, or expressing an emotion by learning to define these problems from different perspectives, trying out different ways to resolve them and evaluating them critically.
- Enhancing understanding of the cultural and aesthetic value of the arts throughout history.
- Getting to know the world of the artist.

An example of a series of sample activities formulated to reach these objectives focuses on the world of colors. The world of colors is introduced by taking the children on an imaginary trip to the countries of color. They paint these countries and discuss the different properties and associations of colors, such as warm or cold, passionate or calm. The children then explore what happens when two countries meet, that is, when two colors mix. They also try out different techniques of producing colors, such as oil or water paints, and notice how these change the qualities of colors. Also, they study the use of color in the works of great artists throughout history, such as Rembrandt, Van Gough, Picasso, and Chagall.

In the above activities, the children engage in a series of imaginative experiences, providing chances for success and a sense of competence in the arts. They sharpen their observation and technical skills in art and integrate basic concepts of different kinds of colors and the meanings that they convey into their world view. The students also begin to gain an understanding of how art reflects culture throughout history. In addition, they enhance their verbal skills by discussing their ideas and observations with others.

In the Szold model gifted disadvantaged students interact with the supportive learning environment described in two sequential stages, exposure and selection.

Exposure

All children in the first and second grades of participating schools are exposed to a supportive learning environment that consists of a variety of experiences, skills, and concepts in two curriculum areas, arts and sciences. The exposure is conducted in the regular classroom, as part of the regular curriculum. It consists of two 2-hour sessions each week during the two years of first and second grade. The sessions are conducted by teachers who receive special preparation for the task. One session each week focuses on the arts and the other on the sciences. This arrangement insures intensity of exposure and continuity of experience, skill, and concept formation throughout the two years. Moreover, it enables students to taste a variety of topics in the arts and sciences and to work on projects for longer periods of time. The students are divided into groups of 20, in order to enable small group interaction and independent study and to insure more individual attention by the teachers for learning and identification purposes.

In order to encourage school personnel to adopt some of the learning principles and contents utilized in the demonstration program with their own classes, two kinds of special efforts are made. First, efforts are made to recruit some teachers from participating schools, that is, those who are interested and capable, to be trained as teachers in the demonstration program. In addition, all teachers in the demonstration school are encouraged to observe the sessions and to examine materials used in the project.

Teachers in the demonstration project receive ongoing guidance on counseling and identifying gifted learners from members of the Szold Institute staff with special training and experience on these topics. They also receive close guidance from scientists and artists affiliated with universities, research institutes, and art museums. These consultants put special emphasis on orienting the teaching and counseling staff of the school to the unique needs of the gifted-disadvantaged that were articulated earlier in this chapter. By combining efforts of experts from various disciplines, teachers and counselors are helped to create a learning environment replete with ample opportunities to integrate concepts and skills into the students' world view and to enhance their sense of competence. It seems reasonable to expect such an approach to provide a fair chance for hidden talent to surface.

Selection

At the end of the second grade, those students who demonstrate signs of excellence during the two years of the exposure stage will continue to participate in the program.

Which signs of excellence are we looking for and how are they measured?

From our previous discussion of tests of general ability, it is clear that these tests supply partial, indirect information concerning excellence in adulthood. In the search for more direct signs of excellence in the arts and sciences, researchers such as Blum-Zorman (1983), Feldman (1980), Gardner (1983), Goldsmith and Feldman (1985), Hatch and Gardner (1986), Luca and Allen (1971), and Tuttle and Becker (1980) focused on a host of observable behaviors denoting excellence in these fields. These behaviors were mainly gleaned from biographies of gifted individuals. Observation-based rating instruments assessing these behaviors in children were developed.

Adapted versions of the Blum-Zorman (1983) mathematical immersion instrument and the Luca and Allen (1974) inventory will be used to identify signs of excellence in science and plastic arts, respectively, among children participating in the program. The Blum-Zorman (1983) mathematical immersion instrument is a teacher-rating instrument designed to identify potential in mathematics. The items on the instrument were constructed according to psychosocial behaviors characteristic of highly able mathematicians. These include obsession with math, independent thinking, perfectionism, getting to the essence of math problems and being able to represent the school in math contests. Blum-Zorman found that this instrument offered a better differentiation of mathematical potential among intellectually gifted preadolescents than standardized math achievement tests. Luca and Allen (1974) developed an inventory of characteristics of highly able students in art. In the inventory a checklist of behaviors under four major headings: interest in art, learning behaviors, social behaviors, and performance patterns is presented.

Expert judgment represents another approach taken by educators in the search for signs of excellence that may provide an approximation of potential performance later in life. Judgments by professional experts have been used frequently to evaluate work samples or auditions in the performing arts and in competitions.

The criteria for judging science projects initiated in the program such as scientific collections or investigations, are mainly based on those developed for the science model competition conducted in the Youth Activities Department of the Weizmann Research Institute, Rehoboth, Israel.

1. Degree of independent thinking exhibited in planning and performing the project.
2. Degree of involvement exhibited by the student.
3. Examining how well-integrated and systematic the project is.
4. Assessing the general scientific approach utilized.
5. Evaluating the degree of innovation exhibited by the work.

Art portfolios will be judged according to the following criteria based on the Cleveland Studies (Lark-Horovitz & Norton, 1959, 1960) and on those employed for entrance into the Bezalel Art Academy in Jerusalem. The main judging criteria include:

1. Assessing the quality of colors, lines, symmetry, shapes, style, and motion exhibited by the work samples.
2. Examining how imaginatively elements are organized into wholes.
3. Assessing the ability to cope with concepts and utilize appropriate media to convey messages.

In the Szold model, real-world behaviors in the spheres of science and the plastic arts will be assessed at the beginning, middle, and end of the exposure phase. The data pertaining to each child's performance during the course of exposure will provide two kinds of valuable information:

1. *Group comparison information.* Information regarding each child's performance and behaviors in comparison with the performance and behavior of other children in the group.
2. *Individual comparison information.* Information concerning the initial and subsequent level of each child's behavior and performance, that is, comparison of each child's performance and behavior at the beginning, middle, and end of the exposure stage.

The group comparison information will enable us to identify those children who show clear signs of excellence. The individual comparison information will help us to know which of these children "turn on" during the exposure phase and progress the most, even though their work may not stand out in relation to the group. This method will increase the effectiveness of our identification process and will be able to include many more promising talents among our students in the selection phase.

We realize that all children cannot excel in art or sciences and may not even be interested in these fields. Moreover, at this stage, there is a large gap between children who demonstrate a high potential to excel and those who do not. The students selected to continue in the program need a special learning environment with expert teachers and special facilities. Students with potential for excelling in the sciences can engage in explorations and projects that will deepen and broaden their understanding of scientific thinking processes and concepts and their implications for our lives. Students with potential for excelling in the arts can engage in activities that will enhance their ability to deal with artistic problems and their understanding of the cultural and aesthetic value of the arts.

What Next?

During the exposure stage, all learning activities take place in the regular classroom. In the selection phase learning activities may take place in a wide variety of alternative environments. In the opening chapter of the current volume Milgram described the wide variety of delivery systems used to implement special education for gifted children. Accordingly, the Szold model could be used to identify and nurture the abilities of gifted-disadvantaged youngsters within the framework of many administrative arrangements. Delivery systems such as magnet schools specializing in the arts or the sciences, afternoon courses conducted in universities and museums, part-time special school (pull-out programs), and resource room arrangements are examples of the large number of administrative arrangements that could be used in the implementation of the model presented in the chapter above.

If the delivery system used during the selection phase is outside of the regular classroom, contact with the regular classroom teachers will be maintained. The contact will be kept by reporting to teachers about the activities and projects that the students engage in. In addition, special opportunities will be provided for students to share their projects and knowledge with other students in their regular classrooms. These opportunities include, for example, exhibits of science and art projects and peer tutoring in the domain of the students' specialty.

These activities are designed to (a) harness the special talents of students for the benefit of their peers in the regular classroom, (b) create a community that enjoys and appreciates the special talents of the students, (c) enhance the sense of competence and worth of the students participating in the program, and (d) provide added reinforcement for them to persist in developing their potential.

REFERENCES

Alvino, J., McDonnel, R., & Richert, S. (1981). National survey of identification practices in gifted and talented education. *Exceptional Children, 48,* 124–132.

Baldwin, A.Y. (1978). Curriculum and methods—what is the difference? In A.Y. Baldwin, G.H. Gear, & L.J. Lucito (Eds.), *Educational planning for the gifted* (pp. 37–49). Reston, VA: The Council for Exceptional Children.

Bernal, E.M. (1978). The identification of gifted Chicano children. In A.Y. Baldwin, G.H. Gear, & L.J. Lucito (Eds.), *Education planning for the gifted* (pp. 14–17). Reston, VA: The Council for Exceptional Children.

Bernal, E.M. (1980). *Methods of identifying gifted minority students* (ERIC Rep. No. 72). Princeton, NJ: ERIC Clearinghouse, Educational Testing Service.

Bloom, B.S. (1985). *Developing talent in young people.* New York: Ballantine.

Blum-Zorman, R. (1983). *Cognitive controls, cognitive styles and mathematical potential among gifted preadolescents.* Unpublished doctoral dissertation. Teachers College, Columbia University, New York.

Bruch, C. (1972). *The ABDA: Making the Stanford-Binet culturally biased for disadvantaged black children.* Athens, GA: University of Georgia Press.

Colangelo, N., & Lafrenz, N. (1981). Counseling the culturally diverse gifted. *Gifted Child Quarterly, 25,* 27-30.

Colangelo, N., & Zaffrann, R.T. (1979). Special issues in counseling the gifted. *Counseling and Human Development, 11,* 1-12.

Cox, C. (1926). The early mental traits of three hundred geniuses. In L.M. Terman (Ed.), *Genetic studies of genius* (Vol. 2). Stanford, CA: Stanford University Press.

Feldman, D.H. (1980). *Beyond universals in cognitive development.* Norwood, NJ: Ablex.

Feuerstein, R. (1979). *The dynamic assessment of retarded performers.* Baltimore, MD: University Park Press.

Frasier, M.M. (1979). Counseling the culturally diverse gifted. In N. Colangelo & R.T. Zaffrann (Eds.), *New voices in counseling the gifted.* Dubuque, IA: Kendall/Hunt.

Gallagher, J. (1973). *Talent delayed—talent denied, the culturally different gifted child.* A report of a conference held in Rougemont, NC.

Gardner, H. (1983). *Frames of mind: The theory of multiple intelligences.* New York: Basic Books.

Goertzel, V., & Goertzel, M.G. (1962). *Cradles of eminence.* Boston: Little, Brown.

Goertzel, M.G., Goertzel, V., & Goertzel, T.G. (1978). *Three hundred eminent personalities.* San Francisco: Jossey-Bass.

Goldsmith L., & Feldman, D.H. (1985). Identification of gifted children: The state of the art. *Pediatric Annals, 14,* 709-716.

Guilford, J.P. (1967). *The nature of human intelligence.* New York: McGraw-Hill.

Hatch, T.C., & Gardner, H. (1986). From testing intelligence to assessing competences: A pluralistic view of intellect. *Roeper Review, 8,* 147-150.

Karplus, R., & Thier, H.D. (1969). *A new look at elementary school science.* Chicago: Rand McNally.

Krantz, B. (1978). Multi-Dimensional Screening Device (MDSD) for the identification of gifted/talented children. *Bureau of Educational Research and Services Publication No. 9.* Grand Forks, ND: University of North Dakota Press.

Lark-Horovitz, B., & Norton, J. (1959). Children's art abilities: Developmental trends of art characteristics. *Child Development, 30,* 433-452.

Lark-Horovitz, B., & Norton, J. (1960). Children's art abilities: The interrelations and factorial structure of ten characteristics. *Child Development, 31,* 453-462.

Lehman, H.C. (1949). Young thinkers and great achievements. *Journal of Genetic Psychology, 74,* 245–271.
Lehman, H.C. (1953). *Age and Achievement.* Princeton, NJ: Princeton University Press.
LeRose, B. (1978). A quota system for gifted minority children: A viable solution. *Gifted Child Quarterly, 22,* 394–403.
Linn, M.C. (1986). *Establishing a research base for science education: Challenges, trends and recommendations.* Berkeley, CA: University of California Press.
Luca, M., & Allen, B. (1974). *Teaching gifted children art in grades one through three.* Sacramento, CA: California State Department of Education.
McKenzie, J.A. (1986). The influence of identification practices, race and SES on the identification of gifted students. *Gifted Child Quarterly, 30,* 93–95.
Mercer, J.R. (1978). *SOMPA Technical Manual.* New York: The Psychological Corporation.
Mercer, J.R., & Lewis, J.F. (1978). *Student Assessment Manual.* New York: The Psychological Corporation.
Minkovich, A., Davis, D., & Bashi, J. (1977). *An evaluation study of Israeli elementary schools.* Jerusalem: The School of Education, Hebrew University of Jerusalem, Israel.
Passow, A.H. (1972). The gifted and the disadvantaged. *The National Elementary Principal, 51,* 22–31.
Renzulli, J.S. (1978). What makes giftedness? Re-examining a definition. *Phi Delta Kappan, 60,* 18–24.
Robinson, H.B., Roedell, W., & Jackson, N. (1979). Early identification and intervention. In A.H. Passow (Ed.), *The gifted and the talented: Their education and development. The Seventy-eighth Yearbook of the National Society for the Study of Education* (Part I, pp. 138–154). Chicago: University of Chicago Press.
Roe, A. (1953). *Making of a scientist.* New York: Dodd & Mead.
Sears, P.S. (1979). The Terman studies of genius, 1922–1972. In A.H. Passow (Ed.), *The gifted and talented: Their education and development. The Seventy-eighth Yearbook of the National Society for the Study of Education* (Part I, pp. 75–96). Chicago: University of Chicago Press.
Tannenbaum, A.J. (1983). *Gifted children: Psychological and educational perspectives.* New York: Macmillan.
Terman, L.M. (1925). *Mental and physical traits of a thousand gifted children.* Stanford, CA: Stanford University Press.
Terman, L.M., & Oden, M.H. (1947). *The gifted child grows up.* Stanford, CA: Stanford University Press.
Terman, L.M., & Oden, M.H. (1959). *The gifted group at mid-life.* Stanford, CA: Stanford University Press.
Tuttle, F., & Becker, L. (1980). *Characteristics and identification of gifted and talented students.* Washington, DC: National Education Association.
Wallach, M.A. (1976). Tests tell us little about talent. *American Scientist, 64,* 57–63.
Wechsler, D. (1974). *Manual for Wechsler Intelligence Scale for Children-Revised.* New York: The Psychological Corporation.

Chapter 10
Differentiating Instruction for Preschool Gifted Children

Merle B. Karnes
Lawrence J. Johnson

Attention to the young gifted child is long overdue. Gallagher (1986) asserted that "one of the most neglected issues in the field of gifted children is the development of meaningful programs for the preschool or early childhood ages" (p. 1). Although there are no data to support one organizational plan over another for educating young gifted children, the data that do exist for gifted children of other ages indicate that most gifted children spend the greater part of their day in the regular classroom (Cox & Daniel, 1984). Since most gifted children are in regular programs, this chapter focuses on programming for the young gifted child in regular preschool settings. In rare instances these classes are in the public schools. More often they are in private schools, day care programs, and Head Start classes.

This chapter is devoted to defining and describing the process of differentiating instruction for preschool children in regular classroom settings. It is divided into the following eight sections.

1. *The Status of Gifted Education at the Preschool Level.* The extent of programming at the preschool level is reported. Existing preschool programs for the gifted in the literature are identified. Barriers to identification and programming are briefly discussed.
2. *Characteristics of the Gifted at the Preschool Level.* Major characteristics of the gifted and the problems that gifted children may encounter are discussed.
3. *Differentiation of Instruction in the Regular Classroom Setting.* Differentiation of instruction is defined. The importance of teacher attitudes and competencies, the need for support from administra-

tors, parents, and the lay public, the environment of the classroom, and effective teacher strategies are considered, as are some of the pitfalls in programming for the gifted. This section culminates in examples of how differentiation of instruction can be achieved for gifted children in the regular preschool classroom, through three approaches which represent varying roles for teachers and children.

4. *Teachers for Preschool Gifted: Attitudes and Competencies.* The importance of fostering the appropriate attitude toward gifted children in teachers and characteristics of effective teachers of the gifted are discussed.

5. *Involving Parents of Preschool Gifted Children in Providing a Differentiated Curriculum.* A rationale for involving parents in gifted programs is presented and methods for involving parents are discussed.

6. *Support of the Administration and the Lay Public.* The importance of obtaining both administrative and community support for addressing the needs of gifted children is examined.

7. *Pitfalls in Differentiating Instruction.* Potential pitfalls in attempting to differentiate curriculum are delineated and discussed.

8. *Conclusions and a Look to the Future.* This chapter ends with some concluding remarks and projections of future considerations to facilitate appropriate programming for young gifted children.

STATUS OF GIFTED EDUCATION AT THE PRESCHOOL LEVEL

More often than not, the gifted in preschool settings go unidentified and underserved (Karnes, 1983). It is rare nationwide to find a program for preschool-age children in which the staff are deliberately identifying the gifted or potentially gifted among their charges and then providing an appropriate instructional program for these children which will ensure that they receive a truly differentiated curriculum.

Three preschool programs that serve the young gifted nonhandicapped child are reported in the literature: The Astor Program conducted by the Gifted Child Studies Department of the Board of Education of New York, initiated by Virginia Z. Ehrlich; the University of Washington Child Development Research Group directed by Nancy Robinson; and the University Primary School (ages 3–8) at the University of Illinois, directed by Merle Karnes. Also reported are three programs for preschool gifted/talented handicapped: one at Chapel Hill Public Schools directed by Anne Sanford, the RAPYHT (Retrieval and Acceleration of Promising Young Handicapped and Talented) at the University of Illinois directed by Merle Karnes, and a rural preschool gifted/talented handicapped model developed by the Panhandle Child Development Association, Inc., located at Coeur D'Alene, Idaho. In 1985 Karnes and Johnson conducted a program in the Champaign County Head Start Program entitled BOHST (Bringing Out Head Start Talents), which concentrated on nourishing the higher-level thinking processes of all Head Start children, identifying the top 10-20 per cent who are potentially gifted/talented, and programming for these children in their areas of talent. The model programs for nonhandicapped gifted children all utilize segregated classes, whereas the three gifted/talented handicapped programs use a mainstreaming approach.

It is baffling why so little attention is given to the young gifted child, since it is generally believed that the earlier we discover gifted children and nourish their abilities, the greater the chances of their maximizing their potential (Cox & Daniel, 1983; Gallagher, 1985; Karnes, 1983; Karnes & Johnson, 1986). Early identification and programming for the gifted is not a new concept. Many experts over the years have urged us to attend to these children early. In *The Gifted Child in the Regular Classroom,* for instance, published over 30 years ago, Marion Scheifele (1953) wrote: "It is generally agreed that identifying the gifted child as early in his life as possible is highly desirable from the standpoint of both the full development of his abilities and his personal adjustment" (p. 1). Hollis L. Caswell (1953), a renowned educator in his time, notes in the editor's introduction to Scheifele's book that "provision for gifted children is a much-discussed subject about which all too little is done." He goes on to explain that where programs do exist, they usually involve special groupings. "This procedure is not feasible in many schools with small enrollments; it implies a social point of view which many people resist, and it adds to educational costs. This discussion strikes directly at the problem of providing for the gifted in the regular classroom."

In 1979 Jenkins conducted a study to determine the status of programming for the young gifted child and found only five programs below the kindergarten level and only 20 at kindergarten age. A few years later Karnes, Shwedel, and Linnemeyer (1982) surveyed programs for gifted preschoolers under 5 years of age and identified only 18 programs. Telephone contacts with these programs led the investigators to conclude that few could be considered stable or ongoing. A later report of a survey to determine the status of gifted education in the nation conducted by the Richardson Foundation (Cox, Daniel, & Boston, 1985) revealed that most programming for the gifted is not initiated until they are in the middle grades.

There appear to be several reasons for our lagging behind in identifying and programming for the gifted at the preschool level.

1. It is not legal in most states for the public schools to identify and program for gifted/talented children below age 5.
2. Parents have not advocated for legislation to permit public schools to make such provisions, as have parents of handicapped children. As Gallagher (1986) put it: "We remain short of policy initiatives in this area."
3. Universities have not been training personnel—administrators, supervisors, teachers—to work with the young gifted child. "The demand for such teachers is negligible, and the cycle is self-perpetuating" (Karnes, 1983, p. 3).
4. Since administrators of private schools—day cares, preschools—are usually not trained in gifted education, they do not make provisions for this segment of their population.
5. Preschool teachers rarely have formal training in gifted education and thus are not likely to identify such children and differentiate instruction for them.

CHARACTERISTICS OF THE GIFTED AT THE PRESCHOOL LEVEL

Critical to teachers' differentiating instruction for gifted children is their understanding of what gifted children are like. In describing gifted children, it is important to remember that we are talking about a group. When we consider a specific gifted child, not all of the characteristics mentioned are likely to appear.

Gifted children differ markedly from their regular classroom counterparts of the same chronological age. It is commonly believed that the differences between gifted children and their peers not identified as gifted are confined to the intellectual sphere and that they are "kids like all other kids" in other domains. While it is undeniable that gifted children require acceptance and sensitive handling as do all children, it is becoming increasingly clear that they may have exceptional needs in the psychosocial domain as they do in the intellectual domain. In a recent authoritative and comprehensive review of the literature on the psychosocial development of intellectually gifted children, Janos and Robinson (1985) concluded that these children are, for the most part, characterized by higher levels of psychological and social maturity, including relationships with adults, especially parents, and with peers. They point out that evaluation of adjustment is much influenced by normative, age-related expectations (Rutter & Garmezy, 1983; Wenar, 1982). Children who deviate from these expectations because they are exceptionally mature or verbally expressive may be seen as poorly adjusted (Manaster & Powell, 1983).

Despite their generally favorable conclusions, Janos and Robinson (1985) cite three instances in which giftedness may be associated with problems in personal-social adjustment. When the child's giftedness becomes the major focus of the relationship with parents, teachers, and other children, adjustment difficulties may occur. Various personal-social problems have been reported in children who are profoundly gifted— that is, characterized by very superior intellectual ability. Finally, gifted underachievers are likely to evidence special adjustment problems.

Several authors have written on characteristics of gifted children (Clark, 1983; Gallagher, 1985; Howley, Howley, & Pendarvis, 1986; Karnes, 1983; Kitano & Kirby, 1986). The following two lists were developed based upon their writings. Although these authors focused on older children, most of the descriptions apply equally to preschool gifted children (Karnes, 1983). The first list consists of positive cognitive and personal-social characteristics often noted in gifted children, the second of problems that sometimes occur in school settings, particularly if the needs of gifted children are not recognized and met.

Before summarizing the findings, two caveats are in order. First, it is unlikely that all of the positive characteristics or problems cited below will be present in a particular gifted child. Second, in describing problems of gifted children in school, most authors do not differentiate among types of giftedness, that is, general/specific intellectual ability, general/specific creative abilities, or among levels, that is, profound, moderate, mild, nongifted, as described by Milgram in an earlier chapter in this book. Most empirical data about the personal-social characteristics of gifted children are limited to those who are advanced in general intellectual ability, high in IQ. Far fewer studies have been done with children with more specific intellectual abilities or creative talents.

The following positive personal-social characteristics are often seen in gifted preschool children:

- Are healthier and larger.
- Are more energetic; seem to need less sleep.
- Are more alert and interested in a variety of things.
- Ask more questions and of a higher order.
- Are thirsty for knowledge and are constantly and compulsively learning.
- Like to pursue a subject in great depth.
- Show a keen interest in books and frequently learn to read at an earlier age.
- Are more task-persistent.
- Are more curious and observant.
- Have larger vocabularies.

- Infer cause and effect at an earlier age and more quickly.
- Have a broader base of knowledge.
- Learn material more rapidly and with fewer repetitions.
- Have a keen sense of humor.
- Think more abstractly.
- Solve problems more readily, often finding more than one solution to a problem.
- Are adept at generalizing learning.
- Have a longer attention span.
- Have more mature interests.
- Are flexible; adjust more readily to new situations and tend to be more stable.
- Are apt to have talent in a number of areas—leadership, academic and intellectual, music, art, other fields of creativity.
- Can engage in more than one thing at a time.
- Are more independent and nonconforming.
- Are sensitive to unfairness and moral issues.

The following problems have been noted in some preschool gifted children:

- Gifted children may grow to dislike school and develop a negative attitude toward learning if they are expected to conform, are restrained from learning what they want to learn, or are unable to pursue their interests.
- Gifted children may become frustrated when a discrepancy in growth interferes with reaching goals they set for themselves. For example, a child wants to write a story, but his creative and intellectual development is far ahead of his fine motor development; thus, he is unable to write what he can think.
- Boredom may develop if they are not challenged or are required to learn what they already know.
- Sometimes children with behavior problems are not being challenged. When the classroom becomes challenging, their behavior may become acceptable.
- Lack of identification and appropriate programming may result in a pattern of underachievement that will be difficult to reverse as the child becomes older.
- Children of lesser ability may reject gifted children because their advanced vocabulary and greater knowledge may make other children feel inferior.
- Gifted children may not enjoy the same games as their less able peers; thus, it is desirable for a classroom to have more than one

gifted child so that each will have a child of comparable ability with whom to work and play.

- Gifted children tend to be intolerant of those who are less capable; they have to learn to be more accepting.
- Gifted children resist conformity and may be regarded as difficult.
- Gifted children are self-critical and tend to be dissatisfied with their work. They want to excel, and feel inadequate if their work isn't perfect.
- Gifted children often set unrealistic goals for themselves and become frustrated if they are unable to meet their goals.
- Some gifted children are sensitive to the feelings of others and perceive rejection readily.
- Because preschool gifted children are often highly dependent on adults for helping them obtain answers to questions, they are more demanding of attention; because they tend to monopolize adults, they may be resented by other children.
- Exploitation of the child's gifts on the part of the parent may cause resentment in siblings and friends and may even engender discord between parent and child.

These lists of characteristics of gifted children are not exhaustive.

The approach to the identification of the gifted that is generally accepted today is the use of multiple procedures. These may be standardized tests, criterion-referenced measures, questionnaires for parents to complete, checklists for teachers and parents to use, sociometric techniques, or panels of experts to judge products. A more in-depth discussion of identification measures and procedures can be found in Karnes and Shwedel (1983), Shwedel and Stoneburner (1983), and Karnes and Johnson (1986). Although Whitmore (1985) did not concentrate on the preschool child, her chapter "New Challenges to Common Identification Practices" applies to the young gifted children as well as to older children and is especially valuable because it covers some important considerations and appropriate procedures for identifying the gifted among minority, culturally different, and handicapped individuals.

DIFFERENTIATION OF INSTRUCTION IN THE REGULAR CLASSROOM SETTING

Teachers of young children are usually warm and accepting and as a general rule try to respond to the needs of all children in their program, especially to their social and emotional needs. They are, however, usually trained to serve children who in most respects are progressing normally.

They may recognize that some children have more problems than others and that some are more capable, but deliberately assessing the needs of all children in their class and appropriately programming for them on an individualized basis are often not emphasized in their training and are thus typically omitted from practice. The charge of this chapter is the differentiation of instruction within a regular classroom. The focus is the assessment of individual needs and the linking of curriculum to that assessment rather than assessment for identification purposes. When such a plan is followed, the need to give a large battery of standardized tests to identify preschool gifted is reduced because the teacher can determine where each child is functioning well developmentally and with adequate resources and support can provide a program that meets the unique needs of each child whether that child is developing slower or faster than comparable age peers.

Definition

Differentiating the curriculum for children means providing each child with offerings that are compatible with her stage of development, her specific needs, and her interests, irrespective of what is considered a standard curriculum for children of her chronological age.

How does the curriculum for the gifted differ from that of the regular child of the same chronological age? There seems to be general agreement that differentiating the curriculum means not teaching the child what she already knows and does not mean giving her more of the same or merely increasing the pace of learning. Maker (1989) stressed the critical importance of providing a curriculum for gifted learners that is qualitatively different from that usually included in the basic curriculum for all children and specified the required adjustments. Karnes, Shwedel, and Williams (1983), in considering how the University of Illinois Preschool Gifted Program differentiates the curriculum for young gifted children, noted the following characteristics:

1. Offerings not usually a part of the standard curriculum for young children.
2. Encouragement to pursue a chosen interest in depth.
3. Learning based on needs rather than on predetermined order or sequence of instruction.
4. Activities more complex and requiring more abstract and higher-level thinking processes.
5. Greater flexibility in the use of materials, time, and resources.
6. Higher expectations for independence and task persistence.

7. Provision of more opportunities to acquire and demonstrate leadership abilities.
8. Greater encouragement of creative and productive thinking.
9. More emphasis on interpreting the behavior and feelings of self and others.
10. More opportunities to broaden the base of knowledge and enhance language abilities. (pp. 129–130)

All of the above can be implemented in a regular classroom setting. Examples of differentiated instruction in a regular setting with children of vastly different abilities will be presented later.

Several studies have suggested ways of modifying the standard curriculum to meet the needs of gifted children (Gallagher, 1985; Howley, Howley, & Pendarvis, 1986; Karnes, 1983; Maker, 1986). These suggestions center upon the following issues: (a) changing the *content* of what is learned, (b) using appropriate teaching strategies, and (c) changing the learning environment. Discussed below are several strategies that teachers may find useful.

Questioning. The purposes of questioning are many: to evaluate the child's understanding, to determine the extent to which the child can generalize and make inferences, to direct the child's attention to a certain aspect of a problem. In differentiating instruction, however, the overriding purpose becomes the encouragement of critical and higher-level thinking processes within lessons.

Questioning is an excellent strategy for differentiating instruction, but must be used with caution. Some questioning techniques can actually inhibit children's formation of abstract concepts. Rowe (1973) studied the effects of rapid-fire questioning which involved two or three questions per minute with short waiting periods. The results indicated that children who were not achieving well volunteered very little, that children who did respond tended to give fragmentary answers and failed to elaborate, and that their grasp of the concepts presented was limited. On the other hand, Rowe found that when children were given additional time to think they asked more questions, volunteered more often, and elaborated on their answers. Even low-achieving children tended to participate more. Robinson and Feldhusen (1984) found that additional questions or probes help children focus on relevant dimensions of a problem. In addition, probes help children achieve insight.

Therefore, it is important for teachers to be well grounded in the use of effective questioning techniques. They need to plan carefully so that their questioning is compatible with the interests and abilities of the children in their class. By using questions that require gifted children to expand upon their responses or to examine an issue further, the teacher can provide challenges for children within a lesson.

Projects. The open classroom or informal approach to teaching lends itself especially well to differentiating instruction for gifted children in a regular classroom. Since this approach is one in which the teacher and children together determine the curriculum, it is unlikely that the whole class would become interested in the same project. Typically, a number of projects are in progress concurrently.

In one classroom a dinosaur project was launched as an outgrowth of a 4-year-old gifted child's reading a book in the library corner on dinosaurs. He told a few children around him what he had read, interest in dinosaurs began to take shape, and soon five children were talking to the teacher about learning more. Among them was the one gifted child, two children with above-average intelligence but not gifted, and one who had average intelligence but was talented in art. The fifth child was average in most respects. The teacher and children sat around a table and discussed what they would like to know about dinosaurs. Where did they live? Are there dinosaurs living today? What has happened to them? How large were dinosaurs? What did they eat? Would a dinosaur be a good pet? Does a baby dinosaur grow in the mother? The teacher brought books from the library to answer their questions and to give them additional information.

The child who was talented in art suggested that the group make a wall hanging of the various kinds of dinosaurs. The group dictated information they learned from the books, which were read by the teacher or a volunteer or the 4-year-old who could read. He needed help with some of the names of dinosaurs.

The child with average ability suggested that they make a dinosaur. After brainstorming about the size of the dinosaur, the color, and the material, it was decided that the gifted child would work with the teacher to draw a dinosaur to a scale, because a dinosaur as large as the one they would have liked to make would not fit in the room. When the drawing was done, the group determined—with questions and comments from the teacher—what needed to be done to make the dinosaur. With the help of the teacher, each child chose work compatible with his or her ability. They soon got underway with enthusiasm and confidence; however, from time to time the teacher needed to help them solve a problem that was interfering with progress.

The project culminated with a program for the parents and the other members of the class. There was a panel of experts on dinosaurs made up of the five children involved in the project. A mother who had been working in the classroom served as the interrogator of the panel (who had several practice sessions, so they knew what they were going to be asked and what they were to answer). The gifted child had dictated an original story about a dinosaur, and he read it to the audience. Each child had made a mask of a dinosaur from a paper sack, each representing a different kind of dinosaur, and each wore his or her mask and responded to music as they felt a dinosaur would respond. At last came the papier-mache dinosaur the children made. Each child told at least one thing about the dinosaur. There was considerable variation in what the children contributed, but each responded at the level of which he or she was capable, as had been the practice throughout the project.

One of the parents suggested a field trip to a museum in Chicago to see exhibits of dinosaurs. The trip was scheduled with parent input and with the gifted child taking an active part in the planning.

Units. Curriculum units are used in most preschool classrooms. These units differ from projects in that they are teacher-initiated and all the children participate in them. However units can also provide opportunities for teachers to differentiate instruction. Young children enjoy participating in a unit on "Pets," for example. Average children of 3, 4, or 5 years of age are easily able to name some common animals that make good pets, can learn about the needs of a pet and how to care for them, and can take responsibility for the care of a pet in the room such as a rabbit, guinea pig, or hamster. They also enjoy listening to stories about pets, and can understand and contribute to a discussion of why pets should not be allowed to run free. More able children can investigate more unusual animals or birds that make good pets, where they come from, the cost, and why they make good pets. These children are interested in learning what kind of special care these animals require and how long they live. Teachers can get volunteers to read this kind of information to the children who are interested.

In one classroom a parent provided a pregnant white rat for the children to observe during a unit on pets. The rat was introduced to the classroom in a discussion that included information as to whether or not such an animal was a good pet. The children decided upon observing the strong white teeth that this animal would not be a good pet in the usual way. The rat was a laboratory animal that had been recently impregnated so the children were able to observe the changes in appearance as the pregnancy progressed. Children in the room who were gifted were eager to pursue such interests as the length of the gestation period and how many rats were usually in a litter. When one child reported that rats were rodents, interest was aroused in what other animals belonged to this family. Parent volunteers were recruited to assist the teacher in taking the class to a pet shop. Before the trip took place, the class brainstormed questions that they could ask about rodents in the pet store. More average children in the class were interested in what the rat should eat and how often it should be given water.

A feeding schedule was established with different children sharing the responsibility of caring for the rat. Every day the teacher weighed the rat on laboratory scales and a gifted child in the class wrote down the weight on a weight chart. The children were increasingly excited as they saw the weight increase as reflected by the larger numbers on the weight chart. One child volunteered to find out when rats usually gave birth. He reported to the class that the event ordinarily took place at night. To the excitement of the class, however, the rat gave birth during the day when all the children were present. The children who wished to do so were able to observe the birth process and see the difference in appearance between newborn and adult rats. All the children counted to see how many rats were in the litter. One of the children dictated a story entitled, "Rosie the Rat." The artistically talented children in the room drew pictures of the babies and two musically talented children in the class spontaneously composed a "birth" song to celebrate the occasion, using various musical instruments such as tone bells, water filled jars, and percussion instruments. The teacher assisted in taping the song and then transcribed it into musical notation. The next day the children performed their birth song for the rest of the class.

Another successful activity that differentiated instruction in the preschool classroom was the inclusion of a book about pets. Each child brought a picture of his pet or drew a picture of a pet that he wished that he could own. Then the child dictated a story about the pet. Some children were capable of dictating a very short story of a simple sentence or two or even just a phrase, while other children dictated more complicated sentences with much information. All children participated in this activity at a level that was comfortable for them.

Lesson plans. Some teachers may develop specific lesson plans to teach skills and concepts to children. These lesson plans are teacher-directed, but can be modified to meet individual needs. For example, one teacher was working with a group of six children who varied considerably in intellectual ability from slow to gifted, and she wished to facilitate divergent thinking. She brought in a box which she referred to as a "mystery box" and said, "There is something in this box, and I want you to tell us what it is." She explained that she would answer "Yes" or "No" when they would ask a question, but she would not tell them anything more to help them. One can readily understand why the below-average child asked very simple, concrete questions while the brighter child came up with more insightful, complicated questions. All engaged in the same activity in a regular classroom, but the teacher was differentiating instruction. Each child responded according to his abilities and was encouraged to do his best irrespective of the kinds of questions other children asked.

Independent study. Another strategy that is useful for some gifted children is independent study, which allows the child to develop an interest that differs from those of his classmates. For example, in a preschool of young gifted children, one 5-year-old became very interested in China because his family was planning to spend a year there. Where would he go to school? What was the climate in various parts of China, especially in the part where he would be living? What clothes would he be wearing? What games did Chinese children play? What pets did Chinese children have? What did a Chinese house look like? What food would he likely be eating? The teacher located a number of books about China which would answer many of the child's questions, and a volunteer read the relevant portions. In the community were Chinese who had come to the United States recently and spoke English well. The teacher arranged for the child to interview two of these people. In addition, the teacher obtained two films on China that gave the child further insights. After several weeks of learning about China, the child decided to write a book on *What I Know About China.* He dictated the story to the teacher, who recorded it on large newsprint and later typed it on a large-type typewriter. The child then illustrated parts of the book, and since he was able to read, he shared it with his peers.

Another independent project was that of a 4-year-old gifted girl who decided to plant an avocado seed. First she had to learn how to plant the seed and how to make it germinate. Then she kept a record of what happened week by week. When the plant began to grow, she kept accurate records of its growth. She became so interested in avocados that she had the teacher bring books on the subject to answer her many questions. Because she wasn't reading fluently, a parent of another child in the room read to her for about half an hour once a week. The project continued for several months. One day she decided to make an avocado salad and serve it to her classmates. With the help of a volunteer, she made the salad from ingredients she brought from home, and while the children were eating it, she shared with them some of the interesting things she had learned about avocados.

In both of these examples the children had interests that were not shared by other children. Of course, they could not carry out the projects with complete independence, because they had to rely on adults for information and assistance.

Grouping. There are several grouping arrangements that teachers may use to address the needs of gifted children in the regular classroom. When several gifted students exist within the same classroom and they have talents in similar areas, they can be grouped together for instruction. If we are aware of which children are gifted prior to their entering the preschool, we can purposely cluster them together in the same class. Teachers can also group children according to interests. As Renzulli (1978) points out, many children manifest gifted behavior at various times given the right conditions. Grouping gifted children with other children of like interests could be beneficial to all. Having regular children work with gifted children in their areas of interest may help facilitate the gifted behavior in these children. Conversely, gifted children can benefit from working with other less gifted peers who are interested in a topic and willing to examine it in greater depth. Another useful grouping is to have gifted children of comparable abilities from several classrooms gather in one room several times a week to collaborate on a topic, a project, or some academic work. These groups would cross age levels in most schools but could consist of children of one age level in very large schools.

Lastly, there will be times when the needs of a gifted child cannot be met within the confines of the regular classroom. For example, there was one gifted preschooler who functioned at a secondary level in math, which was beyond the instructional capability of the preschool teacher. Children who are this advanced usually need a mentor to work with them, and in this case a math professor in the community was contacted and became interested in the child and worked with him several times a week. A teacher, no matter how competent, cannot be an expert in everything. She or he need not feel apologetic about locating a mentor who is better able to work with a child in a given area of talent than he or she.

Microcomputers. The introduction of the microcomputer to the classroom can be a powerful tool for the differentiation of curriculum. Although educational software and applications are in their infancy, the potential even at the preschool level for providing gifted children with opportunities for independent exploration and study is virtually limitless. Children can create stories and pictures, solve problems, and invent problems. As their acquaintance with the computer grows, the sophistication with which they can interact with it increases correspondingly. When the child's skills increase, the challenge to the child correspondingly increases and in turn the reinforcement increases because the outcomes of the child's effort become more sophisticated and impressive. In one preschool gifted program, children found that they can use the computer to publish a class newspaper. Creation of the newspaper has provided many creative opportunities for these children, from leadership experiences to creative writing. The fact that the children lack the fine motor control to be fluent at writing is circumvented by the computer.

TEACHERS FOR PRESCHOOL GIFTED: ATTITUDES AND COMPETENCIES

The teacher is the key person in differentiating instruction for children. To be effective, however, besides having the competencies to differentiate instruction for all children in her room, she must be committed to the approach. As Karnes (1983) asserted, "Not everyone loves a gifted child. For a long time we have suspected that many teachers would rather have the gifted child in someone else's classroom" (p. 61). While no research is reported on the attitudes of preschool teachers toward gifted children, it has been found that some teachers of older gifted children actually feel hostile toward them (Rothney & Sanborn, 1968; Wiener, 1978). It would not be surprising to discover that some preschool teachers hold similar attitudes.

A partial explanation for negative attitudes may be that teachers are intimidated by the abilities of gifted children (Gallagher, 1985). Although it can be exciting to have children who are consumed with the desire to learn and are able to go beyond most children of comparable age, these same qualities can have an unsettling effect on some teachers. If, as Gallagher suggests, these teachers enter into competition with the gifted in their classroom, they are bound to be frustrated and will likely confuse the gifted in the process, because the child will not understand why he or she has upset the teacher.

Heavy emphasis is often placed upon the requirement for teachers of gifted children to have an appropriately high intellectual level. While it is undoubtedly important that teachers of gifted children be academically able, their approach to the challenge and their attitudes toward gifted children are also critical. To teach gifted children, teachers must be in touch with their feelings about gifted children, and their ability to deal with such feelings is related to their self-esteem and maturity. There is much evidence to suggest that the more positive teachers feel about themselves, the more positive they will feel about their charges (Combs, 1965; Coopersmith, 1967; Jerslid, 1965). Clearly, teachers with poor self-esteem will be easily intimidated by the talents of gifted children, while teachers who are mature and confident in their abilities are more likely to be exhilirated by the challenge (Karnes, 1983).

The first step in developing an appropriate attitude toward gifted children in the regular classroom is a commitment to meeting identified needs. This is a difficult goal that requires added effort from the teacher, and without such a commitment it is unlikely that the regular classroom teacher will rise to the challenge.

As Karnes (1983) stated, it seems discriminatory to ask for the best teachers to work with the gifted, but mediocre teachers are more likely to be threatened by gifted children, intolerant of them, and possibly hostile toward them. Although mediocre or poor teachers are a problem for all children, the problem increases when these teachers are expected to teach gifted children. As a child's abilities deviate from the norm, high or low, the inability of mediocre teachers to meet diverse needs increases. It is therefore critical that teachers be highly skilled if they hope to meet the needs of gifted children in the regular classroom.

On the basis of the above argument, it seems clear that we must be careful when selecting teachers who are expected to teach gifted children within the regular classroom. They must be mature individuals with high self-esteem, they must be free of negative preconceptions about gifted children, and most importantly they must be committed to finding a way to address the needs of gifted children and provide them with an opportunity to reach their fullest potential.

Teachers must be willing to make modifications in the environment to provide adequate instruction for the gifted. They must be flexible in the amount of time they allow a child to continue an activity. If we want to encourage more in-depth study on the part of gifted children, we must allow them the time to accomplish this goal. Flexibility and awareness on the part of the teacher are important in the encouragement of independent and in-depth study of topics. The teacher must be aware that a child is indicating interest in exploring a topic, must encourage the child to do so when the opportunity arises, and must then allow the child to do so even at the expense of the classroom schedule.

Universities training prospective teachers to work with young children should incorporate courses which promote an understanding of gifted children and of strategies for differentiating instruction for all children, including the gifted. Since most young gifted children will be in a regular classroom or day care, it is important that prospective teachers of young children learn how to integrate gifted children with those who are progressing at different rates.

Although inservice activities are vital to the development and reinforcement of such attitudes and competencies, it is doubtful that inservice alone will overcome negative attitudes. We have to rely on our ability to select teachers who can develop and hold a positive attitude toward gifted children and a commitment to them. We may, however, be able to foster such aptitude by providing preservice teachers early in their training with information on the importance of meeting the needs of gifted students within the regular classroom. Naor and

Milgram (1980) demonstrated that a one-semester preservice training program increased knowledge about the four kinds of exceptional children most frequently encountered in regular classrooms (mentally retarded, emotionally disturbed, learning disabled, and physically or sensorily handicapped) and improved general attitudes toward them. It is reasonable to assume that preservice training could lead to a similar increase in knowledge about gifted children and the acquisition of more positive attitudes toward them.

INVOLVING PARENTS OF PRESCHOOL GIFTED CHILDREN IN PROVIDING A DIFFERENTIATED CURRICULUM

Although the notion seems to prevail that parents are too biased to provide reliable information about the giftedness of their children, research disputes this point of view. In fact, the findings of several research studies indicate that parents are much more accurate than teachers in identifying giftedness in their children (China, Harris, Hoffman, & Porter, 1974; Jacobs, 1971; Martinson, 1974). Specifically, Jacobs found that parents were able to identify 61 per cent of a group of gifted kindergarten children, while teachers identified only 4.3 per cent.

There is no better resource for ensuring high-quality differentiation of programming than the parents. They can be trained to assess the children, both their own and others. They can be trained to observe and collect data under supervision, thereby facilitating formative and summative decisions. They can be trained to do direct teaching and to interact with the children informally.

It was once thought unwise for a parent to work in the same classroom where his or her child was enrolled. Experience clearly disputes this notion. Parents of the gifted, who are often gifted themselves, understand what gifted children are like and are eager to provide services to the class. Parents and volunteers need an orientation to the program and inservice training on such matters as child management, the philosophy of the program, ways of facilitating learning, how to encourage the development of interests, and the implementation of a curriculum that capitalizes on these interests. Together with the parent or volunteer, the teacher should identify their training needs and develop a plan which will prepare these persons to work with the gifted in a regular classroom.

Parents vary as much as the children enrolled in the program. The entry level of parents who wish to become involved is based on the parents' interests, desires, and time. Parents should have input in assessing their needs and developing individual plans for meeting those needs. All parents, however, should learn to be advocates for their children, but this is especially true of parents of the gifted because there is comparatively little concern for the special needs of the young gifted child. The general feeling among professionals and nonprofessionals is that these children have more of everything to begin with. Although such feelings are far from the truth, they hinder the gifted child in securing the opportunity to develop his or her potential.

Parents need training on how to advocate for their children. This can probably best be accomplished by organizing themselves and providing their own training. Bringing in experts to help them learn to be better advocates can be very beneficial. After all, the parents of these children will be their managers for a number of years and the quality of their child's education will largely rest on their ability to see that their child is placed in the most appropriate classroom and receive the most appropriate programming. An advocate does not need to be "pushy" or "offensive" but does need to be knowledgeable and assertive. The sooner parents are able to begin their advocacy, the better the chances of their gifted child having a consistently challenging program as he or she proceeds in school (Karnes, 1983). By conducting advocacy training in an integrated program, all parents could receive such training, and without a doubt all children could benefit if parents were better advocates for their children.

The support, input, and guidance of parents are assets for the professional staff. After all, the parents are the most significant persons in the young gifted child's life. Most parents sincerely want the very best for their children and benefit in a variety of ways when they are an integral part of the program. Often parents attribute a child's behavior to the fact he is a slow learner or is exceptionally bright when in fact the child's behavior is typical for his chronological age. Being a part of a program for all children helps parents see what is typical. Parents of young gifted children need to be trained to identify the developmental level of their children more precisely and to determine whether or not their children are functionally or potentially gifted.

Parents also profit from interacting with parents whose children are similar. They enjoy sharing information about their child and soliciting opinions on how best to manage their child. It is not easy to rear a gifted child, and sharing information with other parents seems to lighten the load and help parents cope with problems. It behooves the professionals to join forces with these very important persons in young children's lives. Working together the professionals and parents can accomplish much more than working separately.

SUPPORT OF THE ADMINISTRATION AND THE LAY PUBLIC

Gallagher (1986) explains that a successful plan for educating young gifted children is contingent upon both policy and program. "The function of *policy* is to get the right resources to the right place at the right time so that the child has an environment for effective learning. The function of *program* is to fill the environmental space provided by the policy with exciting and constructive curricula" (p. 1).

To develop a program policy which has differentiation of instruction as one of its major goals, the policy must have the support of the administration, teachers, parents, and lay public. An essential ingredient is a high adult-child ratio, no more than eight children to an adult, but this ideal does not mean that all adults in the classroom need to be salaried. In every community there are people in addition to parents who will give their time to an improved program for all children. Some of these volunteers may be especially proficient in working with gifted children, and some gifted children are so talented that they need a mentor. Consider, for example, a 5-year-old gifted child in a special program who scored at the ninth-grade level in math. Since the teacher did not feel competent to meet this child's needs in that area, a professor with expertise in teaching math became the child's mentor. An artist served as a mentor for those children who demonstrated unusual talent in art. Senior citizens can often be recruited to work with gifted children. This arrangement frequently results in significant satisfaction on both sides.

Perhaps the most important variable for meeting the needs of gifted children in the regular classroom is support from the administration. As indicated, teachers must have the flexibility to provide alternatives within the regular classroom for gifted children. This usually includes such simple things as allowing gifted children to go to the library when the need arises and more complex arrangements like letting them go to another classroom to receive instruction with children of similar abilities. With embarrassing frequency one hears the complaint that a teacher at a lower level allows some children to read, thus making it difficult to teach them at the next level. Somehow this lock-step attitude has to be combatted and eliminated. At the same time, differentiation of instruction requires commitment from all teachers to ensure continuity of instruction from level to level. A kindergarten child may be so advanced in a given area—reading for instance—that his needs can best be met by sending him to a first or second grade to join a group who are accelerated in reading. All such arrangements will require flexibility not only on the part of teachers but also on the part of the administrator. Without support from the administrator such a plan can never be implemented.

Related to support are the resources available to a teacher. A teacher who has access to another teacher who is trained in gifted education and also has consulting skills can receive advice on ways to modify instruction for gifted children. The consulting teacher may also lend support by listening to special problems that result from having gifted children integrated into the regular classroom and because of his or her knowledge about educating gifted children can promote insight into solutions.

Differentiation of instruction requires a larger budget for equipping the classroom. Meeting the wide range of abilities and interests of gifted children requires instructional materials that vary widely in difficulty and in content. Moreover, equipment not usually found in preschool programs may need to be purchased. For example, providing a teacher with a computer requires a substantial commitment of resources. Not only must the school provide money for the hardware, it must also be willing to continue purchasing software as the children's needs dictate. The school must, of course, also ensure that someone with the training to facilitate the gifted child's exploration with the microcomputer is available. Making a commitment to purchasing additional materials, however, can substantially improve a teacher's ability to provide alternatives and enhanced instructional opportunities within the regular classroom.

The Physical Environment

The size of the room for a regular preschool class depends on the number of children enrolled, the adult-child ratio, and the approach to education. If instruction is to be differentiated using an open or informal approach, with children engaged in a number of projects, an oversized room is preferable. In fact, a large classroom and two or three small rooms provide the setting for an excellent program.

The atmosphere should be stimulating and inviting, conducive to the pursuit of current interests and the development of new ones, and favorable to independence. Furniture should be light enough that teachers and children can move it about as their needs dictate. Centers of interest, well equipped to meet varying interests and developmental stages, give all children, including the gifted, an opportunity to develop special interests and learn at the rate with which they are most comfortable. Children must be provided with materials and opportunities to explore topics independently. Each classroom should have a sink where children can mix their own paints or clean up, and shelves should be low enough that children can reach for materials they wish to use and put away materials when they have finished with them. A library that preschool children are allowed to use can do much to provide children with both the materials and support they require for independent study. A well-designed playground adjacent to the classroom is highly desirable. Such a playground offers many opportunities for children of varying abilities to play together, especially if encouraged by the adults working in the program.

PITFALLS IN DIFFERENTIATING INSTRUCTION

In meeting the curricular needs of the gifted in the regular classroom, one should avoid anything detrimental to their attitudes toward learning, their habits, or the full actualization of their potential.

Avoid being inflexible. A teacher committed to meeting the needs of all children in the class must not be rigid. For example, a gifted child may have a longer attention span than his less able peers. He may be working on a project with children who have not been identified as gifted. He wants to continue working on the project at a time when small group math lessons are scheduled. Since he is already accelerated in math and since his project involves math concepts, the flexible teacher will allow that child to continue working on his project.

Don't teach them what they already know. This is a common complaint of parents of bright and gifted children. The gifted child who is reading, for example, does not need to engage in reading readiness activities. It is not only boring to such a child but a waste of time to make her do so.

Don't expect a child to be gifted in all respects. One gifted child may have a large vocabulary, use higher-level thinking processes, and be able to dictate complex stories but be progressing in math similarly to the other children. Another gifted child may be highly creative, may think of many different ways to solve problems, but may be no better than average in large motor development and unable to print the stories and poems he develops because his fine motor development is not on a par with his cognitive and creative development.

Don't allow the gifted child to involve himself in more activities than he can handle. Since many gifted children have wide interests, it is easy for them to take on so much that nothing is pursued in depth and the quality of the work suffers. Gifted children, like all children, need reasonable limits set for them. It is the adult who must monitor the activities in which the gifted child becomes involved and see that she doesn't overload.

Don't allow the gifted child an exorbitant share of adult attention. It is true that young gifted children rely heavily on adults to answer questions, to obtain materials, to arrange field trips, and so on. Nevertheless, gifted children must be considerate of others, and the teachers must also be sure to meet the needs of other children. The teacher must ensure that a disproportionate amount of their time is not spent with gifted children. Such a situation can lead other children to become resentful of the gifted child. The teacher may have to develop techniques to help gifted children be patient when he or she is unable to help them and find ways to increase the number of adults available to help the gifted child. Having volunteers and parents working in the classroom is one way that teachers can provide more opportunities for gifted as well as other children to receive increased adult attention.

Don't feel you have to be a walking encyclopedia. It is not uncommon for a 4-year-old gifted child to know more about a given subject than a teacher who is bright himself. If a child asks a question a teacher can't answer, the teacher should simply say: "I don't know, but we can find out," or "I know someone who can answer that question, and I'll try to arrange for you to talk to him." Bluffing is likely to make the teacher feel uneasy and be seen through by the child. Eventually bluffing is likely to result in hostility between the child and the teacher.

Don't be of too much assistance to the gifted child. The teacher's goal is to help each child be as independent as possible. A teacher who always steps in and helps children achieve their goals is preventing them from developing skills of independence. It is better for the teacher to guide the child through questions and comments that will encourage critical thinking and to determine the steps to be taken to solve a problem or achieve a goal. Even when a child sets an unrealistic goal, it is more effective for the teacher to help the child set more realistic goals than it is for the teacher to step in and achieve the goal for the child. At times it may be appropriate for the teacher to let the child attempt a goal that appears unrealistic. We have often been surprised at the things these children are able to accomplish.

Don't allow the child to have gaps in his learning. Cognitively young intellectually gifted children are not likely to have gaps in academic skills, but it does occur. It is not uncommon for gifted children to be poor spellers even when they are reading at the fourth-grade level at 4 years of age. They may also have gaps in learning that are related to interpersonal skills—politeness, willingness to listen, tolerance of those with lesser ability. Teachers should not ignore such gaps, because later such gaps may hinder the child's ability to reach his or her full potential.

Don't belittle gifted children when they make mistakes or fail. Gifted children are often supersensitive. If a teacher calls attention to mistakes in a demeaning way, the gifted children's self-esteem may be in jeopardy. Although such an action is detrimental to children in general, those who deviate from the norm are particularly susceptible to being hurt by the negative attention. When things do not turn out exactly as hoped, the teacher should consider it a learning situation. She should let children know she is on their side and will help them overcome the failure.

Don't hold the gifted child's work up for comparison with that of regular classroom peers. Such a comparison is injurious to the acceptance of the gifted child by his peers. The accomplishments of all children should be recognized by the significant adults in their lives. The teacher can find something that will allow her to give each child positive feedback. Elevating one child's accomplishments as a standard to which others should aspire is often counterproductive. Less-able children resent such comparisons and are apt to give up rather than to put forth more effort.

Don't exploit the talents of gifted children. Having gifted children tutor their peers can be a rewarding experience to both the tutor and tutee. However, if it escalates to the point where the gifted child has become a teacher's aide, something is wrong. Others will resent what they perceive to be unfair privileges and the gifted child will feel used.

CONCLUSION AND A LOOK TO THE FUTURE

There is no doubt that many gifted children are unidentified and underserved at the preschool level. To facilitate understanding of the gifted and their unique needs among administrators and supervisors, teachers, parents, legislators, and the general public, it is imperative that greater effort be made.

First, the general public has to become more aware that for the good of our society it is important to nurture the gifts of our most able children. There must be a commitment to seeking, encouraging, and supporting these children. We cannot afford the loss of any talent. In addition, in a democratic society we owe it to the potentially or functionally gifted children to support their development for their own well-being.

Awareness of the needs of gifted children can be facilitated through television and radio, through articles in popular magazines, and by financing demonstration sites to interpret innovative and effective ways of differentiating instruction for the gifted in the regular classroom setting. Support of research is needed to generate data to reinforce what we believe to be true, that early identification and programming for the gifted can "pay off" on short-term and long-term bases. These results must be widely disseminated so that policy makers can make valid decisions.

We need legislation which makes it legal and provides financial assistance to establish programs in the public school for all children down to age three. Currently it is federally mandated to identify and program for handicapped children as young as age three, but only the handicapped have the opportunity to participate in an organized program at such an early age.

An adoption or adaptation of a blueprint to identify and program for the handicapped which has been developed by the federal government can serve as a model for encouraging the federal government, states, and local communities to serve the young gifted segment of our population. This plan was the result of the passage of the Children's Early Assistance Act in 1968. At that time few programs existed nationwide for the young handicapped. Through financing of demonstration projects, outreach projects, technical assistance, research institutes, and financial assistance to states, this country is well on its way to identifying and programming for all of its young handicapped children.

We are advocating the development of individualized programs designed specifically for each gifted child. This does not mean, however, that gifted children should be educated in isolation (Karnes, Linnemeyer, & Denton-Ade, 1983). Some data indicate that gifted children may become social isolates within the regular classroom (Belcastro, 1987). This is a problem that teachers must recognize and face if they are going to meet the needs of gifted children. Every effort should be made to integrate gifted children into the activities of the general classroom while differentiating curriculum and instruction within these activities. On the other hand, gifted children need to interact with peers of comparable ability; therefore, the wise principal makes certain that the gifted child is not the only gifted child in his classroom.

Many of the principles we use in differentiating the curriculum for preschool gifted children apply equally well to those not identified as gifted. We are often prone to believe that only the gifted have the ability to acquire higher-level thinking skills. Most children, however, can learn to think at a higher level if encouraged to do so. For example, Karnes and Johnson (in press) found, that among low-income preschool children, all benefitted from activities typically used with gifted preschool children. The reason for special classes is the stark realization that in many regular classes children are not challenged with a curriculum that facilitates their full development. Teachers typically gear instruction to the middle, hoping that in this way they will meet the needs of most children. Unfortunately, the needs of many children are not addressed. If, on the other hand, curriculum was differentiated according to the individual requirements of each child, not only would it be possible to integrate gifted preschoolers with their same-age peers, but the educational environment for all children should be improved. It is imperative that we move toward an educational system more concerned with meeting the individual needs of children than assimilating children into society.

REFERENCES

Belcastro, F.P. (1987, May). Elementary pull-out program for the intellectually gifted—Boon or bane? *Roeper Review, 9*(4), 208–214.

Caswell, H.L. (1953). Editor's introduction. In M. Scheifele (Ed.), *The gifted child in the regular classroom.* New York: Bureau of Publications, Teachers College, Columbus University.

China, T.E., Harris, R., Hoffman, C., & Porter, M.W. (1974). Parents as identifiers of giftedness, ignored but accurate. *The Gifted Child Quarterly, 18,* 191–195.

Clark, B. (1983). *Growing up gifted* (2nd ed.). Columbus, OH: Charles E. Merrill.

Combs, A. (1965). *The professional education of teachers: A perceptual view of teacher preparation.* Boston: Allyn & Bacon.

Coopersmith, S. (1967). *The antecedents of self-esteem.* San Francisco: W.H. Freeman.

Cox, J., & Daniel, N. (1983). Specialized schools for high ability students. *G/C/T, 28,* 2–9.

Cox, J., & Daniel, N. (1984). The pull-out model. *G/C/T, 34,* 55–61.

Cox, J., Daniel, N., & Boston, B. (1985). *Educating able learners.* Austin: University of Texas Press.

Gallagher, J.J. (1985). *Teaching the gifted child* (3rd ed.). Boston: Allyn & Bacon.

Gallagher, J.J. (1986, Spring). The need for programs for young gifted children. In R.R. Fewell, S.G. Garwood, & J.T. Neisworth (Eds.), *Gifted preschoolers* (pp. 1–8). Austin, TX: Pro-Ed.

Howley, A., Howley, C.B., & Pendarvis, E.D. (1986). *Teaching gifted children: Principles and strategies.* Boston: Little, Brown.

Jacobs, J. (1971). Effectiveness of teacher and parent identification of gifted children as a function of school level. *Psychology in the Schools, 8*(2), 140–142.

Janos, P.M., & Robinson, N.M. (1985). Psychosocial development in intellectually gifted children. In F.D. Horowitz & M. O'Brien (Eds.), *The gifted and talented: Developmental perspectives* (pp. 149–195). Washington, DC: American Psychological Association.

Jenkins, R.C.W. (1979). *A resource guide to preschools and primary programs for the gifted and talented.* Mansfield, CT: Creative Learning Press.

Jerslid, A. (1965). Voice of the self. *NEA Journal, 54,* 23-25.

Karnes, M.B. (Ed.). (1983). *The underserved: Our young gifted children.* Reston, VA: The Council for Exceptional Children.

Karnes, M.B., & Johnson, L.J. (1986). Early identification and programming for young gifted/talented handicapped. In R.R. Fewell, S.G. Garwood, & J.T. Neisworth (Eds.), *Early childhood special education* (pp. 50-62). Austin, TX: Pro-Ed.

Karnes, M.B., & Johnson, L.J. (in press). Bringing out head start talents: Findings from the field. *Gifted Child Quarterly.*

Karnes, M.B., Linnemeyer, S.A., & Denton-Ade, C.N. (1983). Differentiating the curriculum. In M.B. Karnes (Ed.), *The underserved: Our young gifted children* (pp. 75-117). Reston, VA: The Council for Exceptional Children.

Karnes, M.B., & Shwedel, A.M. (1983). Assessment of preschool giftedness. In D. Paget & B.A. Bracken (Eds.), *The psychoeducational assessment of preschool children* (pp. 473-509). New York: Grune and Stratton.

Karnes, M.B., Shwedel, A.M., & Linnemeyer, S.A. (1982). The young gifted/talented child: Programs at the University of Illinois. *Elementary School Journal, 82,* 195-213.

Karnes, M.B., Shwedel, A.M., & Williams, M. (1983). Combining instructional models to develop differentiated curriculum for young gifted children. *Teaching Exceptional Children, 15*(3), 128-135.

Kitano, M.K., & Kirby, D.F. (1986). *Gifted education: A comprehensive view.* Boston: Little, Brown.

Maker, C.J. (1986). Suggested principles for gifted preschool curricula. *Topics in Early Childhood Special Education, 6,* 62-73.

Maker, C.J. (1989). Curriculum content for gifted students: Principles and practices. In R.M. Milgram (Ed.), *Teaching gifted and talented learners in regular classrooms* (pp. 33-61). Springfield, IL: Charles C. Thomas.

Manaster, G., & Powell, P. (1983). A framework for understanding gifted adolescents' psychological maladjustment. *Roeper Review, 6,* 70-73.

Martinson, R.A. (1974). *The identification of the gifted and talented.* Ventura, CA: Ventura County Superintendent of Schools Office.

Naor, M., & Milgram, R.M. (1980). Two preservice strategies for preparing regular class teachers for mainstreaming. *Exceptional Children, 47,* 126-129.

Renzulli, J.S. (1978). What makes giftedness? Re-examining a definition. *Phi Delta Kappan, 60,* 180-184.

Robinson, A., & Feldhusen, J. (1984). Don't leave them alone: Effects of probing on gifted children's imaginative explanations. *Journal for the Education of the Gifted, 7,* 156-163.

Rothney, J., & Sanborn, M. (1968). *Promising practices in the education of superior children: A demonstration program.* Madison, WI: University of Wisconsin.

Rowe, M. (1973). *Teaching science as continuous inquiry.* New York: McGraw-Hill.

Rutter, M., & Garmezy, N. (1983). Atypical social and personality development. In E.M. Hetherington (Ed.), *Handbook of child psychology, Vol. IV: Socialization, personality, and social development* (4th ed., pp. 775-911). New York: John Wiley.

Scheifele, M. (1953). *The gifted child in the regular classroom.* New York: Bureau of Publications, Teachers College, Columbus University.

Shwedel, A.M., & Stoneburner, R. (1983). Identification. In M.B. Karnes (Ed.), *The underserved: Our young gifted children.* Reston, VA: The Council for Exceptional Children.

Wenar, C. (1982). Developmental psychopathology: Its nature and models. *Journal of Child Clinical Psychology, 11,* 192-201.

Wiener, J. (1978). Attitudes of psychologists and psychometrists toward gifted children and programs for the gifted. *Exceptional Children, 44,* 531-534.

Whitmore, J. (1985). New challenges to common identification practices. In J. Freeman (Ed.), *The psychology of gifted children* (pp. 93-115). New York: John Wiley.

Chapter 11
Educating the Learning-Disabled Gifted Child

Paul R. Daniels

Do learning-disabled/gifted children really exist? For a large segment of the educational and psychological community this is not a rhetorical question. Serious doubts about their existence persist even though sections of professional meetings are devoted to examining and planning for the identification and remediation of learning disabled/gifted children. Lack of academic success by a gifted child is almost always attributed to lack of motivation, personality and adjustment problems, or faulty educational programs. Using such familiar concepts to explain underachievement in gifted children is comfortable and easy to live with. LD/Gifted, by contrast, is an unfamiliar concept that is often difficult to accept and evokes conflict and discomfort in many people.

Teachers and parents can usually understand learning disability and giftedness, two exceptionalities that are essentially cognitive, when they obtain separately. The two exceptionalities, however, are often viewed as a contradiction in terms. Can a learning-disabled child really be intellectually gifted? Can a gifted child really be learning-disabled? As more and more attention is devoted to this group, it will become increasingly apparent that the answers to these questions are affirmative.

This chapter on teaching and counseling the LD/Gifted child in the regular classroom is divided into three sections. The first section deals with the discovery of learning disabled/gifted children through systematic diagnostic evaluation; the second with identification of the specific cognitive and personal-social characteristics of a particular learning-disabled/gifted learner by means of diagnostic teaching activities and other multidisciplinary diagnostic procedures; and the third with practical information and suggestions for teaching and counseling learning disabled/gifted children.

DISCOVERY OF LEARNING-DISABLED/GIFTED
CHILDREN: SYSTEMATIC OBSERVATION

To discover may be defined as to be the first to find, to learn of, to uncover, or to disclose. One major problem has always been the discovery of learning disabled/gifted children. Usually it is easier to find something one is looking for rather than to hope for a chance discovery. So it is with gifted children having learning disabilities. One reason so few of them have been identified might well be that until recently their identification happened mostly by chance. Someone happened to be impressed with the thinking or knowledge of a child not noticeably successful in academic areas. If LD/Gifted children are to receive the attention they deserve, the current haphazard approach will have to be replaced by a genuine desire to discover them and serious efforts to do so. The discovery and identification of children who are *either* gifted or learning-disabled is fraught with well-documented difficulties. When children are *both* gifted and learning-disabled, the processes of discovery and identification are compounded and especially difficult. Systematic diagnostic observation is the first step in the process of discovering LD/gifted learners.

Daniels (1983) suggested the following four behavioral characteristics to serve as landmarks to guide teachers in initial diagnostic observation when there is suspicion that a child may be LD/gifted:

Vocabulary Development

On standardized grade-level tests LD/Gifted children tend to score at grade level or slightly above on vocabulary. They usually learn what is taught. Nevertheless, their problems will be evident if their vocabulary skills are subject to diagnostic observation. They tend not to be able to handle semantic variations, nuances, sarcasm, and so on. Figurative language will often be surprisingly difficult for them even though they have been labeled gifted.

Speed of Reaction

Gifted children are usually spontaneous. They tend to respond in many instances in a manner that might even be called impetuous. However, this spontaneity is noticeably lacking in LD/Gifted children. These children seem to ponder everything. They often appear unable to differentiate between elements that are worth pondering and those that require only a superficial perusal. They find it difficult to skim, often expressing a fear that something might be missed or overlooked. Assurances that skimming is required on a particular task seldom help. This attitude is not changed by simple assurances. The tendency to waste time and effort pondering is often a major element in lowering their scores on achievement tests. They often will not skim to get an overview of a test item. They usually give each word in the problem statement as much credence as any other. They almost always pay a price because of the time constraints of most tests.

Performance on classroom tasks usually reflects their slow "speed of reaction." Assignments are not completed on time. Notes are incomplete. Discussions pass them by. Many of these children become the "slow-pokes" of their classes. Their behavior is frequently misinterpreted as being deliberately negative to gain attention, to disrupt the class, or to harass a teacher. Such accusations often lead to deteriorating behavior and/or poor self-image, especially since these children are being blamed for personal failings for which compensatory or remedial services have not been provided.

Flexibility

As noted above in the earlier discussion of vocabulary, LD/Gifted children usually learn what they are taught and rely on this learning. These children will often develop a single characteristic approach to tasks. As long as the approach works, things go well. However, when a problem requires a different approach or a pronounced modification in their behavior, they often falter intellectually and/or behaviorally. They seem unable to modify their customary approach to fit the new requirements of the tasks. One youngster was devastated when he discovered that the concept *multiply* means more and *divide* means less, only applied to whole numbers. When he tried to multiply fractions and decimals, he immediately rejected the correct answers since they violated the basic concept he believed to be correct. The time devoted to helping him overcome this lack of flexibility was time taken away from furthering his academic growth. This lack of flexibility can be modified but it can seldom be totally controlled.

Adaptability

LD/Gifted children also have a serious lack of adaptability. They seem totally unable to "roll with the punches." New situations, new demands, new ideas are often frightening. When new things are proposed, in some instances, these children will reject them outright. New things seem to disrupt their basic equilibrium. Even the contemplation of anything new is disturbing. They will often ask, why this or why that, not for information purposes, but as a type of plea to maintain their homeostasis.

This difficulty is often evidenced in their intense and intensive efforts in very specific and often narrow areas of interest. A child nearly obsessed with dinosaurs could not understand or accept the idea that one might use the excellent information acquired about dinosaurs to expand one's understanding of reptiles. All he really wanted was further elaboration of dinosaurs. One might feel that parents and educators should live with this obsessional interest, but the child was under tremendous social pressure from peers who no longer viewed his interest as "such a big deal." Many times during the day he was chided for his lack of knowledge about and interest in other age-appropriate topics. He was not accepted into games in school or at home since he did not know how to play them. The usual protestation, "I don't care," was, obviously, a poor defense mechanism against real suffering. He was driven deeper into his interest area so that he could try more and more to impress adults. This, of course, exacerbated the peer relations difficulties and further diminished his self-concept.

With some children this vicious cycle becomes so problematic that psychotherapeutic intervention is required. Often the therapy is quite helpful in improving peer relationships and approaches toward adults, but does little to ameliorate the adaptability problem. This is best handled by a sensitive teacher or learning therapist (Daniels, 1983).

In summary, discovery of LD/Gifted children will occur most often through directed diagnostic observation. If a child is thought to be gifted yet nonachieving by a parent or teacher, then a professional worker in the school—teacher, counselor, school psychologist, or administrator—should observe the child's behavior in light of the four criteria noted above. If most of these behavioral tendencies are evidenced, then the possibility of LD/Giftedness should be explored more intensively. If none of the four tendencies are discerned, then the label nonachieving gifted would appear to be a more accurate designation.

IDENTIFICATION: DIAGNOSTIC TEACHING ACTIVITIES AND OTHER MULTIDISCIPLINARY DIAGNOSTIC PROCEDURES

If diagnostic observation provides evidence supporting the suspicion that the child may indeed be both learning-disabled and gifted, the next step is to pinpoint the nature of the child's learning problem. In this section we will discuss the diagnostic teaching activities and other multidisciplinary diagnostic procedures used to identify the strengths and weaknesses of learning disabled/gifted children.

To identify is to ascertain whether cognitive and personal-social characteristics generally believed to obtain in learning disabled/gifted children are evidenced in a given child so that he/she may be considered a member of that group. LD/Gifted children require a differential diagnosis which by necessity must be multidisciplinary in nature. Some of the diagnostic activities discussed below can be done by regular classroom teachers. On the other hand, some aspects of the diagnostic program require the cooperation of people with professional training and experience in other relevant disciplines. As noted earlier, one reason these children often go unidentified has been too narrow diagnostic procedures. It is impossible to describe with detailed precision in the current chapter what such a diagnosis should entail. However, certain broad aspects can be discussed.

DIAGNOSTIC TEACHING ACTIVITIES

A number of diagnostic teaching activities can help identify the learning-disabled gifted child. For example, a classroom teacher might use materials which contain a concentration of sarcasm or semantic variations based on a specific context. The effect of these elements on the child's comprehension should be evaluated. Brief exercises in reading and math could be given to the child—the first exercise untimed, the second one rigorously timed. The influence of time pressure should be observed. Whenever possible, these diagnostic teaching activities should be done under the guidance of trained professionals. It is important to terminate diagnostic activities before the child experiences distress. It is unfair to push a disabled child to the limit. The activity is valuable enough when it provides either negative or positive behaviors which can be interpreted diagnostically. There is no value in determining the amount of stress a child can endure.

If at all possible, diagnostic teaching evaluations should be conducted both in group and individual settings. It is often enlightening to notice behavioral change in a LD/Gifted child in a peer situation as opposed to an adult-child instructional situation. The element of peer relations versus adult relations can be an important factor in developing a program of remediation.

Other Multidisciplinary Diagnostic Activities

Assessing intelligence. Evaluation of overall intellectual potential is an important part of a good diagnosis. However, if the only measure employed is an individual intelligence test, useful and important as this measure is, then the diagnosis is diminished in effectiveness. Usually the cut-off score for giftedness is determined by administrative policy. If it is 125 or above, the tests are probably valuable as screening measures. However, the score or scores does not provide enough data for either diagnosis or prescriptive programs. Because of a child's disability the real-world possibility of realizing measured potential may be markedly diminished unless considerable remediation is provided. The child may not have the cognitive and/or personal/social tools that he/she requires in order to reach the high-level potential identified. A language disability or a psychological factor affecting intelligence may require the development of goals often deemed inferior to the child's measured potential. These problems must be addressed. To help a child realize his/her giftedness, every effort must be made to overcome or circumvent the disability.

Special aspects of intellectual assessment. Certain psychological processes must also be evaluated in order to differentiate diagnostically between LD/Gifted and Gifted/Underachievers. One of the most important of these processes is memory span or immediate recall. Many LD children have difficulty recalling data immediately after a presentation. How many numbers or discrete words can be given to a child before a reduced performance is evidenced? For example, a child who can consistently repeat four words correctly but not five. This phenomenon exists for words, letters, numbers, related words (sentences) and especially for directions. A child who might be able to handle two consecutive directions will be unable to fathom three sets of directions. This can be a true disability and very handicapping unless it is discovered. However, even though it might not be remediated, compensatory activities can be developed in a prescriptive program that will permit improved functioning (Galanis, 1984).

The ability to concentrate on a task is vital for learning and many LD/Gifted children have difficulty concentrating. On a Wechsler profile of subtest scores, most of these children will have scores of eight or nine on the arithmetic subtest (Fox, Brody, & Tobin, 1983). This subtest appears to reflect the ability to concentrate (Rappaport, Gill, & Schafer, 1968; Wechsler, 1974). Yet, too frequently, this obvious problem is not addressed directly as an element in the diagnostic-prescriptive program.

Assessing achievement. Standardized tests may not be the best approach to assess academic achievement in LD/Gifted children. One serious problem in using standardized tests is often not considered when they are used with these children. Does one use a grade level-appropriate test or an achievement-level appropriate test? There are problems with both approaches. Can you really rely upon a score on a test designed for fifth-grade level obtained by a fifth grader reading at first reader level? What does it mean if the standardized test used with a fifth-grade child was for first reader-level children?

If one assessed achievement through informal measures and/or criterion-referenced inventories of standardized achievement tests instead, a sound evaluation based upon both objective and subjective data could be made. Such an evaluation procedure would not only support a diagnosis but contribute to a prescriptive remedial program as well. Information about these procedures are found in Betts (1946), Johnson and Kress (1965), and Berk (1984). Informal evaluations are useful in investigating reading, writing, or mathematics. A complete set of criterion-referenced inventories and record sheets for reading has been developed by Daniels and Schiffman (1974).

Assessing potential in reading. The informal reading inventory mentioned earlier provides a good index of a child's present level of functioning in reading. A discrepancy between the listening comprehension level and the instructional level provides a measure of reading retardation. More importantly, the informal reading inventory process allows one to measure this relationship when the curriculum content of the inventory selections is varied. In this way one could determine the level of instruction based on a child's interest and background. A child's ability might be higher in sciences but lower in literature. The necessary skills development program in reading could be planned using the material from the child's strong experiential background.

An informal reading inventory would also permit an analysis of a child's present language functioning when compared to the IQ score. For LD/Gifted children this is vital. Sometimes the discrepancy between actual and potential levels of functioning is so great that the words so often hurled at these children, "You should be able to do better!" are completely meaningless and harmful.

Assessing writing ability. When informally assessing writing ability, three or four samples of writing should be evaluated. One sample should always be in the child's subject matter area of strength. This compare and contrast activity across three or four writing samples permits the examiner to decide if the skills are really missing from the child's repertoire or simply unused in areas in which the child feels inadequate. Generally one should evaluate spelling, handwriting, punctuation, grammar, syntax, and composition. With all LD children but especially the LD/Gifted children, the prescriptive approach should be directed toward specific areas of difficulty rather than the entire writing process itself. The lack of flexibility in these children requires that one approach these tasks with great care.

Assessing ability in mathematics. In mathematics organized material should be presented in an ascending order of mathematical difficulty. The samples used for evaluation should have clearly observed processes for which level of competence may be ascertained. The evaluation should use only a limited number of items each day and the evaluation should be spread over a number of days. A total mathematical evaluation is not necessary. Once enough information has been gathered to begin an instructional program, further evaluation should be held in abeyance until there is a demonstrated need for more information. It is vitally important to begin instruction to provide some degree of academic success in order to increase the learner's self-confidence and to improve the attitude toward the remediation program.

Almost all of the activities designed to assess specific abilities cited above should be carried out as part of a diagnostic observation or diagnostic teaching experience. The problems and caveats noted about standardized tests are applicable in these procedures as well.

Personality assessment. Finally, if the child demonstrates adjustment difficulty, socially or academically, a thorough personality assessment should be obtained. This assessment should not be based on paper and pencil inventories. These measures are not valid for children with reading problems or comprehension difficulties. Even though many school systems shy away from the use of projective techniques, they can be very useful. A serious personality or adjustment problem can so influence a child's perception of reality that many diagnostic instruments do not provide valid data. Because of the conflicts inherently produced by being gifted and learning-disabled, special attention should be given to possible emotional handicaps as a further compounding element in the lives of these children. Too frequently, this possibility is ignored or skirted because of parental sensitivities or due process considerations, yet the emotional aspect may have to be ameliorated before any academic progress can be expected. There is little doubt that with some academic success, personal adjustment will improve, but in fact, improved personal adjustment can make a significant contribution to academic progress as well (Abrams & Kaslow, 1976).

Two pitfalls: Nonidentification and mistaken identification. The discovery and identification of LD/Gifted children is very demanding, more so than for children with other academic problems. There are, therefore, many such learners who go through their school years unidentified or mistakenly identified. These children generally follow one of two educational paths. Each takes a toll, although often in different aspects of their lives.

Some children proceed through school identified early as learning-disabled but unidentified as gifted. If the child is not impulsive or hyperactive, or does not present some other problem for the classroom teacher, the diagnosis is never questioned and the giftedness is never discovered. It is impossible to estimate how many children in this group are in our schools at this time. It would seem that the number might be substantial. This problem is especially acute if identification is carried out as part of a kindergarten or first-grade search for learning-disabled children. The new attempt at locating "children at risk" will probably increase the number since many of the measures used may be totally insensitive to the giftedness of a given child.

Early identification is probably a worthwhile procedure, but how the identification affects programming then becomes a problem. Many remedial programs for young children are mainly skills-oriented and often nearly devoid of curriculum content. For LD/Gifted children these programs offer little intellectual stimulation which often produces two reactions. One group of children seems to go along with the program, and the personal indicators of giftedness are eroded so that the recognition of high ability is often accomplished only by a chance encounter. It is possible that these children will never realize their potential.

Some children, however, early identified as learning-disabled but not yet identified as gifted, become problem children very early in their schooling. They are frequently placed in remedial programs, but do not cooperate because of the intellectual sterility of the situation. They respond by either acting out or withdrawing. In some instances their behavior problems lead to their intellectual salvation. The acting out or withdrawn child causes enough concern so that more detailed and sensitive diagnostic efforts are made. Often in such situations the giftedness is revealed with the resulting reappraisal of the child and the appropriateness of the educational program that he or she is receiving.

Some LD/Gifted children proceed through school mistakenly identified. These learners are pseudoachievers, children who because of their good basic intelligence compensate, to a large degree, for their learning disabilities. Again, these children may be viewed as victims of accepted school practices just as much as those incompletely identified through early identification procedures. On the standardized tests commonly used to measure achievement these children usually obtain satisfactory scores. Since this level of achievement is satisfactory by most standards, there would appear to be no compelling reason for a school to look further at children who attain these standards.

Pseudoachievers are usually discovered in one of two ways. First, a sensitive adult instinctively feels that the child really could do better and asks for a more detailed evaluation. This chance happening may lead to a more valid evaluation of a given child. Second, as the pseudoachievers move through the school system, the increased academic pressures eventually overwhelm the compensatory techniques they employ. This breakdown becomes most evident for many of these children as the written language tasks increase, and in mathematics, as the type and variety of word problems increase. The difficulties in flexibility and adaptability probably become too great to manage.

Unfortunately, pseudoachievers are often discovered when they enter secondary education. By that time it may be too late to provide remediation. Puberty and its enhanced social consciousness often make this a period in which the best approaches are compensatory or adaptive. These children usually do not demonstrate as much negative behavior as those narrowly identified early in school, but in one respect they may be more difficult to handle.

Their lack of academic motivation may be a serious problem. In most cases these children have had basically satisfactory school experiences and often do not want to face the demands and expectations of giftedness. Even when the academic burden becomes heavier they still often want only "to get by." The handling of these children offers a challenge educationally, psychologically, and socially. Ethical issues must be considered as well: Do parents and educators have the right to make children unhappy in motivating them to reach a higher academic goal consonant with their abilities? Some of these problems and ways of coping with them have been noted elsewhere (Frey, 1986; Jacobson, 1985).

The discovery and identification of LD/Gifted children who have been mistakenly identified or not identified at all will require more effort and take a somewhat different direction. Past test results must be interpreted not only for what was indicated, but, more importantly, in comparison to current findings. The validity of all measures must be challenged as they might be applied to LD/Gifted children. Cumulative record files have often led to prejudice by adults in authority toward certain children. Prejudicial perception of a LD/Gifted child may lead to particularly unfortunate consequences, including the failure of these children to fulfil their potential.

The discovery and identification of LD/Gifted children will continue to be minimal until school systems systematically introduce and utilize diagnostic teaching activities and other multidisciplinary diagnostic procedures. These activities and procedures should generate a diagnostic hypothesis. Those performing diagnostic evaluations must always keep in mind that when they have reached a diagnosis it is still a hypothesis, not a fact. This hypothesis can be verified only when it is tested in the instructional situation. These "educated guesses" must never be so inflexible that the child must conform to them. Programs must adjust to the child, not the child to the program. We now turn to a critically important question: What can teachers do to help these children learn better?

TEACHING AND COUNSELING LD/GIFTED CHILDREN: PROGRAM PLANNING

In planning special education for LD/Gifted children, teachers and counselors are advised to consider the full range of options available to meet the unique combination of needs presented by these children, those that stem from their learning disability and those that stem from their giftedness. LD/Gifted children, like other learning-disabled children, usually receive their instruction in regular classrooms supplemented by instruction in a supportive special education resource room. In addition, these children may be placed in a part-time program for gifted and talented children. In effect, these children sometimes receive their education in three distinct, and unfortunately, frequently uncoordinated settings. Because of the adaptability problem that characterizes many of these children such a situation can be an educational disaster. Gallagher (1983) and Baldwin and Gargiulo (1983) suggested ways of preventing these problems.

In most instances, teachers of the learning-disabled are not well acquainted with the cognitive and personal-social characteristics of gifted learners. By the same token, it is the rare teacher of gifted children who has background and experience with learning-disabled children as well.

The problem of coordinating the child's learning experiences is best resolved by being sure that each LD/Gifted child has a *case manager*. In some schools this responsibility might fall to school counselors, but only those with the requisite background and experience should take on this responsibility. All special needs children deserve this consideration, but because of the inherent possibility of conflict in programming for LD/Gifted children, it is especially important that one person be designated as the case manager to coordinate the various aspects of the remedial program and to reconcile any differences which might develop. The case manager must initiate and support communication among the professionals responsible for educating LD/Gifted children. When opinions differ, the case manager must make final decisions about the child's program. The very demanding responsibility of functioning as case manager requires the strong support of the school administrator and the parents.

Many LD/Gifted children feel isolated. They tend to have trouble establishing satisfactory peer relationships. When they receive their education in three settings, the problem of satisfying interactions with peers is even more severe. In the regular classroom, because of the need to receive special instruction, the LD/Gifted child misses many activities that provide opportunities for interaction with peers simply by not being there. In the LD resource room the child usually cannot find a peer to identify with intellectually. During gifted and talented classroom activities, the LD child is usually unable to make the quick responses the others do; language subtlies are not understood or are misunderstood. Any of these occurrences further weaken a poor self-concept.

The case manager must be constantly alert to signs that negative behaviors might be developing. In the regular classroom the child might act out to divert attention from perceived inadequacies. In the LD classroom the child might seek a peer relationship by identifying with negative behaviors of others. In the gifted and talented setting the child may lose status by denigrating the interests and ideas of others in a distorted perception that this is the way one achieves status and recognition.

Because of these potential difficulties, the case manager needs to have regular communication with parents. Parents will often be able to provide the first clues of impending maladjustment. Abrams and Kaslow (1976) and Bricklin (1983) offered many suggestions for working with LD/Gifted children that will be helpful to case managers.

Individualized instruction. LD/Gifted children can derive much benefit from individualized instruction based upon their cognitive and personal-social characteristics, especially their learning style. By the same token, counseling gifted learners based upon their learning styles was described elsewhere in this volume by Griggs (see Chapter 4). Although the author did not write about LD/Gifted learners, specifically, the application of the principles and practices are evident. It is not a simple matter to assure that the individualized instruction required by LD/Gifted children in regular classrooms will indeed be provided.

What is called individualized instruction in many classrooms is, in effect, teaching in small groups. Efforts are made to provide for individual differences within heterogeneous classrooms by organizing small somewhat homogeneous groups within the class. Learning in relatively small homogeneous groups can be beneficial for the LD/Gifted learner. This approach also has the added advantage that most regular classroom teachers have more training and experience with this procedure than they do with true individualized instruction as described by Dunn (1989) and Griggs (see Chapter 4). Unfortunately, the small homogeneous groups within the heterogeneous classroom are usually organized by achievement level exclusively. It would probably be more useful to organize the small groups on the basis of discovered needs, with the teacher providing instruction on the basis of a common need or problem (Duane, 1973, p. 258).

In the model of learning style described by Dunn (1989), the empirical evidence demonstrating the importance of identifying the preferred modality or modalities of each learner and of matching teaching strategies to them was summarized. This is especially important when teaching the LD/Gifted child. Materials can be learned via visual-auditory, visual-auditory-kinesthetic, or a visual-auditory-kinesthetic-tactile (sometimes called haptic) manner. It is surprising how frequently children who have failed with word recognition or number recognition continue to have materials presented in a visual-auditory manner exclusively. For many of them their failure occurred because they could not learn using only these two sensory modalities.

It is beyond the scope of the current chapter to describe educational techniques in detail. Readers interested in a thorough, practical, and comprehensive discussion of instructional techniques that will be useful for teaching LD/Gifted children are referred to Daniels (1983), Daniels and Schiffman (1974), Fox, Brody, and Tobin (1983), Johnson and Kress (1966), as well as other references cited at the end of this chapter. The case manager and the teachers of LD/Gifted children must have a variety of instructional techniques with which they are familiar and skilled. We will, nevertheless, cite a few examples of teaching strategies that seem particularly useful to be used by the regular classroom teacher in meeting the needs of these children.

One excellent approach to reading and writing instruction is a language experience approach, modified to use the gifted child's interest and strong knowledge background (Daniels, 1983, pp. 44, 45; Johnson & Kress, 1966, p. 16). When using a conventional approach of directed reading activities, the content should be adjusted for LD/Gifted children. One can use reading materials in science, social studies, fables, and so on. Progress can be continually monitored using criterion-referenced inventories (Daniels & Schiffman, 1974).

The instructional program for LD/Gifted children should not be content-bound. Emphasis should be placed on helping the children develop abstracting skills. They must be able to see the parts of a whole, so that as experiences are provided that contain a number of examples of sameness (percepts), the students will be able to develop the appropriate concepts. Anderson (1985, p. 372) and Brown (1985, p. 501) provide the classroom teacher with guidance on how to help LD/Gifted children develop vitally important metacognition and metamemory techniques. A complete program in developing classification skills is found in Daniels (1983, p. 95). Systematic exercises of this kind on a daily basis in school will provide an opportunity to present new ideas and understanding. This approach allows for discussion and the opportunity to use a large number of "what-if" situations in which outcomes are handled verbally rather than in reality. It is an easy and safe way to help the child see the alternatives in life, on what they depend and to what they lead. These are fundamental learning needs for most LD/Gifted children.

Consideration might be given to having children learn to use a multisensory approach, especially a Fernald Procedure (Fernald, 1943; Johnson & Kress, 1966; Daniels, 1983). This procedure allows the teacher to use a language experience approach for reading instruction, provides a systematic way to learn words, permits the instructor to be flexible in the development of reading skills, and encourages immediate and longer-term monitoring of success and failures. Since the Fernald Procedure is essentially a psycholinguistic approach to learning words and reading instruction, the basic abilities of LD/Gifted children are brought to bear on the learning situation and varied levels of thinking are fostered. The Fernald procedure is valuable in mathematics also. A child having problems with number recognition or number reproduction can use this technique to improve ability in this area. This multisensory procedure is also useful when number facts must be mastered. The Fernald procedure is especially helpful with children with short concentration span.

Recent technological advances can provide important help in remediating the learning difficulties of the LD/Gifted child. Small hand calculators are inexpensive, widely available, and easily portable. Many LD/Gifted children seem to have problems in mathematics when, in effect, their problems are in the areas of memory span and recall of number facts. Many of these children, when permitted and encouraged to bypass their handicaps by using a calculator, do well in mathematical processes and problem solving. Unfortunately, many school administrators view calculators as a crutch that would not have to be used if the child "simply learned the facts." They can, however, come to understand that the calculator for the LD/Gifted child is like a crutch for a lame child.

The wide availability of microcomputers in homes and schools can be of enormous help to LD/Gifted learners. Children with reading and writing problems should be given the opportunity to learn to use word processing and other computer programs that will help remediate their handicap. It is surprising how well the personal computer can help meet the needs of some handicapped children. LD/Gifted children usually have pronounced success with the computer. The frustration of rewriting, incorrect spelling, and the physical strain of handwriting is ameliorated by a machine that does not criticize, accepts what is presented, and provides help when needed. The special needs of LD/Gifted children in a regular classroom will require teachers to adjust some procedures and management for them on an individual basis. This sometimes leads to resentment from the other pupils. The classroom teacher will need to develop ways to explain to the other children what is being done without singling out the LD/Gifted child for undue special attention.

We have limited our discussion in this chapter to the LD/Gifted learner when giftedness is defined as high overall intellectual ability. In her 4 × 4 Model of the Structure of Giftedness, Milgram (1989) cited three additional kinds of giftedness—specific intellectual ability, overall original or creative thinking, and specific creative talent. Moreover, she argued that in educational planning for gifted and talented children, it is important to consider not only type but also levels of giftedness, that is, profound, moderate, and mild. The classroom teacher should bear in mind that learning disability may obtain in the other types of gifted children just as it does in gifted children of the high-IQ type.

It is unrealistic to expect teachers in regular classrooms to meet the needs of LD/Gifted learners singlehandedly. On the other hand, these children, like all other children, deserve a systematic, well-thought-out instructional program carried out by a caring, sensitive teacher supported by parents and colleagues. It is an ethical as well as an educational responsibility for society to discover the potential in all children and to provide the opportunities for each child to realize it. We conclude with a call to teachers to demonstrate understanding in attitude and creativity in practice as they face the daily, often difficult, challenges presented by the LD/Gifted child in the regular classroom.

REFERENCES

Abrams, J.C., & Kaslow, F.W. (1976). Learning disability and family dynamics: A mutual interaction. *Journal of Clinical Child Psychology, 5*, 35–40.

Anderson, R.C. (1985). Role of the reader's schema in comprehension, learning and memory. In H. Singer & R.B. Ruddell (Eds.), *Theoretical models and processes of reading* (3rd ed.). Newark, DE: International Reading Association.

Baldwin, L.J., & Gargiulo, D.A. (1983). A model program for elementary-age learning-disabled/gifted youngsters. In L.H. Fox, L. Brody, & D. Tobin (Eds.), *Learning-disabled/gifted children* (pp. 207–221). Baltimore, MD: University Park Press.

Betts, E.A. (1946). *Foundations of reading instruction*. New York: American Book.

Berk, R.A. (1984). *A guide to criterion-references test construction*. Baltimore, MD: The Johns Hopkins University Press.

Bricklin, P.M. (1983). Working with parents of learning-disabled/gifted children. In L.H. Fox, L. Brody, & D. Tobin (Eds.), *Learning-disabled/gifted children* (pp. 243–260). Baltimore, MD: University Park Press.

Brown, A.L. (1985). The development of selective attention strategies for learning from texts. In H. Singer & R.B. Ruddell (Eds.). *Theoretical models and processes of reading* (3rd ed.). Newark, DE: International Reading Association.

Daniels, P.R. (1983). *Teaching the gifted/learning disabled child*. Rockville, MD: Aspen Systems.

Daniels, P.R., & Schiffman, G.B. (1974). *Individualized directions in reading: Direction I*. Austin, TX: Stock-Vaughn.

Duane, J.E. (1973). *Individualized instruction programs and materials*. Englewood Cliffs, NJ: Educational Technology Publications.

Dunn, R. (1989). Individualizing instruction for mainstreamed gifted children. In R.M. Milgram (Ed.), *Teaching gifted and talented learners in regular classrooms* (pp. 63–111). Springfield, IL: Charles C. Thomas.

Fernald, G.M. (1943). *Remedial techniques in basic school subjects*. New York: McGraw-Hill.

Fox, L.H., Brody, L., & Tobin, D. (Eds.). (1983). *Learning disabled/gifted children*. Baltimore, MD: University Park Press.

Frey, C. (1986). How one school districts programs for its gifted/ld population. *Spectrum, 4,* 2.

Galanis, S. (1984). *The effects of organizational skills training sessions or a monetary incentive on the short term memory performance of learning disabled adolescents*. Unpublished doctoral dissertation, Johns Hopkins University, Baltimore, MD.

Gallagher, J.J. (1983). The adaptation of gifted programming for learning-disabled students. In L.H. Fox, L. Brody, & D. Tobin (Eds.), *Learning-disabled/gifted children*. Baltimore, MD: University Park Press.

Jacobson, V. (1985, July 24). *The Gifted/learning disabled: Who are they?* ERIC Clearing House, #ED254988.

Johnson, M.S., & Kress, R.A. (1965). *The Informal Reading Inventory*. Newark, DE: International Reading Association.

Johnson, M.S., & Kress, R.A. (1966). *Eliminating word-learning problems in reading disability cases*. Philadelphia, PA: Temple University Press.

Milgram, R.M. (1989). Teaching gifted and talented children in regular classrooms: An impossible dream or a full-time solution for a full-time problem. In R.M. Milgram (Ed.), *Teaching gifted and talented learners in regular classrooms*. Springfield, IL: Charles H. Thomas.

Rapaport, D., Gill, M., & Schofer, R. (1968). *Diagnostic psychological testing*. New York: International University Press.

Wechsler, D. (1974). *Manual for the Wechsler Intelligence Scale for Children, Revised*. New York: The Psychological Corporation.

Chapter 12
Profiles in Giftedness: Fictional Portraits of Intelligent and Creative Children

Shoshana Knapp

Why do we go to fiction to learn about gifted children?

What do we find in literature to help us teach and counsel such children?

Stories, like life at its best, provide a coherent view of experience; they focus not on isolated items of information, but on pattern and meaning. For the teacher of the gifted and creative child, they can supply an image of what it would be fully to know the child, who has— in addition to intellectual qualities and traits, as manifested in the school setting—a personality, a home life, a community environment, and a life story in which the school years, and the teacher's contribution, are only a part.

Without a full story, testimony such as IQ tests can appear to be, as Harold Brodkey (1989) puts it, "peculiar witnesses." In an interesting passage in *Stories in an Almost Classical Mode*, the first-person narrator, as an adult, reflects on his inner and outer life as a 13-year-old:

> I was supposed to have a good mind—that supposition was a somewhat mysterious and even unlikely thing. I was physically tough, and active, troublesome to others . . . and I composed no symphonies, did not write poetry or perform feats of mathematical wizardry. No one in particular trusted my memory since each person remembered differently, or not at all, events I remembered in a way that even in its listing of facts, of actions, was an interpretation; someone would say, "That's impossible— it couldn't have happened like that—I don't do those things—you must be wrong."
>
> But I did well in school and seemed to be peculiarly able to learn what teachers said—I never mastered a subject, though—and there was

the idiotic testimony of those peculiar witnesses, IQ test: those scores invented me.

Those scores were a decisive piece of destiny in that they affected the way people treated you and regarded you; they determined your authority; and if you spoke oddly, they argued in favor of your sanity. But it was as easy to say and there was much evidence that I was stupid, in every way or in some ways or, as my mother said in exasperation, "in the ways that count." . . . (Harold Brodkey, 1989)

How much there seems to be to the story of this intelligent boy, and how much one misses if the whole story remains untold.

In *The Call of Stories: Teaching and the Moral Imagination* (1989), Robert Coles, a wide-ranging doctor-writer, describes his own odyssey from Harvard English major to medical doctor, child psychiatrist, writer (most notably of the five-volume series, *Children of Crisis*), and professor of psychiatry and medical humanities at Harvard, where—completing the circle—he introduced a course in "Literature and Medicine." William Carlos Williams, a practicing physician and a major poet, had once said to him: "Sure, if you could get medical students to read certain novels or short stories it might make a difference." Coles went beyond that, not only encouraging students to read (and share with patients) formal literature, but also to elicit their patients' stories and to confide their own. Only through stories, Coles believes, can we see each other as more than inventories of traits and symptoms. One of his students remarked, with surprise: "I've never thought of stories or a novel as a help in figuring out how to get through a working day." But stories are indeed a help in daily life—and not only for physicians (Bevington, 1989). Coles is right. Stories can be the fuel of human interaction: The stories we read that enlighten and inspire us, the stories we tell that convey our longing to make contact, the stories we hear that enable us to feel empathy.

The present chapter—a description of literary works dealing with intelligent and creative children—is an attempt to show what one learns when one seeks, learns, and contemplates such stories. Drawn from 20th-century literature, these children are diverse in abilities, interests, race, class, and national origin. They comprise a gallery of remarkable portraits: Star Holmes, a 3-year-old who discovers the Moebius strip and the capacity for time travel; Morgan Evans, a young Welsh miner who aspires to be a brilliant writer, and perhaps more; Ferdinand R. Tertan, a clinically disturbed adolescent who writes with passionate power; Beulah Lilt, daughter of a gifted philosopher, yet an apparent dullard in her Midwestern elementary school, who grows up to surpass her mother's brilliance; Shevek of Anarres, a physicist on Earth's inhabited moon who endeavors to conquer time, space, and human obstinacy; Beth Harmon, raised in a Kentucky orphanage where the children are controlled by tranquilizers, who becomes the world chess champion; Barry Rudd, a reflective boy, inquisitive and inventive, whose brain is purchased by a corporation after its representative gains the consent of his lower-middle-class parents, his New-England teachers and principal, and the boy himself; Emma "Emancipation" Sheridan, an 11-year-old who wants to be the youngest ever to take the bar exam, choosing the career that enabled her father to transcend his difficult Harlem childhood.

For each, I will discuss the evidence of gifted behavior; the child's personality and the home and community settings; the school environment and the teacher's role; the outcome of the plot, and the conclusions to be drawn. The stories of Barry, Beth, Beulah, and the others are worth telling, and very much worth hearing by people who are personally and professionally interested in a fuller picture of gifted children, not limited to their performance in the classroom.

In "The Man Who Was Present", the science-fiction writer Dmitri Bilenkin (1978) describes Fedyashkin, a retired accountant, who functions as a teacher and counselor for gifted people. He finds himself drawn to people who are about to voice ideas whose time has come. As he explains to one of them: "Around there is a cloud of thoughts. . . . But there are few hot spots nowadays that mark the creation of something new. That's why each jet of flame is so valuable. . . My presence fans the flame. . . . I have this ability, to help others think. That's why I came to you. I go to many people. That's as it should be. It's better for them, it's good for me, for the world" (pp. 34–35).

His sensation of inspirational power is not an illusion, says the narrator.

> "His presence, it seems, really does stimulate the creative capabilities. . . . For millions of people, that's what you would call a profession. Teachers . . . transmit knowledge, and most important, stimulate the mental and moral growth of children—real teachers, of course. That is the great meaning of their profession, to disseminate their thoughts and actions in such a way that they interweave like a golden thread in someone else's life and then come alive unrecognized in the discoveries and achievements of the future. . . . And are teachers the only ones to do this?
>
> Catalysts function in inorganic chemistry—mysterious connections that do not enter the reaction but give it energy and power. Organic processes are catalyzed by enzymes. Why shouldn't there be catalysts and enzymes in psychic phenomena? (p. 37)

The stories of such children as Shevek, Emma, and Morgan can enlighten those who aspire to be the catalysts of discovery and achievement, the golden threads in the life of a gifted child.

STAR HOLMES

The short story "Star, Bright" (Malzberg & Greenberg, 1980) evokes the emotions of a widowed father, raising a 3-year-old girl on his own, who discovers her extreme intelligence when he sees her cutting out a Moebius strip without ever having been told that a half-twist in a paper ring can produce a one-sided surface. In addition to her overall general intelligence (precociousness in reading and mathematics), she exhibits highly original and creative thinking, extending even to telepathy and teleportation. Having suffered himself from the isolation of high intelligence, he sees her as "afflicted," and is prepared to teach her to "compensate," to adjust to the world of her intellectual inferiors, to narrow the gap between herself and others by concealing her own gifts (p. 19). In an adroit comic interlude, Clifton shows Peter Holmes warning Star, after the first day of nursery school, that pretending to be too slow can create as many problems as actually being too swift. Her gifts, as he soon realizes, are immeasurable—although she has developed her own language of measurement, dividing people into Brights (herself), Stupids (e.g., her classmates), and Tweens (e.g., her father). At the end of the story, after a 5-year-old Bright has moved into the neighborhood, she uses the image of the Moebius strip to vanish, somewhere in time and space, with her new friend.

The power of this story springs from its poignant picture of Star's longing for an intellectual peer, and her loneliness and camouflage in the classroom, a setting that mirrors her father's experience in his business life. She tries, at first, to tone down her own brightness, to conform to the expectations for a 4-year-old, to gain the tolerance and acceptance of others. "I guess that's the hard part, isn't it, Daddy—to know how much you ought to know?" (p. 22). Her ultimate recourse—escape through time and space with another Bright—is, in a literal sense, possible only in science fiction. Little Star, however, is not the only gifted child to feel that her true home lies elsewhere, and her father is not the only parent to try, as he does at the end of the story, to follow her into the alternate dimension to which she has escaped. Last line of the story: "Now if, in the folding, I ESP the tesseract a half twist around myself—" (p. 38). Pete Holmes, a Tween, joins his Star, a Bright, believing that he too has been the victim of "the hostility of the world toward intelligence" (p. 20), and choosing, as she does, to be a victim no longer.

MORGAN EVANS

To seek a newer world, however, is not always to leave the present universe, and some gifted children are more fortunate than Star in finding the support, avenue, and environment to develop their gifts. At the conclusion of Emlyn Williams's (1938) *The Corn Is Green*, Morgan Evans, a young Welsh miner with a specific creative talent for language (and the potential for overall general intelligence as well), is headed for an Oxford education and a world of possibilities he has only glimpsed. His story illustrates the shared victory of a dedicated teacher and a bright boy, equally stubborn and equally ambitious, over several formidable obstacles: a closed society, a limited upbringing, and the challenge of educating his character as well as his mind.

The play, we are told, take place in "Glansarno, a small village in a remote Welsh countryside," in the late 1800s. The British residents expect little from the Welsh, who look forward to a lifetime of work in the local mines. As one of them says: "the people in this part of the countryside are practically barbarians" (p. 71). When Miss Moffat comes to town with plans for a school, the Squire, kind, vain, and "obtusely obstinate" (p. 9), is profoundly opposed, afraid of the consequences: "But puttin' 'em up to read English, and pothooks, and givin' 'em ideas . . . If there were more people like you, y'know, England'd be a jolly dangerous place to live in! Whatd'ye want to do, turn 'em into gentlemen?" (p. 51).

This is, in fact, only part of Miss Moffat's plan. "About forty, a healthy Englishwoman with an honest face, clear, beautiful eyes, a humorous mouth, a direct friendly manner and unbounded vitality" (p. 17), she comes to the community because she has inherited a house, and she sees this as an opportunity. Herself a creative thinker, devising unusual and high-quality solutions, she looks at a deserted barn and sees a schoolhouse, looks at Miss Ronberry and Mr. Jones (an unemployed woman still hoping for a husband, a solicitor's clerk—both moderately educated, both unfulfilled) and sees potential teachers. Most importantly, she looks at the Welsh children, whom the British dismiss as unsuited for education, and sees young people who are capable of learning and being more than anyone has expected.

Success is not immediate. Early in the play, she considers abandoning her plan for a school because the Squire has persuaded the barn's owner not to sell. Tired and discouraged, she sits down to read the compositions the children have written on the topic "How I would spend my holiday." She is amazed and impressed by what Morgan Evans has written:

> The mine is dark . . . If a light come in the mine . . . the rivers in the mine will run fast with the voice of many women; the walls will fall in, and it will be the end of the world . . . So the mine is dark. . . . But when I walk through the Tan—something—shaft, in the dark, I can touch with my hands the leaves on the trees, and underneath . . . where the

corn is green. . . . There is a wind in the shaft, not carbon monoxide they talk about, it smell like the sea, only like as if the sea had fresh flowers lying about . . . and that is my holiday. (pp. 57-58)

Ignoring the grammatical and syntactical flaws, she responds to the evidence of his powerful imaginative and linguistic gifts, gifts that match her own ability to infer the potential from the actual. As young Morgan Evans looks at the mine shaft and imagines the corn that will grow above it and outside it, Miss Moffat looks at his writing, sees what she tells him is "exceptional talent for a boy in your circumstances" (p. 63), and asks him how he feels about the news that he is "very clever." He replies: "It makes me that I . . . *(Hesitating, then plunging)* I want to get more clever still. I want to know what is—behind of all them books" (p. 64). He lives alone, ever since his mother died of illness and his father, with his four brothers, died in a mine accident when he was 10. His father had taught him English, and he had taught himself to read. Revived by the spark she sees in him, Miss Moffat opens the school and tutors Morgan privately.

In her efforts to prepare Morgan for what she sees as the first step, an Oxford education, the intellectual task is significant: She wants to provide a compressed background in literature and history while also training him in writing and thinking. Her persistence and his diligence, however, are fully equal to the task, and, for the audience viewing or reading the play, there is never any doubt as to Morgan's ability to learn what he needs to know.

Miss Moffat, moreover, clearly has the versatility to cope also with such practical difficulties as arranging for the Squire to sponsor Morgan's application for a scholarship to Trinity College. When the Squire balks, she begins by stating, with serenely confident emphasis, that the boy is worth every investment.

Miss Moffat: This boy—is quite out of the ordinary.

Squire: Sure?

Miss Moffat: As sure as one of your miners would be, cutting through coal and striking a diamond without a flaw. He was born with very exceptional gifts. They must be—they ought to be given every chance."

Squire: You mean he might turn into a literary bloke?

Miss Moffat: He might, yes.

Squire: I'm blowed! How d'ye know?

Miss Moffat: By his work. It's very good.

Squire: How d'ye know it's good?

Miss Moffat: How does one know Shakespeare's good? (pp. 103–104)

She goes on to play to the Squire's prejudices, flattering him and exaggerating her helplessness ("like a true woman I have to scream for help to a man"), and secures his support for Morgan's application. The toughest obstacle to the development of Morgan's gifts, however, is not the difficulty of classical literature or history, nor is it the impediment of Morgan's late educational start or the Welsh-British conflict. The only real threat Morgan encounters, once he has begun his education with Miss Moffat, comes from himself. By nature impudent and independent, he resents, over the years, Miss Moffat's matter-of-fact approach to him and his studies (an impersonality that masks her fierce ambition and genuine concern), her failure to understand that his education has distanced him from his community and friends, or even to see him as an adolescent with needs beyond those of a learning machine. His resentment explodes into rebellion, as he reasserts his independence by drinking rum in a pub and using, in speech, a double negative. When he complains that his friends mock the way she calls him "Evans" and treats him as if he were a pet dog, she tells him that she cares immensely about him, that his career has been the mainspring of the school, that she has spent on him two precious, irrecoverable years. She thus establishes her own commitment, but does nothing to show respect or understanding. For those responses, he turns—desperately and irresponsibly—to the flirtatious Bessie Watty, who appears some months later, pregnant, on the morning he is to take the scholarship exam.

Although Miss Moffat prevents a confrontation on the spot, she cannot postpone the news forever. In the final act, after competing in both the exam and the Oxford interview, Morgan has had a vision of the world awaiting him in Oxford:

Since the day I was born, I have been a prisoner behind a stone wall, and now somebody has given me a leg-up to have a look at the other side. . . . They cannot drag me back again, they cannot. They *must* give me a push and send me over!

It would be everything I need, everything! Starling and I spent three hours one night discussin' the law. . . . the words came pouring out of me—all the words that I had learnt and written down and never spoken. I suppose I was talking nonsense, but I was at least holding a conversation! I suddenly realized that I had never done it before—I had never been *able* to do it. *(With a strong Welsh accent)* "How are you, Morgan? Nice day, Mr. Jones! Not bad for the harvest." A vocabulary of twenty words;

all the thoughts that you have given me were being stored awy as if they were always going to be useless—locked up and rotting away—a lot of questions with nobody to answer them, a lot of statements with nobody to contradict them. . . . .

Everything had a meaning, because I was in a new world—my world! (pp. 152-154)

When he learns about the child, however, he wants to claim his responsibilities, although he knows it means being dragged back behind the stone wall. Bessie herself, while eager to have him take the child, makes no pretense of loving him or the baby; her current suitor wants to marry her, but has no interest in the child. Her plan is to marry Morgan so that he will take the baby, and then to leave. Morgan is determined to do this—even after the telegram arrives with the news that he has won the scholarship.

A solution, suggested by Bessie's mother, is accepted by all parties. Miss Moffat adopts the child, and Morgan goes to Oxford. She tells him that, on the day of his rebellion, she made an error. "I turned sorry for myself and taunted you with ingratitude. I was a dolt not to realize that a debt of gratitude is the most humiliating debt of all, and that a little show of affection would have wiped it out. I offer that affection to you, today" (p. 178). To all that she has given him, she now adds understanding and one more contribution: the image of his future achievement. Although she told the Squire she expected him to be a writer, and although his gifts have been most specifically evident in writing, she thinks he may be able to become "a great man of our country. . . . Make that light come in the mine and some day free these children" (p. 180).

As Miss Moffat looks forward to teaching at the school she founded and raising Morgan's child, Morgan—the gifted writer who overcame, with her help, his community, his delayed start, and his own immaturity, goes on to become "a man for a future nation to be proud of" (p. 180).

FERDINAND R. TERTAN

If the future career of Morgan Evans can be seen as the joint triumph of a boy and his teacher, the fate of another gifted adolescent, Ferdinand R. Tertan—banished, at the conclusion of Lionel Trilling's (1979) "Of This Time, of That Place" to psychiatric confinement—can be seen as a kind of tragedy. As was the case with Morgan Evans, Tertan's clear and distinct ability becomes apparent in his response to an assigned composition on a routine topic. Joseph Howe, Tertan's instructor in

Freshman English at Dwight College, exhibits far more internal conflicts, however, than did Miss Moffat; himself a poet whose work has met with mixed response, he is engaged in working through his thoughts and feelings about achievement, independence, and conformity, and Tertan becomes, it appears, one of the casualties of his cowardice. Tertan himself, moreover, is unstable and, in significant ways, out of touch with reality. Who, then, is to blame for Howe's decision to tell his Dean about this problem student, and for the Dean's resolve, after consultation with a physician who "had said the word, given the name," to place the boy "into the proper hands" (pp. 104–105)? The story itself explores a question that Howe used to introduce the English class discussion of Ibsen's *Ghosts:* "The question was, At whose door must the tragedy be laid?" (p. 87).

"Of This Time, of That Place" is most directly the story of Tertan's teacher, who begins and ends the narrative. Dr. Joseph Howe, age 26, published poet, a new instructor in literature at a distinguished university, encounters three related challenges: a negative review of his poetry, a brilliant and highly unusual freshman who offers him admiration and gratitude, a manipulative senior who tries to bully him into accepting unacceptable work. On the first day of the term, he asks his students to write a brief, extemporaneous essay telling him who they are and why they have come to college. The assignment is routine, and so are most of the compositions. The following is typical:

I am Arthur J. Casebeer, Jr. My father is Arthur J. Casebeer and my grandfather was Arthur J. Casebeer before him. My mother is Nina Wimble Casebeer. Both of them are college graduates and my father is in insurance. I was born in St. Louis eighteen years ago and we still make our residence there. (p. 78)

Ferdinand R. Tertan, however, is in no way typical. When he hears the assignment, he feels obligated, for the sake of fairness, say that for him the subject would not be extemporaneous: "Sir, the topic I did not expect but I have given much ratiocination to the subject" (p. 76). His "ratiocination," his originality, and his lack of a sense of proportion become evident when Howe reads the essay:

Who am I? Here, in a mundane, not to say commercialized academe, is asked the question which from time long immemorably out of mind has accreted doubts and thoughts in the psyche of man to pester him as a nuisance. . . . Today as ever, in spite of gloomy prophets of the dismal science (economics) the question is uninvalidated. Out of the starry depths of heaven hurtles this spear of query demanding to be caught on the shield of the mind ere it pierces the skull and the limbs be unstrung.

Materialism, by which is meant the philosophic concept and not the moral idea, provides no aegis against the question which lies beyond the tangible (metaphysics). Existence without alloy is the question presented. Environment and heredity relegated aside, the rags and old clothes of practical life discarded, the name and instrumentality of livelihood do not, as the prophets of the dismal science insist on in this connection, give solution to the interrogation which not from the professor merely but veritably from the cosmos is given. I think, therefore I am (cogito etc.) but who am I? Tertan I am, but what is Tertan? Of this time, of that place, of some parentage, what does it matter? (p. 77)

Nothing in Howe's background has prepared him for responding to this blend of wisdom and absurdity, bombast and eloquence. What is a teacher to do with a student who tries to answer the question "Who are you and why are you here?" as if it really mattered? He is similarly bewildered, later that day, by a negative review, in a prestigious publication, of his recent book of poetry, a review that, without providing specific criticism of his actual work, uses him as the classic example of a modern trend the reviewer wishes to attack. During office hours, a week later, he meets a third challenge, an affable and dishonest senior who intends to "con" him into rewarding incompetence. Theodore Blackburn, vice-president of the Student Council, is too busy with extracurricular activities to do the reading for the course, too incompetent as a writer to conceal his ignorance, and too stupid to see that the instructor cannot be fooled.

In the course of the story, both students refer to the review; Blackburn, who tries to use it as part of a blackmail campaign, is contrasted with the gifted Tertan, himself a putative author, who dismisses the critic with "absolutely certain contempt" (p. 84). Howe, although deeply moved by Tertan's support and affection, turns coward, giving Blackburn an undeserved passing grade (in order, he says, to pass him out of the school), allowing him to be graduated on time and become the first man of his class to be placed in a job. Tertan, too, is to be passed out of the school; as a result of Howe's conversation with the Dean, Tertan is diagnosed as a "classic case," not to be readmitted for his sophomore year. And Howe experiences guilt and relief at his release from contact with, and accountability for, a gifted boy whose strangeness threatened him, perhaps because it betokened a strangeness in himself that, in his craving for acceptance, he refused to admit.

In what way is Tertan strange, and is he, as Howe and the Dean would have it, "mad"? His language and attitude, as evident in his composition, are extravagant and incoherent, and his behavior peculiarly remote. Looking at him, Howe reflects on "the thrice-woven circle of the boy's loneliness," his "majestic jauntiness, superior to all the scene" (p. 115); in the classroom, the other students silently mock him for his disproportionate seriousness, for his excess, for his failure to remember, halfway through the term, that one does not need to rise in order to speak. Meeting with Tertan to discuss assigned work, Howe experiences frustration, puzzlement, and the surprise of admiration. With Tertan, Howe

> had never been able to communicate to Tertan the value of a single criticism or correction of his wild, verbose themes. Their conferences had been frequent and long but had done nothing to reduce to order the splendid confusion of the boy's ideas. Yet, impossible though its expression was, Tertan's incandescent mind could always strike for a moment into some dark corner of thought. (pp. 90–91)

Tertan's immediate, unquestioning dismissal of the negative review, saying that disapproval is "the inevitable fate" of genius, reassures and revives Howe, as does Tertan's bizarre, Baroque, unsolicited letter on his behalf to the Dean, which Howe reads after having told the Dean he suspects Tertan of instability:

> The Paraclete, from a Greek word meaning to stand in place of, but going beyond the primitive idea to mean traditionally the helper, the one who comforts and assists. . . .

> Here is one chosen, in that he chooses himself to stand in the place of another for comfort and consolation. . . . But not in the aspect of the Paraclete only is Dr. Joseph Barker Howe established, for he must be the Paraclete to another aspect of himself, that which is driven and persecuted by the lack of understanding in the world at large, so that he in himself embodies the full history of man's tribulations and, overflowing upon others, notably the present writer, is the ultimate end.
>   This was love. There was no escape from it. Try as Howe might to remember that Tertan was mad and all his emotions invalidated, he could not destroy the effect upon him of his student's stern, affectionate regard. He had betrayed not only a power of mind but a power of love. And however firmly he held before his attention the fact of Tertan's madness, he could do nothing to banish the physical sensation of gratitude he felt. He had never thought of himself as "driven and persecuted" and he did not now. But still he could not make meaningless his sensation of gratitude. The pitiable Tertan sternly pitied him, and comfort came from Tertan's never-to-be-comforted mind. (pp. 99–100)

While deciding what to do about Tertan, Howe had looked into his background and found that he was poor, but not penniless. His father, born in Budapest and trained as engineer in Berlin, had been employed by a local factory, but was employed no longer; mother, a housewife, had trained as a teacher in England. Tertan, who wears shabby clothes (perhaps his father's, perhaps his own) lives with them in one of the small apartments into which once-elegant houses had long ago been divided. This sad glimpse of Tertan's home is the only picture the story offers of a world outside the academy—a world which is, in fact, large enough for a drama of betrayal and shattered opportunities.

The one extended classroom vignette shows Howe leading a discussion of *Ghosts*, fielding the usual student witticisms and solecisms, finally allowing Tertan to show his combination of incoherence and brilliance. To answer the question, "At whose door can the tragedy be laid?" Tertan asks another question, "From the sense of determinism, who can say where the blame lies?" (invoking an inappropriate metaphysical context), then shifts to epistemological skepticism ("Flux of existence produces all things, so that judgment wavers. Beyond the phenomena, what? But phenomena are adumbrated and to them we are limited" p. 89).

When asked to come to the point, he does so, "at once" and "brilliantly."

> "This is the summation of the play," he said and took up his book and read, " 'Your poor father never found any outlet for the overmastering joy of life that was in him. And I brought no holiday into his home, either. Everything seemed to turn upon duty and I am afraid I made your poor father's home unbearable to him, Oswald.' Spoken by Mrs. Alving."
>
> Yes, that was surely the "summation" of the play and Tertan had hit it, as he hit, deviously and eventually, the literary point of almost everything. (p. 90)

But in spite of his awareness of Tertan's gifts, in spite of his gratitude for Tertan's admiration and affection, he finds himself in the Dean's office, seeking the conventional solution to his unconventional student, doing exactly what he thought he must not do.

> He must not release Tertan to authority. . . . One way or another the Dean could answer the question, "What is Tertan?" Yet this was precisely what he feared. He alone could keep alive—not forever but for a somehow important time—the question, "What is Tertan?" He alone could keep it still a question. Some sure instinct told him that he must not surrender the question to a clean official desk in a clear official light to be dealt with, settled and closed.
>
> He heard himself saying, "Is the Dean busy at the moment? I'd like to see him."

But it would always be a landmark of his life that, at the very moment when he was rejecting the official way, he had been, without will or intention, so gladly drawn to it. (p. 94)

Trilling's story does not unequivocally condemn Howe, nor does it suggest what he should have done instead. With a reach that exceeds his grasp, Ferdinand R. Tertan walks alone: bemused, bewildered, and beleaguered. To deal with such a student, is beyond Howe's ability. In resorting to an official solution, to be implemented by someone else, he moves the problem to someone else's desk—as he does not fully believe that the critic who attacks him is wrong until Tertan says so, or as he pushes off on the outside world the problem of the lazy student whose amiability was designed to replace hard work. Tertan's gifts and Tertan's troubles exemplify the issues Howe refuses to confront independently, with Tertan and in his own life. Much of the story is an answer—not just for Tertan, but for Howe himself—to the question Howe asked Tertan on the first day of class: Who are you and why are you here?

BEULAH LILT

If the outcomes for Star, Morgan, and Ferdinand are very different, the beginnings of their stories are similar: In each case, an observer identifies them as gifted and must then decide what to do. For Beulah Lilt in Cynthia Ozick's, *The Cannibal Galaxy* (1983), on the contrary, there is no early identification. The creative ability that makes her an internationally known painter in her twenties astonishes Joseph Brill, principal-founder of the elementary school Beulah attended for eight years.

As was the case with Miss Moffat and Joseph Howe, the educator, rather than the gifted child, is the center of the narrative. Here, however, there is no educational process to follow, no record of an attempt to instruct. Beulah learned nothing at school, and the school learned nothing from her. The teachers at the school did not notice Beulah while she was there, nor do they remember her; Beulah herself, in a television interview, says that she does not recall being educated in the American Mid-West. For Brill, who founded the Edmond Fleg Elementary School in a spirit of love and dedication, his school's failure with Beulah—which he perceives as his personal failure with Beulah—becomes emblematic of the disappointments of his complicated life.

Growing up in a crowded Jewish area of Paris, not far from his father's fish store, he studies astronomy at the Sorbonne, but his incipient career is interrupted by the war. He loses his parents and several of his siblings to the death camps, but is hidden himself in the cellar of a convent (where he spends his days reading the books left behind by a heretical priest), then in a farmer's hayloft. After the war, when he sees he has lost his interest in astronomy, he leaves for the United States, where he founds a school inspired by his reading of the (fictitious) philosopher Edmond Fleg, based on a "Dual Curriculum," a combination of secular and religious studies, the "fusion of scholarly Europe and burnished Jerusalem" (p. 27). When we meet him in his fifties, roughly 30 years into the great experiment, we encounter a man with powerful dreams and wrenching disappointments. Intensely aware of the significance of education, "he felt himself not so much a schoolmaster as a man of almost sacral power. He knew what lay in his hands: the miraculous ascent of lives, the future implicit in the present, the very goodness of humankind" (p. 4). Along with his awareness of his responsibilities, however, is the suspicion that he has succeeded only in achieving the ordinary. "He saw himself in the middle of an ashen America, heading a school of middling reputation (though he pretended it was better than that), beleaguered by middling parents, and their middling offspring" (p. 5). The experience of Beulah Lilt— or, rather, the nonexperience, the fact that she and his cherished school had no impact on each other—confirms his worst fears. As he tells one of his veteran teachers: "The fact is, we grow pygmies here" (p. 153).

For Beulah was the child he ought to have been able to foster, instruct, and enjoy, he who cherishes the extraordinary, whose motto (in an allusion to the career in astronomy he felt compelled to abandon) is "Ad astra." Her paintings, he learns, are acclaimed and endorsed by both the traditionalists and the avant-garde. Seeing them in the Guggenheim, he tries to analyze their distinctive qualities. "You could fancy amazing scenes in them: but when you approached, it was only paint, bleak here, brilliant here, in shapes sometimes nearly stately, sometimes like gyres" (pp. 147–148). The talent that is now evident to him and to all the world was entirely invisible during her years at his school, as she was evaluated negatively by the school psychologist (who recommended that she not be admitted), by each of her teachers, by Brill himself, by everyone with the single exception of her mother.

Her mother, in fact, is the crux of the story. Had Brill not seen Hester Lilt on television, had he not known her to be "an imagistic linguistic logician," had he not bought (if not read) her books *(The World as Appearance, Metaphor and Exegesis, Interpretation as an End in Itself)*, he would never have admitted her charmless and unpromising daughter to his school. He becomes fascinated with Hester Lilt, drawing her into long conversations, going to hear her lecture, trying to see her extraordinary mind in the child who appears extraordinary only in her blank dullness and impassivity. When Hester, rejecting his pity for Beulah's limitations and his apologies for failing to teach her child, tells him that Beulah is an original whose gifts he cannot recognize, he sees Hester as bizarrely deluded.

Apart from the mother, the testimony appears to be unanimous. The admission report by Dr. Glypost, the school psychologist, reads as follows:

> Beulah is a tense, anxious child, constricted in her approach to tasks, lacking in spontaneity, withdrawn in her relationships to others. Although she is right-handed, she is not well-integrated and she did not use the testing time in an efficient or assured manner. There is a rigidity about her and a weakness in adaptability. She sat through the entire testing period without smiling once. She was slow, like a sleepwalker. She had dead eyes. Shown a Rorschach card expressing ominous darkness, she responded with Storm Cloud. The popular response among children of her age is Bird or Bat. Non-achiever, not recommended for Dual Curriculum. (p. 46)
>
> Her first-grade teacher is similarly unenthusiastic, consigning her to the "slow beginners," saying that she is "hopeless. A deaf-mute. She doesn't talk. She never volunteers."
> "You don't need a crystal ball to know about this one. Nothing much there, nothing much to come," Mrs. Bloomfield said.
> "Could you try harder," he intoned. "Because of the mother."
> "It's not the mother who's in my first grade. . . . Principal Brill, you want a silk purse out of the wrong animal's ear." (pp. 57–58)

Six and seven years later, when she arrives in the upper grades, the teachers are different, but no more inspiring:

> Gorchak and Seelenhohl ministered only to the upper school—they taught the seventh and eighth grades—and Beulah was now in their hands: in the hands of Gorchak, who wanted only right answers exactly memorized; in the hands of Seelenhohl, who wanted no answers at all, only tactics and guesswork. (p. 77)

And no more insightful:

> On Beulah Lilt's report card Seelenhohl wrote: "Beulah is a quiet child who should try harder." Gorchak wrote coldly: "Beulah looks out of the window too much. Therefore you must expect her to remain in the lowest quarter of the class." (p. 80)

As we read the novel, we do not know—any more than Brill knew at the time—that Beulah will be revealed as creatively gifted. The environment of the school, however, along with the description of the conventional parents, teachers, and students hint at the possibility that the mother is likely to be right about her daughter. Consider, too, ironic passages like this one:

> Beulah was an undistinguished child, and worse; it was as if she suffered from an unremitting bewilderment. She sat like a deaf-mute. When the others ran she stood stiffly at the periphery. The teachers thought her dull. And meanwhile there were all the lively ones—how many answers they had, what wit, what a blaze of child-acuity the lively bright ones flaunted! (p. 74)

Hester Lilt, in a lecture that Brill attends without taking to heart its immediate relevance, speaks of the pedagogical error of judging from the first evidence rather than the last. If one stops too soon, she says, one "takes aggressiveness for intelligence, and thoughtfulness for stupidity, and diffidence for dimness, and arrogance for popularity, and dreamers for blockheads, and brazenness for the mark of a lively personaliity" (p. 68).

If his blindness to Beulah's creative ability is a crime deserving punishment, one could say that, in every possible respect, Joseph Brill is punished. Even after Beulah becomes famous, the teachers continue to value the bright ones, the clever ones, the acute ones. (One of Beulah's fellow classmates returns to the school as a teacher, and is considered a "jewel.") Brill marries late, to a quick and clever woman; his son Naphtali is bright, successful, curious, and alert—but not extraordinary. Gently pressured to retire, Brill is succeeded by one of his popular teachers, who changes the school's name to Lakeside Day School. Brill and his wife move to Florida, where Naphtali attends Miami University and plans a business career. On television, in the press, in the galleries, he is perpetually confronted by the life and work of Beulah Lilt.

> He understood she was acclaimed. He understood more: the forms, the colors, the glow, the defined darkness, above all the forms of things—all these were thought to be a kind of language. (p. 156)

She is, as her mother had said she was, an original. Her mother had in fact used Beulah herself as the source of her philosophical ideas, contemplating, for example, Beulah's silence and writing a treatise *On Structure in Silence*. And what Hester Lilt had told Joseph Brill was in fact correct: "It doesn't matter whether you do anything for her or you don't. . . . Nothing like that matters" (p. 100). Joseph Brill's harvest is bitter: He is disappointed by the school he founded, his teachers, his students, even (and secretly) his son. And Beulah Lilt, whom he had seen as a "little crippled creature," becomes distinguished. "She spoke. The world took her for an astonishment. She was the daughter of her mother" (p. 156). Brill, the would-be teacher and founder of a school, is forgotten. Although he need not reproach himself for the cowardice showed by Joseph Howe with Tertan, he has not managed to matter in the life of the gifted child who was placed in his charge. And if irrelevance is not actually a sin, it is surely no great honor either.

SHEVEK OF ANARRES

Shevek, the protagonist of Ursula K. Le Guin's *The Dispossessed* (1975), is different from Star, Morgan, Tertan, and Beulah in two important ways. The first and most obvious is that his universe, although a variation on our own, is not the same as ours. Shevek, a brilliant physicist, lives on Anarres, a socialist community situated on Earth's barren moon and populated by the descendants of the followers of Odo, an Emma Goldman figure who was imprisoned on Urras (Earth) and died there; his goal, as the novel begins, is to reunite Urras and Anarres by making a free gift of his new discovery, the Theory of Simultaneity, which will remove the time lag that accompanies space travel. Shevek, moreover, differs from Star and the others in another way: We see him, for much of the novel, as a full adult, a functioning professional, a husband and twice a father. We are, however, given poignant glimpses of his early years as a gifted child, of his life at home, in school, in the community. These images of the beginnings of a creative physicist who was ultimately to solve the toughest and subtlest problems of time and space entitle Shevek to a place in our gallery of gifted children.

On Anarres, a planet struggling with its scarcity of resources, all comrades, parents included, are posted where they are needed; although "partners" can try to stay together, particularly if both are raising the child together, this is not always possible. When Shevek's mother Rulag is posted to another city, she leaves him with his father Palat. Although Palat brings Shevek "home" fairly frequently for "dom visits," the child spends much of his time in the communal nursery, where the teachers endeavor to inculcate the communal attitudes on which the society is based. (The Anarresti language, in fact, includes no possessive pronouns.) From the start, without trying to be a trouble-maker, Shevek is different. We see him as a knobby baby, sitting in a square of sunlight, pushing away a baby who tries to sit near him, screaming "Mine sun!" and sobbing when he is told that nothing is his, that he cannot use it if he will not share it (p. 22).

As an 8-year-old, meeting with his Speaking-and-Listening group at the learning center, he reinvents Zeno's Paradox, tries to share his discovery with the group, and learns that this sort of sharing is seen as "egoizing" (hence, illegitimate). The incident unfolds as follows:

> "To get from you to the tree, the rock has to be halfway in between you and the tree, doesn't it. And then it has to be halfway between halfway and the tree. And then it has to be halfway between *that* and the tree. It doesn't matter how far it's gone, there's always a place, only it's a time really, that's halfway between the last place it was and the tree—"
>
> "Do you think this is interesting?" the director interrupted, speaking to the other children.
>
> "*Why* can't it reach the tree?" said a girl of ten.
>
> "Because it always has to go half of the way that's left to go," said Shevek, "and there's always half of the way left to go—see?"
>
> "Shall we just say you aimed the rock badly?" the director said with a tight smile.
>
> "It doesn't matter how you aim it. It *can't reach the tree.*"
>
> "Who told you this idea?"
>
> "Nobody. I sort of saw it. I think I see how the rock actually does—"
>
> "That's enough. . . . Speech is sharing—a cooperative art. You're not sharing, merely egoizing. . . . This kind of thing is really directly contrary to what we're after in a Speaking-and-Listening group. Speech is a two-way function. Shevek isn't ready to understand that yet, as most of you are, and so his presence is disruptive to the group. You feel that yourself, don't you, Shevek? I'd suggest that you find another group working on your level." (pp. 23–24)

A society based on identification with the group tries to bring the solitary genius into the fold, preferably by making autonomy unpleasant, shameful, and difficult. With Shevek, they are only partially successful. But although Shevek never apologizes for his independence, never wishes to be other than he is, he does not find his life on Anarres easy.

> Since he was very young he had known that in certain ways he was unlike anyone else he knew. For a child the consciousness of such difference is very painful since, having done nothing yet and being incapable of doing anything, he cannot justify it. The reliable and affectionate presence of adults who are also, in their own way, different, is the only reassurance such a child can have; and Shevek had not had it. His father had indeed been utterly reliable and affectionate. Whatever Shevek was and whatever

he did, Palat approved and was loyal. But Palat had not had this curse of difference. He was like the others, like all the others to whom community came so easy. He loved Shevek, but he could not show him what freedom is, that recognition of each person's solitude which alone transcends it. (p. 86)

As he grows older, Shevek is fortunate in having several close friends, similar to him in their independence. One is Tirin, a dissident playwright, who is later crushed and cowed by the society's pressure. Another is Takver, a creative biologist, who becomes his partner and the mother of his daughters. For the development of his creative gifts, however, the most important people are Mitis and Gvarab, two physics teachers.

In late adolescence, he meets Mitis at the Regional Institute, where she is the senior physicist, age 55. She wins his immediate respect:

There was always a kind of psychological clear space around Mitis, like the lack of crowds around the peak of a mountain. The absence of all enhancements and enforcements of authority left the real thing plain. There are people of inherent authority; some emperors actually have new clothes. (p. 45)

She teaches him what she can, and she has the wisdom to know when he needs instruction she cannot provide. Go to Abbenay, she says— center of research in Anarres. "For the books, and for the minds you'll meet there. You will not waste that mind in a desert!" (p. 46). She also warns him to beware of Sabul, the chief physicist there. (Her warning proves apt: Sabul later tries to appropriate and stifle Shevek's work.) Having given Shevek intellectual training and practical advice, Mitis leaves him, as Miss Moffat left Morgan Evans, with a prediction, and a push. "There's work for you to do. Do it!"

In Abbenay, he meets Gvarab, with an even greater mind than Mitis's.

Mitis, though a splendid teacher, had never been able to follow him into the new areas of theory that he had, with her encouragement, begun to explore. Gvarab was the only person he had met whose training and ability were comparable to his own. (p. 58)

For Gvarab, at the end of her productive life, Shevek is her last and greatest student, the one she has always awaited.

Gvarab . . . soon picked out the thin boy with big ears as her one constant auditor. She began to lecture for him. The light, steady, intelligent eyes met hers, steadied her, woke her, she flashed to brilliance, regained the vision lost. She soared, and the other students in the room looked up confused or started, even scared if they had the wits to be scared. Gvarab saw a much larger universe than most people are capable of seeing, and it made them blink. The light-eyed boy watched her steadily. In his face she saw her joy. What she offered, what she had offered for a whole lifetime, what no one had ever shared with her, he took, he shared. He was her brother, across the gulf of fifty years, and her redemption. (pp. 87–88)

With her training and his own moral and intellectual qualities, Shevek becomes, at Abbenay, the adult who is to create the "ansible," a device, based on the Theory of Simultaneity, "that will permit communication without any time interval between two points in space," a telephone that can be used "to talk between worlds, without the long waiting for the message to go and the return to reply that electromagnetic impulses require" (p. 276). His invention, to be sure, has a certain irony: The man who felt aloof and apart even from his Anarresti comrades has created a device that links and binds, that annihilates interplanetary distance. The boy who could not quite handle a Speaking-and-Listening group now makes possible communication between worlds.

The plot of *The Dispossessed,* which traces Shevek's attempt to bring Urras and Anarres together by offering as a gift his communication device, takes the novel beyond the present focus on the gifted child. Two passages from his adult life, however, are in fact relevant to our interests. The first and most dramatic is a description of the Eureka experience, of the theoretical discovery that ultimately led to the ansible.

The fundamental unity of the Sequence and Simultaneity points of view became plain; the concept of interval served to connect the static and dynamic aspect of the universe. How could he have stared at reality for ten years and not seen it? There would be no trouble at all in going on. Indeed he had already gone on. He was there. He saw all that was to come in this first, seemingly casual glimpse of the method, given him by his understanding of a failure in the distant past. The wall was down. The vision was both clear and whole. What he was was simple, simpler than anything else. It was simplicity: and contained in it all complexity, all promise. It was relevation. It was the way clear, the way home, the light.
The spirit in him was like a child running out into the sunlight. There was no end, no end. . . . (p. 225)

The reader responds not only to the evocation of the joy of creative discovery, but to the subtle reference to the baby Shevek, sitting in a square of sunlight and proclaiming his ownership of "Mine sun!"

Another significant passage in Shevek's adult life is the experience, on Urras (Earth), of meeting his intellectual peers:

With immense pleasure, and with that same sense of profound recognition, of finding something the way it was meant to be, Shevek discovered for the first time in his life the conversation of his equals. . . . It was a revelation, a liberation. . . . . they came to him, or he went to them, and they talked, and new worlds were born of their talking. It is of the nature of idea to be communicated: written, spoken, done. The idea is like grass. It craves light, likes crowds, thrives on crossbreeding, grows better for being stepped on. (pp. 57–58)

We recall Morgan Evans at Oxford, talking through the night with another scholarship candidate, and feeling that at last he is out of prison, over the stone wall, in his own world. From Zeno's Paradox to the communication ansible, from possessiveness toward a patch of sunlight to genius in theoretical and practical physics, *The Dispossessed* portrays the growth of a creative child into a creative adult.

BETH HARMON

Imagine a world without Bobby Fischer, whose triumph over Boris Spassky in the summer of 1972 made chess, for the first time, front-page news. What if the first serious American contender for the world chess championship had been not Bobby Fischer, but an adolescent girl? The growth and victory of Beth Harmon, protagonist of Walter Tevis's *The Queen's Gambit* (1983), dramatizes the triumph of a specific intellectual ability—abstract thought and logical problem-solving in a single area—over highly adverse circumstances. The novel traces her story—with emphasis on her aptitude, training, and motivation for the thinking and stamina chess requires—from her difficult beginnings to the day the reigning champion resigns a game by handing her his king.

When Beth is eight, several years after her father's death, her mother dies in a car crash, and she spends the next four years in the Methuen Home, an orphanage in Mount Sterling, Kentucky, where the children are given demerits for assorted misdeeds (with a leather-strap beating as the penalty for 10 demerits). Growing up awkward, unhappy, and lonely (with only one friend, the rebellious Jolene), Beth is sent to the basement one day to clean the erasers, and there she sees the custodian, Mr. Shaibel, scowling over a chessboard.

Immediately she becomes interested in the game, and demands to watch. "Something about this man and the steadiness with which he played his mysterious game helped her to hold tightly to what she wanted" (p. 14). She learns some of the moves from watching him, and asks him to teach her the rest. They play during the hours she is supposed to be in class, at chapel, at lunch. After a few months, she beats him and his friend, the high school chess coach. Invited to the high school to participate in a simultaneous, blind match, she beats all 12 players.

At this point, however, she encounters a severe setback. When the school is forced to suspend the use of tranquilizers, Beth remains addicted, and cannot sleep without them. When she is caught breaking into the school office to steal pills, no one is interested in her reason (that she can't sleep without them) or her accusation (that they shouldn't have given the drugs to her in the first place). Her punishments include suspension of library and playground privileges, longer attendance at chapel, and no more chess. Several years pass, during which she plays mental chess and works through the games in *Modern Chess Openings,* the chess Bible, a book Mr. Shaibel had given her.

At 12, she escapes the orphanage, adopted by a fluttery, kind-hearted, impractical woman and her grim, distant husband (who soon deserts them both), and takes steps to advance her chess career. She remains hampered by her years at the orphanage, by the errors she learned there. Still addicted to pills, she uses her mother's prescription to acquire a supply. Still willing to steal to get what she wants, she shoplifts a copy of *Chess Review* to learn about tournaments and takes money from a schoolmate's locker to be able to join the Chess Federation. She also retains the persistence that spurred her to play mental chess when she was forbidden the chess board, as well as the brilliance that allowed her to do so. She wins her first tournament, and does so in a way that will maximize her rating. Asking to be placed not in the Beginners Division, but in the Open, she advances undefeated through stronger and stronger players. After the first win, a local contest, she informs her mother, Mrs. Wheatley, who had not before taken Beth's chess seriously. Impressed by the prize, she encourages Beth to enter more tournaments, each time turning a profit that Mrs. Wheatley carefully figures, deducting a commission for herself. Over the next three years, she continues to win prize money, and she is truly launched.

From this point on, the course of her achievement and failures can be clearly charted as a struggle between her genius and her residual internal demons. The difference between international victory and total collapse depends entirely on Beth's capacity to take charge of her mind, body, and opportunities. At 16, she is devastated by her first defeats. Losing a game in the U.S. Open to Benny Watts, the American champion, she becomes only Co-Champion, and this seems almost worse than losing. During her first international tournament in Mexico, she does well for most of the tournament, then loses to Borgov, the world champion, and returns to the hotel room to find Mrs. Wheatley dead.

Back in Kentucky, in her mother's home, she is at first immersed in chess, working with a trainer, reading chess books, playing games, preparing to meet Borgov again. When her trainer leaves, however, she resorts to pills and alcohol—the legacy of the orphanage, and her habitual response to stress. She continues to brood about Benny Watts and Borgov.

At the next U.S. Open, however, she defeats Benny, who serves as her coach for her next encounter with Borgov, scheduled for Paris. She arrives there confident in her improved analytical skills, prepared to play her best chess against Borgov—and again loses to him, in a defeat that overwhelms her and sends her back to the tranquilizers. For a chess player of her caliber, second place is worse than none, and her repeated loss to Borgov threatens to the core her self-confidence and ability to perform even the simplest tasks. Although she is the U.S. Champion, she loses a game in the Kentucky state championship and drops out of the tournament. Even then, she continues to drink, and worries that she may be permanently blunting her gift.

The route to her triumph in her third confrontation with Borgov begins when she seeks out Jolene, her friend from the orphanage, who helps her recover from alcoholism and chemical dependence. She also exorcises the ghost of the past, returning for the first time to the orphanage for Mr. Shaibel's funeral, and seeing his basement room covered with clippings of her victories. Winning the necessary tournament in San Francisco, she goes on to Moscow. Well prepared and strong, she wins all her games, some with more ease than others, and finally meets Borgov. She realizes that she is afraid of him, but also knows that she can make her fear irrelevant; their game is adjourned for the evening, and her confidence remains high. In the interview she gives during the adjournment, she tells the press that she learned the game from Mr. William Shaibel, the custodian (her first attempt in years to talk about him publicly). Benny Watts, her trainer and former rival, calls from New York with advice and support. The next day, Borgov offers a draw, and she refuses. She wants to win, and knows that winning is within her power.

> She did not open her eyes even to see the time remaining on her clock or to look across the table at Borgov or to see the enormous crowd who had come to this auditorium to watch her play. She let all of that go from her mind and allowed herself only the chessboard of her imagination with its intricate deadlock. It did not really matter who was playing the black pieces or whether the material board sat in Moscow or New York or the basement of an orphanage; this eidetic image was her proper domain. (p. 298)

Concentrating on the board rather than her fear, she sees a sequence that will lead to mate in nineteen. After a few moves, Borgov resigns, and embraces her warmly.

The novel offers the thrills of suspense and the satisfaction of victory, without concealing the shadows of the drugs and doubts that jeopardized Beth's success. For those interested in Beth as a gifted child endowed with a specific intellectual ability, there are—along with the observations that have emerged from the narrative of her ability to marshal her emotional and intellectual resources to solve her emotional and intellectual problems—two significant features of interest: Beth's motivations and her deep satisfactions.

Beth's special talent, first of all, is seen to provide self-esteem, a positive self-image, for a child who very much needed one.

> Abruptly she saw herself as a small unimportant person—a plain, brown-haired orphan girl in dull institutional clothes. She was half the size of these easy insolent students with their loud voices and bright sweaters. She felt powerless and silly. But then she looked at the boards again, with the pieces set in the familiar pattern, and the unpleasant feeling lessened. She might be out of place in this public high school, but she was not out of place with those twelve chessboards. (p. 42)

She wants, however, not recognition as such, but recognition on her own terms. She has only scorn for the interview in *Life* that makes her a temporary celebrity in her public high school (where the cashmere-sweater girls, for the first and last time, invite her to one of their boring parties).

> "It talks about the orphanage. And it gives one of my games. But it's mostly about my being a girl."
> "Well, you are one."
> "It shouldn't be that important," Beth said. "They didn't print half the things I told them. They didn't tell about Mr. Shaibel. They didn't say anything about how I play the Sicilian."
> "But, Beth," Mrs. Wheatley said, "it makes you a *celebrity!*"
> Beth looked at her thoughtfully. "For being a girl, mostly," she said. (p. 122)

Beth's chess-playing, moreover, is not only an act of self-affirmation, a means to the end of self-respect, but also—moment by moment—a source of deep joy. From her earliest games to her victory over Borgov, chess is for Beth the fullest use of her powers. In evoking Beth's mind at work, Tevis conveys the concentration and ecstasy of a profoundly gifted child.

Consider the description of her first public victory, her triumph over 12 players in a simultaneous exhibition at the high school:

> Her mind was luminous, and her soul sang to her in the sweet moves of chess. The classroom smelled of chalk dust and her shoes squeaked as she moved down the rows of players. The room was silent; she felt her own presence centered in it, small and solid and in command. Outside, birds sang, but she did not hear them. Inside, some of the students stared at her. Boys came in from the hallway and lined up along the back wall to watch the homely girl from the orphanage at the edge of town who moved from player to player with the determined energy of a Caesar in the field, a Pavlova under the lights. There were about a dozen people watching. Some smirked and yawned, but others could feel the energy in the room, the presence of something that had never in the long history of this tired old schoolroom, been felt there before.
>
> What she did was at bottom shockingly trivial, but the energy of her amazing mind crackled in the room for those who knew how to listen. Her chess moves blazed with it. By the end of an hour and a half, she had beaten them all without a single false or wasted move. (p. 43)

Perhaps even more powerful, however, is the description of her private victory, her discovery, at 13, of an error in a published game. She walks down a street, thinking. And she knows. Oblivious to distractions, she works through a game played by Paul Morphy, "perhaps the most brilliant player in the history of the game."

> *There it was.* One of the little boys across the street began crying. *There was nothing Black could do.* The game would be over in twenty-nine moves at least. The way it was in the book, it had taken Paul Morphy thirty-six moves to win. He hadn't seen the move with the rook. *But she had.*
>
> Overhead the sun shone in a blank blue sky. The dog continued barking. The child wailed. Beth walked slowly home and replayed the game. Her mind was as lucid as a perfect, stunning diamond. (p. 74)

Like the Welsh miner and the Anarresti physicist, Beth Harmon faces a future that—although endangered by difficult circumstances and a hostile community—has been made possible by tenacity, teachers, autonomy, and gifts that bring them intense happiness as well as tangible achievement.

BARRY RUDD

Barry Rudd, the adolescent protagonist of John Hersey's *The Child Buyer* (1961), is the target of Wissey Jones, an officer of United

Lymphomilloid. His company has a long-term, secret contract to change gifted children—through conditioning and sensory deprivation—into thinking machines endowed with vastly increased intellectual powers, but utterly lacking in individual memories or identities. To that end, Jones, the child buyer, has come to the small, smug New England town of Pequot to locate the brightest child and, through bribery and other persuasions, to secure the consent of everyone who has a stake in the child, including Barry himself.

The novel, which unfolds through the transcript of the hearings of the State Senate Standing Committee on Education, Welfare, and Public Morality, moves toward a conclusion that is made to seem inevitable: all the participants—from the parents to his mentor to the boy—agree that Barry should be surrendered to the five-part plan. The child buyer's program, designed to make the most of the purchased "specimens," begins with a Forgetting Chamber that obliterates personal identity and conditions the "specimen" to worship "U Lympho." The next stages include high-level training in problem solving, data feeding through machine, surgical removal of all senses except touch, and, finally, full-time work. In the closing paragraph of the novel, the boy asks a question, perhaps the last question he, as Barry Rudd, will ever ask:

> I was wondering about that this morning. About forgetting. I've always had an idea that each memory was a kind of picture, an insubstantial picture. I've thought of it as suddenly coming into your mind when you need it, something you've seen, something you've heard, then it may stay awhile, or else it flies out, then maybe it comes back another time. I was wondering about the Forgetting Chamber. If all the pictures went out, if I forgot everything, where would they go? Just out into the air? Into the sky? Back home, around my bed where my dreams stay? (p. 229)

From the perspective of the present chapter, *The Child Buyer* offers many features of interest. If *The Dispossessed* gave us the longest time span, if *The Queen's Gambit* provided the most intense analysis of the child's achievement, Hersey's novel supplies the fullest picture of the various environments in which the gifted child lives. We see, for example, his home: a tarpaper apartment, dirty and in disrepair. We meet his mother, once an excellent student planning a career as a surgeon, who sees education as a victory over coarseness, and wants her son to fulfill her abandoned dreams. And we meet his father, a machinist, who tried and failed to make Barry a "regular boy," who is eager to sell him. We see the town of Pequot, suspicious of difference and hostile to intelligence. Mrs. Rudd remembers the day a neighbor saw 4-year-old Barry reading a book:

I looked at Martha's face, and there was a look of horror, as if the monster Godzilla had come up at her out of the Bay of Tokyo, and she said "Holy God, look at little Einstein!" and she coughed and had a hard time breathing, like she had asthma. (p. 81)

This attitude—the gifted as Godzilla—explains why the school superintendent, Mr. Owing, explained at first to the child buyer that the school made no special provisions for gifted children:

I'm afraid of anything too special for these clever children. I'm afraid of it for our community. We don't like anything that smacks of privilege. But don't worry, we'll reach these children. We'll take care of them without enrichment. (p. 21)

The school environment, in the course of the novel, comes in for considerable implicit criticism. One of his teachers is known to mutter that bright kids just aren't normal. The State Supervisor for Exceptional Children—who deals with the retarded, the handicapped, and "a smattering of the gifted, many of whom are emotionally disturbed" (p. 119)— believes that her reading (or misreading) of Pavlov, Thorndyke, Guthrie, and Skinner has qualified her to speak on "maladjustment in deviates at the upper end of the scale"—in a lecture that is disrupted by a mysterious stink bomb.

The school environment, however, also has significant positive aspects, notably a dedicated teacher, who champions Barry and cooperates with his plans for classroom innovation, and a remarkable principal, herself ambitious, intelligent, and energetic, who serves as his mentor. The testimony of Charity Perrin, the teacher, is one of the most delightful episodes in this grim novel. Old-fashioned, enthusiastic, and straightforward, Miss Perrin had denounced, as a fraud, a "talent search" arranged by the guidance counselor, in which talent was measured by familiarity with the children's world of television, sports, toys, and gadgets. Having spent a lifetime with children and a year with Barry, she knows how to evaluate and enjoy his unique gifts. She recalls his developing an interest in geology:

Since then we've had a geology museum full of quartzes and micas and schists, and a tank of guppies—they carry their eggs within and seem to give birth as mammals do, pushing out these tiny folded-up babies; the children loved that—and a bench of cacti, and a display of bugs and beetles with their scientific names, and pressed leaves, and a word-game bank, and—(p. 60)

When asked if she provides enrichment for Barry, she replies:

Oh, yes, with a boy like that you have to. For example, the other day the health officer was coming to the school, and I sent Barry down to the office to straighten out the dentistry record before the health man came, and Barry did a good job, these cards had to be arranged in alphabetical order, a better job than us grownups would do, orderly and neat and accurate, and I asked him afterwards if he'd want to be a doctor or dentist, but no; he was definite about that. (p. 61)

She goes on to discuss Barry's Humor Nook, a failed experiment, and the Word Market that replaced it:

The thing is, last summer Barry's mother thought he was too serious, and Barry, he adores his mother, and he sensed she thought he should be more humorous. So he went in the humor business. He got these anthologies of wit, these Bennett Cerf books, and joke, joke, joke! . . . the first you know we had a Humor Nook on popular demand. It got too much, and I realized I was going to have to stop it. The last thing to do with a joke is put it on display. . . . So we agreed to dismantle the Humor Nook, and in its place we were going to set up a Word Market . . . Barry and his friends have been swapping long words lately, like stamps. . . . It's uncanny the way Barry can decipher these marathon words.

One sees that Miss Perrin, although not herself as gifted as Barry, can be effective as his teacher: With good will and encouragement, she offers him room to grow on his own and to be a classroom leader.

He was fortunate, too, in his close relationship with Dr. Frederika Gozar, an ambitious and creative woman with several doctorates and many interests. One morning at five, he suddenly appeared in the high school biology lab to watch her pursue her research on termites.

Anyway, he was just there, and he said, 'Mind if I watch, Dr. Gozar?' He came the next morning, and he had a piece of paper with a list of questions he wanted to ask me. Mind you, the child was only eight—fourth grade. He's been coming ever since. (p. 54)

Her inspiration has been crucial to him, as the child buyer immediately inferred:

It was evident to me, after some time in the class, that the boy had met and fallen under the influence of a first-class mind, which had dealt with him as if he were an adult. His fantastic inner powers are leashed, disciplined. I felt from the way he opened up each thought and even each rote memory for use that he was always reorganizing, that he has at base one of those minds that can never be satisfied with things as they are.

That's the kind we want at United Lymphomilloid. Of course the topnotch
mind that had influenced this specimen belonged to Dr. Gozar . . . (p.
105)

Dr. Gozar shows insightful understanding of Barry:

Why is he outstanding? Because he has this mood of intensity. That you
don't teach. You don't say, "Flex. Tighten your mind. Have desire." Barry
makes this mood about science more than any child I've ever seen. He
creates a certain tension out of nothing—a sense of excitement. That
comes from within. (p. 25)

Her contribution to his development, moreover, goes beyond her stimulation of his mind; she has served, he says, as his model of concentration
and persistence:

I've seen her marked willingness to stay at a task, to withstand discomfort,
go without food, disregard fatigue and strain, forget a cold or a headache—
above all, to face the possibility of failure, and facing that chance seems
to me to be the first prerequisite of success, or completion. (p. 90)

Of all the people who "sell" Barry out to the child buyer, Dr. Gozar
is the one who most surprises us. Having seen her admiration for
Barry's mind and her personal affection for him—she, it turns out, is
responsible for the stink bomb during the lecture on brilliant deviants—
we do not expect her to capitulate. In her case, the "bribe" is her belief
that Barry will withstand the conditioning, that he will prove the futility
of the U-Lympho program, that his inner strength will enable him to
resist. No matter what Forgetting Chamber he enters, he will never
forget.

The novel, however, does not endorse her optimism, nor does Barry
himself expect to escape the fate of the other specimens. Why does
Barry choose to yield? Because, he says, such an existence will at least
be interesting. And we see—even as we are aware of the naivete of a
child who does not realize that surrendering his identity will make the
question of "interest" irrelevant—that the desire to make life interesting,
to find the interest in his life, has inspired this gifted child as long as
he can remember.

The most striking passages of the novel, in fact, come from reports,
by Barry and others, of what it means to be this extraordinary child.
His testimony reveals a reflective boy, with a sharp and informed eye,
moderate sensitivity about his plumpness and clumsiness, a taste for
the absurd (in himself and in others), a curiosity about the unusual.
He muses on four-dimensional tick-tack-toe, on anomalies in spelling

and punctuation, on the name for the monstrous sea creature in *20,000 Leagues under the Sea* (the movie version, the Viewmaster slide, the French novel, and the English translation), on Linnaean classification, on mathematical shortcuts, on family patterns of greatness (the Adamses, the Roosevelts, the Bachs) and examples of isolated greatness (Lincoln and Carlyle). When someone mentions George Washington, Barry begins to think about Washington's young contemporaries: Bach, Bering, Chien Lung, Voltaire, Watt. He enjoys monitoring his own thinking, his progress from rambling through inspiration to the productive labor of consolidating, verifying, and elaborating. He enjoys, too, putting his ideas to practical use; he is proud of the Rube Goldberg device he has invented for turning his light on and off.

Yet he thinks, too, about his physical awkwardness, and wishes he were as adept as his sister or classmates, whose grace he views with admiration and without resentment. Barry is also a boy, with a child's desire to have fun, to have friends (one of his recruits is a near-illiterate, a near-delinquent, who shares his sense of adventure), and to exist not only as a learning machine. He has, moreover, a keen sense of humor.

> He was using an opaque projector, and at one point, being clumsy, he got his thumb caught in the reflector and it showed on the screen. In a pompous network voice he said: "One moment, please. The picture will be off the air for a few seconds because of technical difficulties. The audio portion of the program will continue. . . ." (p. 105)

Our strongest impression of Barry Rudd, however, is of a boy who pursues knowledge and wisdom with passionate persistence, and whose life would have continued to offer him many rewards.

> But I'll tell you something: no matter how awkward I may be at stickball or volleyball, no matter how much I'm the butt of the beefers on the playground—and no matter how jaggedly I write, nevertheless when I get in the lab, next to Dr. Gozar, and we're sorting Promethea, Cecropia, and Polyphemus moth larvae, or we're mounting beetles or bugs on pins, I can feel an unusual grace flowing into my fingers, like an electric current. I'm transformed. (pp. 90–91)

At the conclusion of the novel, deserted by the adults who might have advised him, misled by his false perception of the U-Lympho program as an attractive alternative to his individual future, he is to be transformed in a very different sense. And this—like the tragic resolution awaiting Ferdinand Tertan—is a tragedy.

EMMA "EMANCIPATION" SHERIDAN

The cover of Louise Fitzhugh's novel *Nobody's Family Is Going to Change* (1976) shows, in the background, a small, slender boy, gracefully tap-dancing in his tennis shoes on a city stairway; in the foreground, a plump girl, somewhat older, with an untidy Afro, grins as she clutches a thick, red book. Although the Broadway version of the novel, entitled *The Tap Dance Kid* features 7-year-old Willie, who longs to be a professional dancer, the novel itself emphasizes the ambitions, struggles, and victories—external and internal—of Emma Sheridan, a bright 11-year-old who plans, after setting a record for the youngest person ever to pass the bar exam, to practice law under the name "Emancipation Sheridan." She has, moreover, the high-level skills in language and logic that she will need to achieve her goals.

Emma encounters numerous obstacles: the strong opposition of her father (without overt justification, but based, apparently, on a deep-seated fear that she might be a better lawyer than he), the mild opposition of her mother (based primarily on lack of empathy and the wish for tranquility in family relations), and her own self-disgust (of which her overeating seems to be more a symptom than a cause). She resents and torments her brother, who has what she lacks: attractiveness, grace, and her father's respect and affection.

Willie too encounters obstacles. Although he has the practical aid of his maternal uncle Dipsey, a professional dancer, and the support of his mother, who tries to persuade her husband to let Willie accept a role in summer stock (after an audition secretly arranged by Dipsey, at Willie's strong urging), his father thinks stage life is trash, especially for a black person in contemporary America, and wants him to be a lawyer instead. At home, too, he feels threatened by the niggling per-secutions of his sister, who seems to hate him without knowing why.

An additional element of the plot is the Children's Army, an un-derground organization (of the children, by the children, for the children) that supplies Emma with a kind of community. The Army is a voluntary association of interested children, led by an adolescent boy of evident political ambitions and skills (who founded it five years ago, when he was 11), divided for convenience into brigades (Emma's is the Anne Frank Brigade), and based on the principle that children come first. As the army's registrar tells Emma: "We believe that if every decision made on this earth were first put to the test of one question, "Is this good for children?" and the decision makers were forced to make decisions that would be good for children, there would only be good decisions made" (p. 75). Relying on numbers rather than force, the

Army—after a public meeting in which child victims air their complaints—arranges for a committee of children to visit the offending adult and to say, simply, that they know what is going on, and that it has to stop.

Investigating the complaints and limiting their jurisdiction to cases of obvious abuse, the Army has been quite successful. To hear their marching orders is to see why the Army works as well as it does:

> Today we are sending out three committees to talk to parents. One will discuss Helen Mason, six times admitted to six different hospitals for fractures of the arms, broken legs, bruises of the abdomen, and a smashed head. Helen Mason is a battered child. Her parents have been getting away with this. She is six years old. A committee will approach the parents to inform them that the police will be notified if Helen has one more bruise. There will be ten in this committee. It will be larger than most committees because of the known violence of the father. If the parents do not respond in a satisfactory way, the committee will go to the police immediately. They will contact Martin Feininger, the father of one of our members, and a fine lawyer, who has prosecuted many parents of battered children. This violence will be stopped.
>
> The next committee will go to the home of Charles Tyson. Charles Tyson is being driven crazy by his mother. His father is dead. His mother will not let him out of the house except to go to school and come back. He has no freedom. He is thirteen years old and he is not even allowed to close the door to his room. The committee will inform Mrs. Tyson that an appointment has been made for her to see a psychiatrist about this situation. If she does not agree to go voluntarily, three committee members will escort her personally to the doctor's office. If she says she will call the police, the committee will say go ahead. If she does call the police, the committee will say they are friends of Charles Tyson's and they will never, under any circumstances, divulge the fact of the existence of the Children's Army. At all times, whenever confronted, each member of this Army must and will say that he or she is only acting out of personal feeling and friendship for the child involved.
>
> The third committee will go to the house of Lois Babson. Lois is the two-year-old sister of one of our army. The parents of this two-year-old have bought a device which rings a terrible clanging bell every time the child wets the bed. Her sister feels and this committee concurs that this is no way to toilet-train somebody, that with sympathy and patience Lois will learn to be toilet-trained, and that this barbaric arrangement should stop immediately. The committee will approach Mr. and Mrs. Babson, tell them that they are confiscating the instrument, and why. They will inform the Babsons that they will take said instrument back to the store, get a refund, and return the money to the Babsons. (pp. 78-79)

Although Emma's experience with the Army is valuable in many ways—she formulates a Children's Bill of Rights, she becomes a leader, and she makes new friends (some already in the group, some recruited from her private school—of which we hear almost nothing, for it and its teachers are not an important element of Emma's life)—she realizes that the Army cannot be the solution to her problems, or Willie's. No one's rights are being violated, and even were she to bring her situation to the Army's attention, it would not be judged appropriate for committee action, any more than the problem of her new friend who wants to be a scientist, and whose mother wants her to marry a doctor. She has to handle this herself, and she can.

The motor of the plot is Emma's discovery that her own growth can become a means to the fulfillment of Willie's dream as well as her own. Emma comes to understand her family better. She sees that Willie, who has always seemed weak because he cannot stand up to her bullying, has had the courage to audition, to defy their father, to persist; she realizes that, although he lacks her skill with language and her aggressiveness, he cares about dancing as much as she cares about her values. She sees that her father's life has been a struggle to escape his childhood poverty and the racial prejudice that hindered his career and blighted his self-image, that his power and self-respect, which she has taken for granted, were earned by effort and remain, for him, fragile and perilous possessions; he wants Willie to be a lawyer rather than a dancer because he wants his son to have, sooner and with greater certainty, the security he won much later in life. She remembers, too, that her father seemed to love her when she was little, before Willie was born; longing ever since for the affection she seems to have lost, she resolved to try to beat him, to become a better lawyer, and sooner— as if competition could replace the lost bond she sees no way to restore. Looking at her mother, who briefly emerges from congenial docility to defend Willie's desire to dance, Emma sees a woman who wants to love her, but understands little about her, and therefore recommends her own life pattern (Don't become a lawyer—marry one) instead of one appropriate to Emma's gifts.

And Emma looks at herself, at her overeating, at her undeserved unkindness to Willie, at her futile, infuriating attempts to ignore her mother and defeat her father—and she decides to act within her powers, to change what she can, and to embrace herself and her chosen future. Although Emma is not confronted by the more usual handicaps of economic hardship and physical abuse, she has, for an 11-year-old (particularly one with gifts demanding scope and development), a lot on her plate. The resolution of the novel is a tribute to her imagination, resilience, courage, and sense of realism.

Acting as Willie's lawyer, she presents his case to her father. The confrontation is amusing, and inspiring:

"May it please the court," said Emma, standing in the middle of the room and facing her father and mother. "I would like to plead a mistrial on the basis of the fact that in this case the complainant, Mr. William Sheridan, Sr., happens also to be the District Attorney."

"Listen, smart-ass," Mr. Sheridan pointed a finger at her. "You think you know so much. I'll have you in contempt of court in three minutes."

"—and is also the judge. My client, William Sheridan, Jr., has, therefore, no possibility of a fair trial."

"But you have a very good possibility of getting your ass whacked," said Mr. Sheridan. "Now, sit down and shut up."

"I'll stand."

"All right, Willie. Since you have a loyal sister who seems to feel you rights to a fair trial are being prejudiced, I will begin again, calmly, to try to find out what you did on the afternoon of the second; that is, today."

Willie had his thumb in his mouth, having fled back into his youth.

"Sit up," said Emma. "Make a more pleasing appearance for the jury." Willie looked around for the jury.

"Finish your story, Willie," said his father.

"I watched this boy dance with Dipsey and he was real bad. He couldn't do it half as good as I could. So when Dipsey come to start again, I went up on stage and did it with him."

"Son, you must have practiced this many times. You must therefore have disobeyed me many times. Did you not know you were being bad?"

"Objection. My client could not be honest about this situation because he would have been incarcerated."

"Emma, get out of the way!" Mr. Sheridan bellowed.

"Willie, dear, what your father wants to know is whether you knew you were being disobedient. Did you, dear?"

"My client takes the Fifth Amendment," said Emma quickly. (pp. 165-166)

When she also enlists the help of her mother, her father agrees to let Willie perform, this time. She recognizes that her family may never change, but that she can change the way she lets their view of her affect her view of herself. In addition to her continued membership in the Children's Army, she suggests to her new friends a different form of action, a discussion group in which they can help each other with the changes they need to make in themselves, the changes they cannot expect adults to make. As she reflects with satisfaction on her accomplishments at home—her success in helping Willie play the role he has won in a summer-stock play, her decision to improve her eating habits, and her continued defiance of her father's opposition to her career plans—she looks forward to sharing her achievements with her discussion group:

That night, at dinner, Emma waited until dessert was served to make her announcement.

She waited patiently, watching Willie try to tell what had happened that day at rehearsal. She watched her mother being nervous. She watched her father retreating more and more into silence, eating faster and faster. She watched her mother watching her father.

When Martha placed a piece of chocolate cake in front of her, Emma pushed it away and said, "I'm going to be a lawyer when I grow up."

"Oh, for Christ's sake! Can't we have a peaceful dinner around here?" said her father loudly. He jerked his cake closer to him and shoved his fork down into it.

"Stop saying things just to upset your father," said Mrs. Sheridan.

"Women lawyers are idiots! They're the laughingstock of any group of lawyers. I think any woman who tries to be a lawyer is a damned fool!" Mr. Sheridan glared at Emma.

"That," said Emma, "is your problem, not mine." To herself she added, And frankly, Daddy, I don't give a damn.

She shook with silent laughter. Wait till I tell them tomorrow how these two looked when I said that. (pp. 220–221)

Architect at eleven of her own emancipation, Emma Sheridan knows that she does not need to hope or wait for her family to change; changing herself, changing the way she responds to the challenges that face her, she advances confidently in the direction of her gifts.

We neglect at our peril what is there in literature for us to learn. William Carlos William (1968, pp. 150–151), the doctor who inspired Coles, who in turn has inspired me, said it years ago:

My heart rouses
> *thinking to bring you news*
>> *of something*

that concerns you
> *and concerns many men. . . .*
>> *It is difficult*

to get the news from poems
> *yet men die miserably every day*
>> *for lack*

of what is found there.

The "news" we get from poems, the value to be found in stories, is essential. It is not, of course, sufficient. What we learn from these fictional stories is to be combined with "news" from other kinds of sources, with values to be found in factual stories, and with the experience and insight we bring to the challenges at hand.

To close my account of profiles in giftedness, I want to quote the conclusion of Kennedy's *Profiles in Courage,* as recited by his own voice, at the end of the popular television program in the 1960s. "These stories of past courage can teach, they can offer hope, they can provide inspiration, but they cannot supply courage itself. For this, each man must look into his own soul."

Author Index

A

Abrams, J.C., 214, *221*
Albert, R.S., 14, *20*, 34, *35*, 42, 43, *51*,
    75, 76, 77, 78, 79, *91*, 132, *135*
Allen, B., 174, *178*
Allen, D.W., 81, *91*
Alvino, J.A., 109, *119*, 165, *176*
Anastasi, A., 12, *19*
Anderson, M.A., 152, *158*
Anderson, R., 97, *120*, 219, *221*
Applebaum, M.I., 105, *120*
Arad, R., 12, *21*
Austin, A.W., 19, *20*

B

Bachtold, L.M., 153, *158*
Baldwin, A.Y., 161, 162, *176*
Baldwin, L.J., 217, *221*
Bandler, R., 64, 69, *73*
Barbe, W., 96, *119*
Barbee, A.H., 156, *160*
Bareford, K., 153, *158*
Barron, F., 12, *20*
Bashi, J., 165, *178*
Bate, J.W., 85, *91*
Baumrind, D., 86, *91*
Beck, L., 133, *135*
Becker, L., 174, *178*
Belcastro, F.P., 202, *203*
Belenkin, D., 225
Bennetts, L., 146, *158*
Berk, R.A., 213, *222*
Bernal, E.M., 161, 162, 165, *176, 177*
Berrington, H., 78, *91*
Betts, E.A., 213, *222*
Beville, K., 39, *51*
Bevington, 225
Birch, J., 97, *120*
Blaubergs, M.S., 146, 148, *158*

Bloom, B.S., 14, 17, *20*, 34, *35*, 43, *51*,
    76, *91*, 127, 132, *135*, 162, 163, *177*
Blum-Zorman, R., 174, *177*
Borman, C., 133, *136*
Boston, B.O., 17, *20*, 30, 32, 34, *35*, 127,
    132, 133, *135, 136*, 181, *203*
Bounous, R.M., 132, *135*
Bricklin, B., 108, *119*
Bricklin, P., 108, *119*, 218, *222*
Brodkey, H., 223, 224
Brody, L., 212, 219, *222*
Brolin, D., 134, *137*
Brooks-Gunn, J., 149, *160*
Brown, A.L., 219, *222*
Bruch, C., 97, *120*, 165, *177*

C

Callahan, C.M., 143, 151, 152, *158*
Carrow, P.A., 131, *137*
Casserly, P., 149, *160*
Caswell, H.L., 181, *203*
Chickering, A.W., 132, *135*
China, T.E., 195, *203*
Clance, P., 109, *119*
Clark, R.M., 83, 89, *91*
Clarke, B., 39, *51*, 183, *203*
Colangelo, N., 99, *119*, 129, 130, *135*, 146,
    158, 167, *177*
Collins, E.C., 24, *36*
Collins, H., 149, 154, *158*
Colon, P.J., 156, *158*
Colson, S., 133, *135, 136*
Combs, A., 193, *203*
Coopersmith, S., 86, *91*, 193, *203*
Cornell, D., 98, 113, *119*
Cox, C.M., 76, 77, *91*, 163, *177*
Cox, J., 17, *20*, 30, 32, 34, *35*, 127, 132,
    133, *136*, 179, 181, *203*
Cox, L., 134, *136*
Cramond, B., 155, *158*

259

Subject Index

C

Career, 75, 121
  development, 4, 5, 87, 123-130
  education, 123
  guidance, 124
Classroom management, 170, 179, 217
Computers, 131, 153, 192, 220
Counseling, 7, 15
  career, 130
  learning style-oriented, 53, 60-65
  needs and concerns, 15, 39, 70
  strategies, 17, 43
  teachers as counselors, 37, 48

D

Differentiation of curriculum content, 43,
    151, 168, 185, 211

G

Gifted
  characteristics, 7, 67, 103-119, 121, 182
  definition, 1, 10-14
  family influences, 86
  fictional portraits, 223
  identification, 10-14, 162
  mentor relationships, 82, 83

  personality development, 75, 79
  with special needs, 139
    disadvantaged gifted, 144, 167
    gifted girls, 143
    preschool gifted, 179
    learning disabled gifted, 207

L

Learning style, 3, 53
  elements of, 54-59
  of gifted, 67

M

Milgram's 4 × 4 Structure of Giftedness
  Model, 16

P

Parents of gifted, 3, 4, 195
  of gifted girls, 145
  parent-teacher conferences, 95-100
  parent discussion groups, 100-118

S

Special education options, 23, 28
  replacement systems, 26
  supplementary systems, 27